MANAGEMENT
OF
COMPUTER OPERATIONS

MANAGEMENT
OF
COMPUTER OPERATIONS

Israel Borovits
Tel Aviv University

Prentice-Hall, Inc.
Englewood Cliffs, New Jersey 07632

Library of Congress Cataloging in Publication Data

BOROVITS, ISRAEL.
  Management of computer operations.

  Bibliography: p.
  Includes index.
  1. Electronic data processing—Management. I. Title.
QA76.9.M3B67 1984   658.4′038   83-21245
ISBN 0-13-549493-1

Editorial/production supervision and interior design: Maureen Wilson
Cover design: Jeannette Jacobs
Manufacturing buyer: Ed O'Dougherty

Printed in the United States of America

10 9 8 7 6 5 4 3 2 1

ISBN 0-13-549493-1

PRENTICE-HALL INTERNATIONAL, INC., *London*
PRENTICE-HALL OF AUSTRALIA PTY. LIMITED, *Sydney*
EDITORA PRENTICE-HALL DO BRASIL, LTDA., *Rio de Janeiro*
PRENTICE-HALL CANADA INC., *Toronto*
PRENTICE-HALL OF INDIA PRIVATE LIMITED, *New Delhi*
PRENTICE-HALL OF JAPAN, INC., *Tokyo*
PRENTICE-HALL OF SOUTHEAST ASIA PTE. LTD., *Singapore*
WHITEHALL BOOKS LIMITED, *Wellington, New Zealand*

To Adi, Einat, Danna, and Yael

Contents

Preface

With the expanding use of data processing, particularly in business, increasing numbers of people in all disciplines are finding themselves involved in acquiring, developing, using, managing, controlling, and auditing data processing systems. Therefore, management of data processing, which includes all those activities, has become an important function in many organizations.

This book is designed for persons interested in the managment of data processing. It is also intended for use as a textbook for students who are majoring in computer science and/or information systems as well as students in business administration who are learning about information systems. This book may also be used as a reference for practitioners, such as policymakers in middle and upper mangement who establish, implement, and monitor policies that affect the data processing activity in the organization.

In view of the diverse backgrounds and interests of the intended readers, the structure of the book follows a logical sequence to ensure a comprehensive treatment of the topics covered. In addition to extensive discussions and explanations of critical topics, we also discuss diverse topics in an integrated manner that stress interrelationships and common themes. The book requires only elementary knowledge of the fundamentals of data processing. It is believed that the nonprofessional will find no difficulty in following much of the presentation.

With its balance between theory and applications, and with broad coverage of topics, *Management of Computer Operations* is divided into ten chapters that cover most of the topics a data processing manager faces. The accompanying chart presents an overview of these topics and the relationship between them.

For better understanding, the book should be read in sequence, since some later chapters assume knowledge of preceding ones.

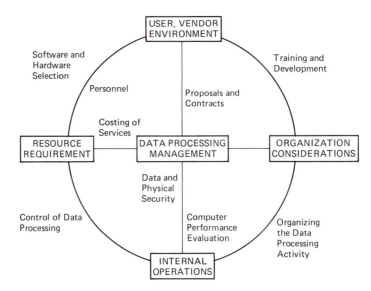

Most of this book was written while I was on sabbatical at the University of Southern California, Graduate School of Business Administration, Department of Management and Policy Sciences. I am much indebted, therefore, to the university's faculty and staff for giving me the opportunity to work on this project. I also wish to thank my colleagues on the Faculty of Management at the Tel Aviv University for providing me with all the help I needed during my work.

This book incorporates a number of articles written by colleagues. I wish to express my great appreciation to these scholars for allowing me to use their material.

Since most of the material in *Management of Computer Operations* has been used in the form of notes in classes at the University of Southern California, I am indebted to many colleagues and students for their helpful suggestions.

MANAGEMENT
OF
COMPUTER OPERATIONS

1

Preparation of Proposals and Contracts

INTRODUCTION

This chapter describes the procedures involved in the computer system acquisition process, starting with the preparation of a request for proposal (RFP) and culminating in the signing of a contract with a chosen supplier. The intention is to present a comprehensive checklist of procurement procedures rather than a model or proposal for any particular decision method. Therefore, alternative methods of performing a given step will be described, but no specific preferences for any one method are given.

The process of computer acquisition is a complex one, necessitating numerous preliminary steps before the actual formulation of the requirements can be accomplished. These preliminary steps include the actual drafting of the RFP, analysis of proposals submitted by suppliers, decisions on supplier selection, negotiations with the supplier selected, and finally the preparation of a contract. Care must then be taken to prepare for conversion to the newly selected system, which requires a follow-up on the supplier's compliance with the conditions agreed upon and system acceptance checks.

In presenting a complete picture of the computer system acquisition process, we begin with a concise description of the initial preparatory steps. The subsequent sections cover the details of each particular step in the process. Figure 1.1 is an overview of computer system acquisition process.

Awareness of Need
for a New System

Performance of Informal
Market Survey

Performance of Feasibility
Studies

Writing the RFP

Publishing the Final RFP and
Assisting Suppliers in Bidding

Receiving Comparing, and
Analyzing Bids

Selecting Vendor and
Specific Configuration

Beginning Negotiations

Writing the Contract

Installing the System

Figure 1.1 Overview of Computer System Acquisition Process

PRELIMINARY STEPS

The steps leading to the actual writing of an RFP, which will generally consume many resources, such as time and money, can be outlined as follows.

Awareness of the Need for Equipment Replacement

As a rule, the procurement process begins with a "feeling" that the current system employed is no longer sufficient. This recognition may either be a vague perception or a well-based result of systematic study and measurement, often performed at the time of installation of the existing computer. Of course, all such "intuitive feelings" must be analyzed for cost-effectiveness, especially if the organization has no prior experience with computer systems.

Factors that Support the Decision to Acquire a New System

The initial awareness of the need for a new computer system, or a first computer, as the case may be, can arise from one or more of the following circumstances:

Unmanageable projected work Load

While a number of applications are being regularly processed by the existing system, it becomes apparent, through studies and projections, that an unmanageable overload on the current system exists or may soon occur. This can be attributed to increases in the number of operations, volume of files, or quantity of output.

Extended requirements projected

New, broader, and more sophisticated client requirements will soon overwhelm or render the existing system obsolete.

Manual information system explosion

The manual systems can no longer cope with the existing work load.

Advent of new technology

Clients may demand services that cannot be performed with the current system (e.g., switching and communication or data-base management), and thus there may be intense pressure to replace the current system, regardless of whether or not it is fully loaded.

Many cases of equipment replacement are due to more than one of these factors, namely, demand for quicker throughput as well as the need for extended and more sophisticated services that can support the decision to acquire a new system.

Determining Specific Needs

Use quantitative yardsticks to measure existing system

After the decision is made to procure a new computer by RFP, the work load of the existing system should be measured for a number of months as a departure point for preparing the RFP.

The chief parameters to be obtained for each application (as monthly averages) are the following:

- Number of jobs submitted
- CPU seconds utilized
- Read/write operations on direct access units
- Read/write operations on magnetic tapes
- Number of records input
- Number of lines printed
- Size of memory required

- Number of direct access devices required concurrently
- Number of magnetic tape devices required concurrently
- Execution frequency

For each file, the following information should be gathered:

- Number of records
- Record size
- Total file volume
- Storage devices
- File organization technique
- Frequency of access
- Average daily hours of use
- Backup arrangement

The utilization of these data will be discussed in the following sections. However, it should be noted that data collection leading to valid and representative averages will take quite a few months.

Determine qualitative requirements

Concurrently with quantitative data gathering, qualitative information is required, especially with respect to future systems. To this end, the analyst should interview both present and potential users or customers to ascertain their demands and needs. From such a survey, analysts will then prepare a forecast of qualitative and quantitative requirements regarding software, hardware, and types of applications. Such a forecast should include the following:

1. Rates of increase of input and output should be measured for existing systems. From these measurements an educated guess can be made about the influence of input and output rates on other load characteristics.
2. For new applications based on existing techniques, the customer should be requested to obtain actual data from similar systems in operation from which an approximation might be made regarding the resulting load on the new installation. Such data are somewhat forced, but nonetheless are still useful.

Perform feasibilty studies

The purpose of an RFP is to provide a uniform, unbiased basis for soliciting bids for a system. Sometimes, it may be that there is no point in preparing an RFP, since there are no feasible alternatives to be compared. In such cases, a formal decision should be made not to go through the expensive process of preparing an RFP. However, if an RFP is to be prepared, a feasibility study should be undertaken first to determine current and future information processing requirements before the actual RFP can be formulated and drafted. By taking the time to examine its present and future needs, the firm is well prepared and is more likely to end up with a satisfactory agreement that ensures that the best possible combination of hardware and services will be obtained at the lowest cost.

The following points outline the preliminary steps leading to the preparation of the RFP.

1. *Justify the system economically.* Economic reasons for system replacement should both be justified and feasible. Cost-benefit analysis may be performed.
2. *Develop the system realistically.* The RFP should be realistic in the sense that the actual potential of both equipment and technology being available will be taken into account.
3. *Estimate the costs of data processing.* An estimate of capital and running costs of data processing should be obtained. These estimates can be used later as a baseline for comparison.
4. *Eliminate unsuitable systems.* Unsuitable systems should be eliminated, allowing effort to be concentrated on those considered acceptable.
5. *Forewarn potential suppliers.* Advance warning should be given to potential suppliers allowing them more time to prepare a serious bid.

Perform informal market survey

After the need for a new system is recognized, an informal market survey is required to become acquainted with the existing possibilities. Such a survey will also help to fine-tune both the quantitative and the qualitative considerations inherent in the procurement of a new system. Only after the completion of this survey can the purchaser's specific needs by efficiently and intelligently matched with available systems. An informal market survey will save time in the long run and should involve the following activities:

1. *Obtain copies of other RFPs.* Getting copies of RFPs prepared by similar organizations is a starting point in developing a checklist of things that are important or that meet your needs.
2. *Visit other data processing managers.* Visiting with those who have been through the procurement process is one of the best ways to get first-hand information regarding system procurement.
3. *Use professional organizations.* Joining a professional organization permits sharing of technical and professional knowledge as well as making contacts through the industry.
4. *Research technical journals.* Publications can provide detailed and comparative information about current data processing systems and the general management problems associated with them.

5. *Use computer vendors as a source of information.* Local computer vendors offer a wealth of information at no cost and can arrange a series of presentations for you on nearly any subject you desire.

Prepare timetable

Preparing a timetable is absolutely essential in developing the RFP. The timetable should be rather rigid, so that the entire process is not too lengthy. The best planning takes place when the need for replacement is perceived to be approximately two years before the time of actual replacement. If such is the case, the second year can be devoted to preparations for physical installation and other preliminary and conversion steps. A suggested schedule for the first year is presented in Table 1.1.

Most of the foregoing discussion relates to organizations that presently have a computer and thus can make comparisons. Totally inexperienced firms are in a different position, however, and therefore some remarks are in order.

The actual decision with respect to feasibilty studies and market surveys involves a longer process. The process generally starts with an explosion of the manual information system and loss of managerial control. The feasibility study, then, is conducted by either the organization's own EDP personnel or by external consultants. If the recommendation is to proceed with an RFP, the first step is to appoint a data processing manager, who will start building a skeleton staff. This process should take about half a year, after which time the market survey can begin.

As there are no data to be measured with respect to existing computerized systems in these cases, the manual system must be measured (e.g., number of cards and types of transactions and their frequency) and a projection drawn for its

Table 1.1   SUGGESTED SCHEDULE FOR FIRST-YEAR PLANNING

Month	Activity
1	Decision is made to start studies toward RFP. Preparation includes discussions of requirements, forecasts, and budgets.
2	Market survey is performed.
3,4	Quantitative measurements are derived. Qualitative requirements and forecasts are formulated.
5	RFP is drafted, including appendices. Committees are appointed. Final tender draft is approved.
6	RFP is published and is distributed to viable candidate suppliers.
7,8	Competing suppliers are guided on their bids by means of adequate information.
9	Bids are received and preliminary investigaton is begun. Unsuitable bids are refused and others are completed according to need.
10,11	Perform analysis of bids (trials and investigations are required).
12	Analysis is completed and final position is taken. Recommendations are made by committees.
13	Negotiations are begun with supplier selected. Contract is signed. Preparations are started to receive and install the equipment.

expansion in the next few years. Quite possibly, part of this information could have been gathered for the feasibility study. These estimates then replace information on work load and file volume.

It will be more difficult for completely inexperienced customers to define qualitative requirements. Therefore, the job of the professional staff necessitates the expenditure of more time and effort and will probably exceed the two-month period alloted in our proposed time frame.

WRITING THE REQUEST FOR PROPOSALS

Introduction

The request for proposals is a document used to solicit competitive bids for special acquisitions (e.g., construction projects, defense systems, computer systems). This section deals exclusively with RFPs for acquisition of computer services, software, and systems (systems are defined as a package of hardware, software, and related services).

The variability of performance characteristics and capabilities for each element (hardware, software, service) of a computer system is immense, and the possible permutations of the total combination are infinite. For this reason especially, a properly composed RFP is critical to the acquisition of a satisfactory computer system.

Although this discussion deals exclusively with an RFP for a computer system, the general guidelines outlined should be applied when acquiring any single element of a system.

When drafting an RFP, the purchaser should proceed with expressed intention that the RFP will be an integral part (in fact, the basic "core") of any purchase contract that results from the RFP. This explicit intention dictates that the RFP contain all necessary disclosure required for the vendor(s) to make informed, binding, viable replies.

In the world of computer systems and their acquisition, Murphy's law (if anything can go wrong, it will) can always be expected to hold. Further, the later one attempts to correct any problems that develop, the more expensive (and difficult) the corrections become. These additional facts provide further substantiation for the investment of time, personnel, and money required to draft a quality RFP. If "shortsighted" management insists on skimping on this investment, it must bear the blame for additional risks (substantial) and extra costs (almost inevitable) resulting from that decision. Such shortsightedness opens the door to possible legal battles, system failures or shortcomings, and so on, and almost always guarantees dissatisfaction with the resultant computer system. A properly drafted RFP is the "ounce of prevention" in the old cliché, "an ounce of prevention is worth a pound of cure."

In summary, a quality RFP is essential to the acquisition of a satisfactory computer system and the proper exercise of management's fiduciary responsibility. Failure to insist on the investment required to draft a quality RFP is, at best, an exercise in futility and can only result in headaches for management (and dire economic consequences implicit in those headaches).

A general outline for an RFP for acquisition of computer system, software, and services is presented in Table 1.2.

THE RFP GENERAL OUTLINE

The following comments are keyed to the outline presented in Table 1.2.

Executive Summary

Although this is the first section presented, it should be the last section drafted. As the title suggested, it is a *summary* of the RFP contents, and it follows that one cannot properly summarize the contents of the RFP until it has been drafted.

The executive summary should contain a short description of your company, its operations, and its system requirements. The summary should explicitly state that it is an overview of the whole RFP and should not be construed by the vendor as a substitute for the whole RFP (or any of its subsections).

Purpose

This section should address three essential topics. First, it should discuss the basic structure and general objectives of the RFP. This discussion should include such items as the major elements of the RFP, explicit major expectations as to vendor response, and the major objectives of the proposed acquisition.

Second, it should identify the department/office/division of your company that issued the RFP, including the name and corporate address to which all proposals and related inquiries should be addressed. It should also identify the department/person(s) responsible for decisions concerning the merits and acceptance of submitted proposals.

Finally, it should state the scope of the RFP. In other words, it should state exactly what the RFP purports to be and any limitations implicit in its structure or contents.

Introduction and general requirements

This section should start with a brief, general description of the business in which your company operates and the extent of your company's operations. For example, Is your company currently operating on regional or national basis? Does management expect to expand operations to a national or international basis in the near future?

Second, this section should discuss the functions to be performed or the operations to be supported by the proposed system. For example, Will the proposed system supply accounting support for portions of the operations or for the

TABLE 1.2 GENERAL OUTLINE FOR RFP FOR AQUISITION OF COMPUTER SYSTEMS, SOFTWARE, SERVICES

Executive Summary

1. Purpose
2. Introduction and General Requirements
3. Organizations Involved
4. Application Description
   a. General System
   b. Subsystems
5. Information Requirements
   a. System Files
   b. System Input/Output
   c. Machine-Readable Input/Output
6. System Design Constraints
7. Statement of Work
8. Information Required from Vendor
   a. Introduction
   b. General
   c. System Software
   d. Application Software
   e. Hardware
   f. Site Preparation
   g. Vendor Support
   h. Financial Data
   i. Installation
   j. Evaluation Table
   k. Site Visit Demonstration
   l. Project Timetable
9. Criteria of Selection
   a. General
   b. Evaluation Methods to be used
   c. Criteria for Technical Evaluation
   d. Criteria for Financial Evaluation
10. Administration and Constructual Information
    a. Vendors' Proposals
    b. Rejection of Proposals
    c. Incurred Costs
    d. Addenda to the RFP
    e. Response Data
    f. Multiple Proposals
    g. Acceptance of Proposal Content
    h. Economy of Preparation
    i. Oral Presentation
    j. Prime Contractor Responsibility
    k. News Releases
    l. Schedule of Activities
    m. Negotiated Standard Agreements
    n. Proposal Lease-Purchase Price Quotation
    o. User Visits
    p. Confidentiality of Information
    q. Public Records
    r. Contract Revisions
    s. Subsequent Revisions
11. Appendix

operations as a whole? What other operations or processing (e.g., order, billing, and inventory processing; management information systems; market analysis) must the system be capable of?

Finally, the general requirements of the proposed system should be identified and defined. In addition to the required functions and/or capabilities, this section should specify the elements (hardware, software, service) of the proposed system that management expects the vendor to supply. For example, Is the vendor expected to supply training, maintenance, implementation planning, implementation supervision, budgeting information, and documentation?

All the major requirements should be identified, although the description may (and probably should) refer the vendor to appropriate subsections of the RFP for details.

Organizations involved

This should identify the departments of divisions of the company that will utilize the proposed system. Included in this discussion should be the general functions and responsibilities of the identified departments and their interrelationships. Such a discussion should implicitly identify the demands that each department will make on the proposed system.

The general objective of this section is to supply the vendor with any and all information about your company's operations that will assist the vendor in supplying a system with maximum operating efficiencies, at the lowest cost. The more information you provide the vendor, the greater your assurance of receiving a system that meets all your expectations.

Application description

This is one of the most important sections of the quality RFP. Great detail is not merely recommended, it is essential. Any and all details that might assist the vendor in completely understanding your operations and requirements should be included. A general rule of thumb to be followed is, "When in doubt, it is better to err in favor of too much detail rather than too little."

You should first present a description of the general flow of information through your company. A recommended approach is to present a flow chart with a descriptive narrative keyed to the flow chart.

This should be followed by a detailed description of each application subsystem (e.g., purchasing, inventory, accounting, forecasting, and management information subsystems). The descriptions should be supported with charts, flow charts, narratives, and samples of inputs and outputs. In addition, calculation methodologies (e.g., forecasting algorithms) and assumptions used in the methodologies (e.g., first-in, first-out product flow assumption used in the inventory subsystem) should be fully discussed.

This section should also describe the system(s) to be used until the proposed system is operational, its limitation, its similarities to and differences from the proposed system, and the way in which the transition to the proposed system is to take place (e.g., gradual or otherwise).

And, finally, any special problems should be fully disclosed. Examples include data and system integrity and security.

Information requirements

System Files.   All the different files required should be identified. For each file, the following information should be supplied:

- Type of file (e.g., vendor file, customer file)
- Purpose of file
- Information to be contained in each file (e.g., customer name, address, phone number, credit limit)
- Number of files required
- Type of information in file (e.g., alpha, numeric, alphanumeric)
- File access constraints (restricted or unrestricted)
- File updating requirements and restrictions
- Frequency of use/updating of file

System Input/Output.   All relevant system inputs and outputs (and related restrictions) should be described in detail.

Machine-Readable Input/Output.   All inputs and outputs that must be in machine-readable form should be identified and their form specified. For example, you might wish to have the daily accounting transaction logs put on tape files.

System design constraints

In this section, you should discuss the current size and expected growth of your company's operations. For example, you might state that "our company currently has 10 sales offices, which we expect to expand to 50 offices over the next two years. Each sales office will initially have 4 to 6 sales representatives, each responsible for approximately 75 customers. Each customer results in about 200 transactions per year. We expect the number of sales representatives per sales office to expand to 20 over the next four years."

The purpose is to quantify and/or qualify expectations of management of the proposed system in terms of growth and flexibility. This information is vital to the vendor in determining hardware sizing and the extent of software requirements and related service requirements (e.g., maintenance and training).

The discussions of these expectations and constraints should be broken down into individual categories such as general performance, hardware (computer mainframe and peripherals), systems and applications software, communications, and so on. These discussions should be broken down further within each category by mandatory, highly desirable, and desirable capabilities. Any parameters used on these discussions (especially qualitative constraints such as reliability, ease of operation, and quality of service) should be clearly defined to avoid possible confusion and ambiguities.

Other possible categories for discussion in this section in relation to design contraints and expectations include training, maintenance (timing and availability), finances, and evaluation techniques.

Statement of work

The purpose of this section is to identify and describe the services we wish to purchase from the vendor beyond the basic system. For example, Is the vendor responsible for managing the project? What training do we expect the vendor to supply, and when? Is the vendor responsible for implementation, installation, writing of systems/application software and system testing?

The point is to identify, specify, and define clearly the scope and limits of the vendor's responsibilities to avoid confusion, ambiguities, and later arguments.

Information required from vendor

Introduction. This is basically an executive summary for this particular portion of the RFP. It is used to describe the information and the general format of the presentation we require vendors to supply in their replies to the RFP. Typically, the introduction addresses

- Whether or not vendors may bid on portions of the proposed system, and which portions
- Whether vendors may supply additional information if they desire
- Whether vendors' replies should address all topics in the RFP, and explicitly their responsibilities
- Whether replies should be "open" or "sealed" bids
- General proposal (reply) format

General. This section specifies the contents of the general reply and includes

- Cover letter
- Brief statement of salient features of the proposal including conclusions and generalized recommendation (executive summary)
- Brief statement indicating vendor's capabilities and experience with projects of this type
- Brief description of how vendor's proposed system meets requirements specified in RFP
- Any additional information the vendor feels would provide a better understanding of the proposal
- Complete statement of costs
- Brief description of the demonstration to be conducted at the site visit

System Software.   Required here is the response of the vendor, including

- Statement of vendor's experience and capabilities including qualifications of staff
- General statement of strategy to be employed in addressing specifications outlined in Application Description section of RFP
- List of former or current clients of vendor with applications similar to those in this RFP, including company name and address, contact name and phone number, and brief description of application

Application Software.   Generally, this section specifies response requirements similar to those listed under System Software.

Hardware.   The response should include the following items:

- Brief description of how proposed hardware meets mandatory, highly desirable, and desirable requirements identified in the RFP
- Identity of each hardware component, including special devices and features
- Description of the existing potential for hardware and software expansion and enhancement that could increase work load capacity
- Detailed equipment list for support of future expansion, which includes additional memory, communications, and peripherals. Other equipment necessary for support of the system must also be provided in the equipment list. (This equipment list is often specified as for informational purposes only, to serve as aid in the overall evaluation of the proposed system)
- Date on which the equipment was made available for general sale or lease (model and year)
- Cost of each hardware component
- List of current users of hardware cited with comparable configuration(s)

Site Preparation.   This section is often included in the hardware section. It usually requires vendor to supply

- Equipment weight and dimensions
- Equipment flooring and space requirements
- Equipment power requirements (electricity requirements)
- Equipment environmental requirements (e.g., air conditioning, water supply for coolant purposes)
- Site security requirements and recommendations

Vendor Support.   Recommended requirements include vendor's discussion of

- Capability to meet training requirements
- Capability to meet maintenance requirements
- Detailed description of maintenance philosophy and practice

- Parts supply and availability on local basis
- Technical personnel support available on local basis, including members, numbers, and skills
- Backup support for personnel in preceding item
- Internal notification procedures
- Problem isolation and identification responsibilities (vendor's or purchaser's)
- System and engineering change procedures
- Operating system and programming maintenance procedures
- Available hours and costs of all vendor support services
- Schedule of maintenance and training support services
- List of appropriate technical literature regarding all hardware and software
- One copy of all items listed in previous item, under separate cover, from vendor reply

Financial.   Recommended requirements include

- Application software design, development, and installation. Estimate of cost by task and an estimate of the total cost of the project including all costs for time, travel, materials, system integration, proprietary software (purchase and/or license), and documentation.
- System hardware and software. Vendor should be encouraged to submit as many financial alternatives as deemed appropriate for lease, lease-purchase, and outright purchase for both single- and multiple-unit acquisitions.

Installation.   Recommended requirements include

- Estimated schedule of application software, assuming hardware and system software will be available 90 days after award of contract
- Delivery and installation schedule for hardware and system software

Evaluation Table.   This usually applies only to hardware and system software. Recommended requirements usually specify a complete evaluation table (content and format of table should be specified in Design Constraints section of the RFP) for each system proposed by the vendor.

Site Visit Demonstration.   Recommended requirements include a description of proposed demonstration and a list of possible sites for the demonstration.

Project Timetable.   Recommended requirements include estimated completion dates for delivery, installation, testing, and implementation of each element of hardware, system software, and application software, with date of contract award considered day zero.

Criteria of selection

General.   This subsection explicitly states that the objective of the evaluation process is to ensure the selection of a system that best fits the needs (present and future) of the company and meets all the requirements specified in the RFP.

Evaluation Methods to be Used.   The purpose of this subsection is to identify the two areas of evaluation, technical and financial, and their relative weights in the final decision (usually assigned equal relative weights).

Criteria for Technical Evaluation

• Proposals are first screened to determine if they meet mandatory requirements.

• Proposals that pass the first phase are then evaluated based on their suitability for the application. The method for evaluation should be specified as should the relative effect of meeting desirable and highly desirable requirements.

• It should be specified whether all vendors, or only those who receive top scores in the second phase, will be awarded on-site visits for the purpose of demonstrating the vendor's proposed system as well as the relative weight in the final decision that demonstration will have.

Criteria for Financial Evaluation.   This subsection should specify the methods used to evaluate the financial implications of the vendor's proposal. The usual methods employed are a combination of present value analysis, capital budgeting impact to the purchaser, and the extent to which the proposal is compatible with the budgetary contraints of the purchaser.

Administration and contractual information

The basic purpose of this section is to state explicitly the legal and contractual implications of the RFP (and/or the vendor's reply) and all the disclaimers of the RFP issuer. This section should address the following topics:

Vendor's Proposals.   This section should specify that the vendor will not distribute copies of his or her reply to anyone other than the issuer of the RFP, that a certain number of copies of the reply should be submitted for evaluation, and that all replies should conform to content and format requirements specified in the RFP.

Rejection of Proposals.   This section should specify that your company reserves the right to refuse any proposal as well as the length of time you will hold the vendor responsible for the contents of his or her proposal (typically six months).

Incurred Costs.   This section should disclaim any liability for the costs incurred by any vendor prior to acceptance of proposal and signing of a contract and any liability to pay for any information solicited or obtained as a result of the RFP.

Addenda to the RFP.   This section should specify procedures for making changes to RFP. For example, you might state "in the event that changes must be made to the RFP, we will submit a written copy of all such changes to all vendors."

Response Date.   This section should specify the deadline for responding to the RFP by vendors and explicitly state that the deadline refers to receipt of vendor's proposal by the RFP issuer.

Multiple Proposals. This section should specify whether vendors may submit more than one proposal and whether additional proposals from same vendor must strictly adhere to the form and content requirements specified in the RFP.

Acceptance of Proposal Content. This section should specify that the contents of the proposal(s) of successful bidder(s) will become contractual obligations if acquisition action ensues. It should specify that failure to accept these obligations in the resultant purchase contract(s) by the successful bidder(s) may result in cancellation of the contract.

Economy of Preparation. This section should specify that the vendors' proposals should be prepared simply and economically. In other words, vendors should concentrate on quality of content, not presentation.

Oral Presentation. This section should specify whether all vendors, or only finalists are required to give oral presentations to management.

Prime Contractor Responsibility. This section should specify that the vendor is primarily responsible for performance of all subcontractors included in the proposal.

News Releases. This section should specify that the vendor may not make any public statements pertaining to this project without prior written approval of the RFP issuer.

Schedule of Activities. This section should provide a schedule of dates, with a specific date (or explicit statement that the date is to be determined later) for each discrete event in the project. Typical events included in the schedule are release of RFP, bidder meeting, response deadline, vendor selection, contract signing, installation of system hardware and software, and implementation of major applications subsystems.

Negotiated Standard Agreements. This section should specify expectations as to compromise between your standard contracts and the vendor's. Also, it should specify that copies of vendors' standard contracts be submitted with their proposal(s).

Proposal Lease-Purchase Price Quotation. This section should specify that the vendor may not increase the prices quoted in the proposal without an approval. Another common stipulation is that the purchaser shall enjoy the benefit of any reductions by the vendor of the vendor's established lease-purchase price that occur prior to delivery or installation.

User Visits. This section should state your intention to visit the sites of previous satisfied clients of the vendor.

Confidentiality of Information. This section should explicitly state that the vendor is responsible for keeping all information made available by the issuer of the RFP to the vendor strictly confidential.

Public Records. This section should clearly state that all vendor proposals (and information contained within) shall be considered public unless explicitly specified otherwise by the vendor.

Contract Provisions. This section should typically express the right of the purchaser to withold contract payments if the vendor fails to meet any contractual obligations.

Subsequent Revisions. This section should specifically state that all subsequent revisions to contracts must be submitted in writing and are subject to approval by both parties.

Appendix

The appendix should include the specification as to content and format of the statement(s) of costs. A separate statement should be required for each financial alternative (lease, lease-purchase, outright purchase) that the vendor proposes. Each statement should be broken down as follows:

Financial Plan. The financial plan should include (as applicable) length of lease term, cancellation period, and purchase price.

Hardware Costs

• Item
• Model number
• Description and quantity
• Monthly rental (gross) and purchase price (gross)
• Education allowance or discount
• Net price (quantity times unit price)
• Monthly maintenance
• Additional cost (if applicable) for first-, second-, and third-shift coverage
• Extent of coverage
• Additional cost (if applicable) for unlimited coverage

System and Application Software Costs

• Item
• Program name
• Monthly price
• Purchase price
• Education allowance or discount
• Net price
• Maintenance cost

Education and Training Costs

- Item
- Course title
- Charge per person
- Recommended number and level of personnel to attend
- Net cost per course

BID EXAMINATION PROCEDURES

Introduction

Both RFP preparation and bid analysis demand large investments of high-quality staff time. This section deals with the procedures used in setting up selection committees—in terms of the functions to be performed by each committee member—as well as the qualifications needed for membership on the committees.

The RFP Preparation Group

As stated previously, the preparation of an RFP entails a long and tedious process of gathering and checking data. This process is handled most efficiently by specialists from the organization's data processing department.

After management has made the commitment to begin the preliminary work, the process can be performed within one of the following frameworks:

A senior executive (such as the head of data processing) would coordinate efforts and delegate data gathering tasks to competent staff members according to their functions; for example, data on work load would be gathered by the head of operations, customer demands are best obtained by the senior programmers, costing and other economic analyses would be jointly handled by an economist and a data processing expert, and market research might be conducted by the specialist, if there is one in the organization, or else farmed out.

A task force would be established to include the head of data processing, senior systems programmers, head of operations, and senior applications programmers. Tasks would be distributed among the members according to their particular expertise, and each member would be responsible for his or her part of the project. The group would meet regularly to exchange information, report on progress, and define approaches. Ultimately, the task force would prepare the first draft of the RFP.

In connection with the RFP preparation process, two critical points should be borne in mind:

First, with regard to progress reports to top management, there should be a firm procedure for reporting progress to nonspecialist management. Management should be kept informed of the trends and developments in the preparations, and there should be a cross-fertilization of ideas and objectives. To this end, a senior executive should be appointed "godparent" to the project (as representative of users or customers). He or she then would act as the principal liaison with the data processing head or the task force.

Second, regarding outside expert assistance, the organization should contract for expert assistance from an external consultant for the preparation period, if necessary. The consultant would be a full member of the group and would both check his or her co-workers' work and undertake special tasks.

Generally, however, the entire preparation process should not be farmed out to a consultant or firm of experts, as there exists a real danger of receiving a recommendation that fails to consider the organization's specific problem. Therefore, it is preferable to integrate the experts in the organization rather than buy the experts' recommendations outright.

Steering and Technical Committees

The final product of the preparation group is the draft of the RFP. This draft is not made available to bidders until its final form has been approved. Approval should be undertaken by two groups within the organization: the technical committee and the steering committee.

The technical committee represents the data processing unit and should include data processing professionals qualified to analyze the bids. These individuals should be experienced in the fields of computer center management and operations, system engineering, software, equipment, computer costing, and economics.

It is preferable that the committee consist of many individuals who represent expertise in different fields. The committee should be chaired by the head of data processing, and should include senior systems and applications programmers as well as the head of operations. Here again, if needed, external consultants should become full committee members, as the process of analysis and selection should not be farmed out as a whole.

The steering committee represents the interests of the total organization. It oversees, directs, and controls the work of the technical committee. It should include representatives of top management, the finance or accounting department, the economics or planning department, legal counsel, and the technical committee (usually as chairperson).

The steering committee need not discuss the actual merits of the bids offered. Rather, its task is to oversee the technical committee, to define criteria, and to make interim decisions on professional questions or policies needing clarification.

Divisions of Tasks Between the Committees

To clarify each committee's field of action and interactions, this section discusses the programs of each in chronological order. As stated previously, the draft RFP is not published before it is approved by both committees.

First, the technical committee should carefully scan the draft, checking and verifying each detail. If need be, the committee can demand further clarification or additional data. Ultimately, the technical committee approves the draft.

The approved draft is then presented to the steering committee, along with an appropriate explanation of technical and professional terms and problems, given by the representative of the technical committee. The steering committee either approves the draft or returns it to the technical committee for improvement or clarification. After the approval of the two committees is secured, a representative of the steering committee then signs and issues the approved draft of the RFP for publication.

The process of maintaining contact with prospective bidders is conducted by members of the technical committee. These individuals should assist bidders in understanding the demands required of the system, which may entail frequent meetings for clarification. Upon receiving bids, the committee analyzes each one individually. During the analysis, the technical committee may reject a bid totally because the bid does not conform to basic requirements defined in the RFP or because implementation of the bid would require significant organizational changes.

The committee may find that several bids are not comparable in the sense that they are based on different conceptions of the organizational structure or of the data processing function. In addition, the committee may find that implementation of a certain bid could affect the internal control processes in the organization. Such differences, however, are outside the technical committee's competence.

The steering committee should meet less frequently than the technical committee. The following items, as a bare minimum, should be included on the agenda:

1. A report from the technical committee describing progress and plans for further action
2. A report from the technical committee on significant deviations from the timetable
3. A presentation of policy problems raised at technical committee meetings with explanation of the roots of each problem and the foreseeable consequences of each alternative solution
4. A decision on policy problems that had been raised at the previous meeting

CONTACT BETWEEN CUSTOMER AND SUPPLIER

Introduction

After the final RFP has been approved, it can be sent to each potential vendor for submission of formal bids. This discussion describes the process from the publication of the RFP up to the formal submission of bids.

Distributing the RFP

The importance of conducting a preliminary survey among possible suppliers has already been stressed. If this survey was performed, and assuming that the number of potential suppliers were somewhat limited, there would be no need to advertise the RFP through communications media. The best method of contacting potential vendors is to invite each prospective supplier to a meeting, where he or she would receive a copy of the complete RFP as well as other necessary information.

In these meetings the organization would be represented by the following officers: the chairperson of the steering committee, the chairperson of the technical committee, and one or two members of each committee.

The following items should be included on the agenda at each meeting:

- A formal invitation to bid on the RFP
- A review of the legal requirements to be fulfilled by bidders
- A review of the timetable for supply and installation
- An explanation of the organization's plans, policies, and expectations regarding the system
- An explanation of the criteria used to rank the bid
- An explanation of the working relationship expected between customer and supplier during the preparation of bids
- A detailed explanation of the actual selection process including a tentative timetable, a statement regarding the membership and power of the selecting committee, and a statement of the organization's requirement that the vendor perform field trials and the importance of these results in the selection process.

Assisting the Supplier in Preparing the Bid

Usually a serious competitor in the bidding process will find the information contained in the RFP to be incomplete for his or her purposes and, therefore, will request further clarification of certain points. For example, one might ask to become acquainted with the organization's computerized systems and development plans and might well require additional details on the flow of activities, records, and applications.

When the RFP is given to a particular supplier, a senior data processing staff member should be appointed as liaison with that supplier. The staff member will see that the bidder receives all the help necessary, be it from the liaison officer or from the individual best qualified to assist the bidder. If a meeting is required, the liaison should arrange for one and be present as well.

It is advisable to appoint a separate liaison officer for each individual bidder. Although one might think it feasible to appoint contacts for each field or subject instead, this latter method has certain disadvantages:

1. It is generally not desirable for the supplier to contact different people in the organization
2. Often suppliers are not well acquainted with the organization, so they might not contact the person qualified to help them with a particular problem.
3. One of the main advantages of the liaison officer system will be lost, namely, that one person in the organization becomes well acquainted with

one bidder, understands the bidder's methods, abilities, and intentions, and is therefore able to explain fully to the selection committee the advantages and limitations of a particular supplier's proposal.

The liaison officer should avoid reinterpreting the RFP. Questions of principle should be discussed directly with the chairperson of the technical committee.

Contact Between the Supplier and the Committee

Most of the contacts between suppliers and committees will be channeled through the liaison officer. However, with respect to questions of principle or organizational policy, direct contact between the supplier and the committee might be necessary. Also it may be desireable at some time for the committee to communicate directly with the suppliers, for example, to monitor the supplier's progress, understanding of requirements, and adherence to the timetable.

It cannot be overemphasized that the RFP for installation of a computer system is not a standard RFP, with the submission of a sealed envelope before a stated date followed by secret deliberations. Rather, the business of computer supply requires an interactive process whereby the customer seeks the best equipment possible within the firm's budget; thus, the more the bidder knows about what is required and expected, the better equipped he or she will be to submit a satisfactory offer. Therefore, communication between the organization and the supplier is essential.

It is recommended that regular meetings be scheduled between the supplier and the technical committee, or some of its members, in the presence of the liaison officer. The bidder, then, can ask the committee all questions that may have arisen, and the supplier can also describe his or her progress and plans.

While this "open" system of bidding may contain the danger of possible leading suppliers to interpret certain explanations as promises, commitments, or expressions of preference, this system is still much preferred to the sealed bid system.

There is no need for the supplier to meet the steering committee. Any questions, whether technical or otherwise, should be brought before the technical committee. The technical committee will contact the steering committee whenever necessary and will also keep that committee informed of developments that might significantly affect the timetable.

This stage of the computer system selection process ends with the submission of final bids by the suppliers to the technical committee chairperson.

RECEPTION AND COMPARISON OF BIDS

Introduction

All bids should be submitted in writing. It is expected that all bids will conform to the style indicated in the RFP and be stated uniformly, so that the manner and modes of expression and other selling terms do not influence the selection process. In addition, bids should concentrate on relevant facts and details of hardware and software.

The Influence of Externalities

Proposals are sales devices for vendors, and as a result, there is the natural tendency to emphasize the strength of one's system and not the weaknesses. Often this tendency is reflected in the preparation of nicely packaged bids, with attractive folders, mulitcolored artwork, and so on. It may also lead to nebulous formulations and oftentimes results in unwarranted attention to irrelevant information. Information that the supplier may use to advance his or her cause might include size and market share of the supplier's organization, quality of hardware and software, experience with similar systems in this country and in the world, or the excellence of the supplier's service, support, and training.

Often the supplier undermines the competition and makes claims of superiority that are unwarranted. Although the value of qualitative information in connection with general characteristics should not be totally discounted, it is to be remembered that such information is basically self-serving and therefore should be placed in proper perspective.

Often bids are accompanied by presentations and demonstrations of the equipment involved. While such demonstrations are helpful, the buyer should beware of attempts to dazzle with externalities and visual effects that distract attention from the more substantive points.

Techniques to Aid in Selection

Proposals may be compared using the following techniques.

Comparative tables

To overcome the adverse influence of externalities, the buyer should prepare comparative tables in which different bids are actually compared against each other, item by item. This assures the buyer that all details thought to be important are objectively assessed with respect to all bids. Generally, the sheer bulk of information dictates preparation of a separate table for each logical field, which is yet another reason for insisting on a uniform format for presentation of bids.

One of many possible methods of classifying fields and items into technical comparison tables is the following (a partial listing):

- Memory
    Suggested size
    Size of memory in existing equipment
    Maximum memory expansion feasible with the hardware offered
    Memory unit and number of bits per unit
    Average number of units per command
    Memory access time

- Connections between memory and peripheral devices
    - Type of connection (channels, BU, PP)
    - Maximum number of channels feasible
    - Number of channels recommended with the configuration suggested
    - Channel characteristics (for each channel separately)
        - Interrupt priority
        - Compatible peripheral devices
        - Devices that can be attached simultaneously
- Slow peripherals
    - Card readers
        - Types
        - Read rate
        - Bin capacity
    - Line printers
        - Types
        - Print rates
        - Line length
        - Fonts available, languages
- Magnetic tapes
    - Types
    - Number of units
    - Read/write rates
    - Density
    - Number of channels and parity
- Magnetic disks
    - Types
    - Number of units
    - Capacity in bytes or characters
    - Number of characters available on line
    - Read/write rates
    - Access time
    - Plate structure
    - Size of block/record
    - Number of read/write heads
    - Availability and compatibility of disks packs
- Other magnetic devices
    - Diskette, cassette, and so on
- Terminals and communications network
    - Characteristics, types, transfer rate, transmission technique, type of lines and their regimes and so on.
- Additional peripherals and communications equipment
    - List of peripherals and telecommunications equipment that can be added and supported later on as well as changes required to accommodate them, such as added memory or channels

Miscellaneous tables

The foregoing examples are certainly not the only methods of comparing data; other tables might be needed according to the type and characteristics of devices required. With respect to software, similar tables should be prepared as follows:

Programming Languages. The supplier should specify the languages to be supplied with the system. For each language, the supplier should give data on the compiler, compilation speed, options and extensions, adherence to standards, memory requirements, and other relevant characteristics.

Service Programs (Utilities). The main utilities (such as sort-merge, file record manager, copy, edit, trace) should be listed. For each supplier, existence of those utilities as well as the main characteristics of added facilities supplied should be indicated.

Operating Systems. The technical description of the operating systems offered should be given in full (e.g., memory requirements, disk requirements, dynamic memory allocation, multiprogramming ability, priorities, communication with the operator, dayfile, catalog, dump and retrieval, and time and manner of installation).

Additional Software. Macro facilities, file management, data-base management, statistical and technological application software, and so on should be listed and described in the manner indicated.

Cost comparison tables

In addition to technical comparison tables, cost comparison tables should be arranged (along the lines given in the RFP) by items of expenditure such as purchase, rent, lease-purchase, maintenance, and other services. Details of the support offered by the supplier should also be listed, such as numbers and qualifications of personnel, training, software updating and support, frequency and duration of supports, and whether cost is included in the price quoted or is to be charged separately.

Timetables

If a supplier proposes to supply part of the equipment later, all the relevant conditions and processes should be carefully noted. Timetables should allow comparison of supply between different suppliers, and all expenditures presented as net present worth. Capital and financing costs for computer acquisition should be handled similarly to those for any other project or investment.

It should be stressed that to arrive at complete and comparable pictures for each supplier, all costs must be supplied, including alternative costs for equipment delayed or support withheld. For instance, if the supplier does not offer programmer support, the cost of hiring alternative programmers should be computed. The same reasoning applies to extra costs specific to a given offer, such as added insurance, special technical features and fixtures, and unusual conversion efforts.

Qualitative tables

A separate table should compare individual bidders in terms of characteristics such as company size, experience with similar equipment in this or other countries, similar installation, support facilities, and comparable applications. As stated, the arrangement of all data into comparison tables allows for a more precise and unbiased analysis in that irrelevant items capable of influencing the judgment of the technical or steering committees will be isolated and eliminated. In addition, the utilization of comparison tables assures that all relevant data are examined and integrated into the decision underlying the selection of the supplier.

Questionnaires as an aid in analysis

Another approach for analyzing a proposed system's capabilities is to include a questionnaire with the RFP. The questionnaire would seek information as to speed, capacity reliability, and capability for the proposed system, enabling the firm to obtain desired and uniform information from each vendor. This also compels vendors to submit information that otherwise might be omitted or withheld.

Analysis of Bids

With the help of clear and complete comparisons tables, the technical committee should be able to make a competent selection and to pass it on to the steering committee for confirmation. There are two approaches: one can select the "best" proposal or one can prepare a short list ranking the potential suppliers. In the second case, a final decision is reached after negotiations with each of the bidders, in the order of their ranking.

Another selection method is to point out the best system for each organizational policy alternative. Thus, if a proposal is obviously inadequate or incomplete, and cannot be fairly compared with the competition, it should be immediately eliminated from consideration. This allows for easier analysis of serious proposals.

THE CONTRACT

Introduction

The following are the principle subjects to be included in the contract. Again, this presentation is meant to be a general one and, as such, is intended to cover wide ranges of equipment contracts.

Equipment and Software

The contract should describe in detail (either in the body or in the appendices) the hardware and software. These components should be clearly identified, because generally similar components can have different characteristics. The description of the components could be given in a table, listing the following for each component:

1. Identification or supplier's catalog number
2. Description and function
3. Model and type
4. Specification or technical document identification (where the characteristics of the component are given in detail)
5. Agreed price of sale, rent, or lease-purchase
6. Maintenance fee, specifying shift and overtime hours
7. Dates of supply and installation
8. Timetable of payments
9. Additional details that may be component specific

The importance of having the characteristics, features, and promised performance of each component of hardware or software specifically set out in a written contract cannot be overstressed.

In addition, there sould be a similarly detailed written statement of the expected capability and performance of the complete system when installed. For instance, it is conceivable that each component offered could satisfy its specification, whereas the system as a whole might not meet expectations as a result of faulty installation, unjudicious juxtaposition of components, or lack of essential items. If the written agreement is complete, there will be no unfortunate surprises on the part of the buyer.

Provision should be made for replacement of equipment or software that becomes obsolete. Obsolescence frequently occurs in the rapidly changing computer field as technological innovation may occur before the equipment is installed. Since the period from time of order to time of delivery is generally long, it is important to anticipate one's needs and to place the orders for new equipment as soon as practical.

If the equipment or any part thereof is used, this should be specified in the contract, as should the length of time and nature of the previous usage. The buyer is certainly entitled to an appropriate adjustment in price in these cases.

There should be an agreement between the buyer and the supplier regarding new software developed by the supplier during the life of the system, to the effect that such new technology will be made available to the buyer at a given time and at a reasonable price.

In addition to prices of equipment, the contract should provide for the payments of other charges involved in handling the hardware, such as taxes, customs charges, dues, packing, handling, hauling, cartage, and overseas freight charges as well as insurance, other fees, and commissions. The details of each payment to be made should be clearly spelled out—that is, how payment is made, to whom payment is made, and who makes the payment. Generally, the problem is handled in either of two ways: (1) the supplier sees to the transportation from source to customer's premises, or (2) the customer is responsible for the transportation. In the latter case, handling costs and other dues need not be mentioned in the agreement. Still, to be helpful, the supplier should give information to the buyer regarding the details involved, especially those details to be handled at the place of origin. Separate provisions should be made for transportation and other costs involved in replacing equipment at any time after installation, in cases of equipment breakdown or equipment substitution.

Supply and Installation Timetable

The contract should contain a detailed timetable for equipment supply and installation. Provision should be made for anticipating supply under certain eventualities as well as for customer-induced delays. Compensation for lost usage or other damages incurred as a result of delayed delivery should be clearly stated. The buyer should also have an option to cancel the agreement and receive compensation in the case of delays beyond a certain stated time limit; these provisions should cover both hardware and software. In cases where the equipment cannot be used because of delays in supplying the software, the loss to the entire system should be considered.

An alternative to renting or purchasing alternative equipment or software from other suppliers in cases of such delays should be integrated into the contract. This option assumes that replacements are compatible with the system. The supplier certainly should be required to compensate the customer for cost and inconvenience of seeking replacements.

There should be a clear statement in the contract of what exactly constitutes "events of force majeure" or "acts of God" that justify deviation from the agreed schedule for which the supplier incurs no liability.

It should be stated in the contract that components that fail their acceptance tests shall be regarded as being delayed, until such time as acceptable components are delivered.

On the other hand, the supplier should be entitled to some compensation for losses caused by customer tardiness (e.g.., in preparing the computer room, its flooring, or utilities). Such losses may be reflected in increased costs of storage, interim rises in prices, or extra handling charges and may be charged to the customer in the contract.

Terms of Acceptance and Usage

Payments due the supplier should be made conditional upon the equipment passing the customer's performance test. To avoid any ambiguity or misunderstanding, provision should be made in the contract for the exact tests that will be performed on the equipment before payment is made.

These tests and inspections should be conducted both at the source and at the buyer's place of business. The supplier should provide adequate evidence of test results conducted at the source, and the buyer, or a representative, should be present, at the supplier place of business during the tests. The system should be accepted only after successful tests have been made and after the system has been in operation for a prescribed period of time.

If the tests are not successful, the contract should provide that the supplier compensates the customer for the loss of usage and time. Provisions similar to those recommended in regard to delays in delivery should be included for replacing faulty equipment or for canceling the contract completely.

As a rule, acceptance trials are not predicated on 100 percent efficiency, since troubles and downtime are normal in computer operation. A threshold of efficiency (e.g., 95 percent) should be set. The remaining percentage are computed as the ratio of downtime to total run time. Unambiguous definitions for these terms should be clearly drafted into the contract.

Costs of repair and replacement during the trial period should be covered by the supplier. If part of the equipment is to be supplied later, separate trials for those components, as well as for the entire configuration when installed, should be conducted. In such cases, rental and maintenance for the part of the system already installed should be conducted.

Another condition to be fulfilled is optimum operation under the environmental conditions prescribed by the supplier, assuming that they have been implemented by the purchaser. If energy requirements (e.g., for air conditioning or for running the system) are higher than those indicated by the supplier, due compensation should be made, either in a cash payment or as deductions from rental and maintenance costs.

During the selection process, the advantages and disadvantages of renting equipment as opposed to purchasing equipment are considered. In the case of rentals, the contract should clearly define "usage hours" for rented hardware, allowing for downtime, as well as repair and maintenance time. A tariff for overtime wage should be effected, and the customer should receive credit for regular hours not utilized. If the parties agree to "carry over" hours from month to month, this should be clearly stated in the contract.

Warranty and Maintenance

A period of perhaps one year should be allowed during which time the vendor is responsible for correcting production defects in the system and/or in individual components. Provision, therefore, should be made in the contract for distinguishing between production defects and those arising from improper usage.

A shorter warranty period of perhaps three months should be stated in the contract during which time the vendor is responsible for providing system maintenance and repairs at no cost, provided that the customer is utilizing the equipment correctly. Of course, the vendor should provide both training and assistance to the customer's personnel with respect to installation and operation of the system to avoid any incorrect usage thereafter.

The supplier's responsibility for maintenance should extend to equipment both new and used, which the customer may add at later stages, and is found to be compatible with the system. Of course, different charges will be made in each case. The vendor should assure that there is available backup for equipment being produced and supplied.

The vendor is responsible for storing the required replacement parts, even after they are no longer in regular production. A maximum repair and supply time should be set, and if the equipment is disabled for a longer period, the supplier should replace the complete component with a new one and compensate the customer for loss of usage.

Maintenance may be provided for in the main agreement or in a separate contract. In the case of rentals, there might be a combined charge for rental plus maintenance. Individual charges should be listed for the repair and maintenance of each separate component and for repairs conducted at different times. For example, the different charges for repairs needed during a regular shift, overtime, late hours, or a special call should be clearly spelled out.

For rented systems, the contract should offer the customer an option to purchase, stating the terms for crediting the customer with all or part of the rental payments. Rental contracts should be for a fixed term and should be renewable according to clearly stated conditions. As a rule, longer contracts are more advantageous for the vendor as they offer both stability and guaranteed rental period. With the present high rate of computer equipment obsolescence that exists, this gives the customer an undoubted advantage. However, it may also result in lower tariffs, unless provision is made for pegging the payments to some index.

If the customer intends to plug in equipment from a separate source, such as a printer from a producer other than that of the mainframe, it should be stated whether the mainframe vendor is responsible for establishing and maintaining the connection between the components within the terms of the contract or whether the vendor is entitled to additional consideration. In any event, the customer is expected to supply the vendor with all relevant information.

Conditions should be set for changes in the system or in its environment at any time during the life of the contract as well as for the eventualities of adding equipment or moving the installation to a different site.

The contract should describe the ancillary equipment to be placed at the customer's disposal during the life of the system (similar to that done for replacement parts), and it should also state whether the customer is entitled to use compatible ancillary equipment from other vendors.

Assistance with Training and Operation

The contract should clearly define the extent to which technical assistance is to be provided by the vendor. For example, the following should be specified:

1. Number of experts needed, their qualifications, and their expected time of service

2. Subjects and activities covered
3. Special fees for the service of an extra number of experts or for a longer time than originally agreed upon
4. Monitoring, supervising, and evaluating experts' work

In addition, the training and operating aids and documentation to be supplied with the system should be described. For example,

1. Technical literature of each component
2. Guides and reference manuals for programmers
3. Guides and operating instructions for operators
4. Items that may be published at a later time by the vendor

The vendor's commitment to provide training to the customer should be spelled out in detail. The contract should make clear whether this training is included in the agreed-upon price, or whether it involves additional payment. On the other hand, rates will be quoted for later courses and extensions as well as for assistance with special tasks and projects.

As stated, the purchase price or rental price includes the use of the equipment for a stated period of time to conduct tests either on the system supplied or on a comparable one. Extra charges should be made if the customer requires use of the equipment for a period of time in excess of that stated.

Legal Considerations

Application software and sophisticated hardware often involve substantial investments of money and effort. If the software and hardware are not developed and delivered as promised, or if vendors do not perform according to standards set in the agreement, it is quite possible that litigation will ensue. Therefore, the user must protect the firm with a comprehensive written agreement. In this way, expensive future misunderstandings can be avoided as the vendor will know exactly what is expected of it by the user. Thus a well-prepared and solidly drafted agreement is the foundation of the development and implementation of a successful installation. As with any investment decision, the acquistion of a data processing system has some unique considerations.

Negotiation of contracts

Problems may occur during the negotiation and drafting of a complex agreement for computer acquisition. The contract should explicitly state everything the user wants. The user should insist on an agreement that clearly spells out the obligations of the vendor in terms of data processing performance, delivery, warranties, responsibilities, penalties, and prices. Provisions should also be included that cover data and coding security, copyright, and availability of software to other users. In the event that the vendor breaches the agreement, the user can exercise any remedies available.

Both hardware and software specifications should be described in the contract.

Software acquisition

If software is to be acquired, the user should take certain precautions to protect the firm's interests. The contract should spell out the costs and personnel required as well as the level of quality to be produced. If the software does not perform as promised or is not delivered on time, the result can seriously affect the company's operations. A meticulously detailed written contract can therefore minimize the inherent risks.

Software ownership

Ownership of programs should be defined in the text of the agreement. For example, if the user is the owner of any software that has been developed, the user then has legal remedies available if a question of ownership arises or in the event that the vendor breaches the agreement.

Hardware acquisition

The agreement should clearly define the obligations in terms of hardware performance. If the hardware does not perform in accordance with specifications, the user firm will be able to avail itself of legal remedies. Warranties should also be specified and penalties for delivery delays should be listed.

Protection of proprietary software

At present, software is protected by copyright laws or by the concept of confidentiality of trade secrets. Therefore, unless adequate safeguards are incorporated in the contract, either party may find itself in breach of contract, either for infringing upon the other's copyright instructions or for using the software in non-permissible manner.

The contract therefore should include a provision to protect the business secrets and proprietary rights of both parties. This provision should cover disclosures both of equipment or software characteristics and descriptions of the customer's applications. Specific sanctions should be drafted into the contract, and such provision should be effective even upon termination of the relationship.

As the user may incur financial liability in the event of a breach of confidentiality, the user should ensure that the commitments in the contract are realistic.

Documentation

Documentation should be maintained in the form of correspondence and memos throughout the development of the system. In the event that the vendor breaches the agreement, a well-documented history can help to resolve any dispute.

Conclusion

This section contained a general discussion of the items to be included in the contract. In essence, it does not claim to be more than a general checklist. As each vendor-customer relationship is different, however, the language to be contained in the contract must be tailored to the specific situation. The contract is the end product of extensive negotiations that will find expression in the terms finally agreed upon.

The principle that should be firmly kept in mind, however, is that a contract is only good insofar as it is explicit and reduces the need for litigation. Therefore, important points should not be left open, and to the extent possible, every detail should be reduced to writing; there should be no reliance on oral representations. In the absence of clearly defined requirements or obligations, the danger that misunderstandings will occur and litigation will result is increased.

SELECTED READINGS

AUER, JOSEPH, AND JOHN SCOGGINS. "Contracting for EDP Maximum Protection at Minimum Cost—Are You Getting What You Are Paying For?" *Governmental Finance,* Vol. 6, no. 3 (August 1977).

———, AND CHARLES EDISON HARRIS. "Negotiating Computer Contracts Effectively." *Infosystem,* Vol. 25, no. 4 (April 1978).

BELL, THOMAS E. "Twenty-one Money-Saving Questions." *Financial Executive,* Vol. 45, no. 12 (December 1977).

BERLINER, THOMAS H. "Early to Bid—Evaluating Computer Procurement Proposals." *Computer Decisions,* Vol. 7, no. 11 (November 1975).

BOROVITS, ISRAEL. "Computer Selection and Acquistion." *Data Processing Journal,* Vol. 17, no. 2 (March–April 1975).

———, AND SEEV NEUMANN. *Computer System Performance Evaluation.* Lexington, Mass.: Lexington Books, 1979.

BURSTYN, H. PARIS. "Maslow's Laws Guide Computer Negotiation." *Minicomputer News,* April 27, 1978.

"Buying EDP Intangibles: A Guide to Software Acquistion." *Modern Office Procedures,* Vol. 23, no. 9 (September 1978).

CHENEY, PAUL H. "Selecting, Acquiring, and Coping with Your First Computer." *Journal of Small Business Management,* Vol. 17, no. 1 (January 1979).

CORTADA, JAMES W. *EDP Costs and Charges.* Englewood Cliffs, N.J.: Prentice-Hall, 1980.

"Don't 'Get Taken' When Negotiating Computer Contracts." *Savings and Loan News,* Vol. 98, no. 10 (October 1977).

FREED, ROY N. "Computer Contracting Is Changing for the Better." *Computer Decisions,* Vol. 2, no. 6 (June 1976).

———. "Unhappy Computer Users Have Themselves to Blame." *Infosystem,* Vol. 26, no. 2 (February 1979).

HOUSLEY, T. J. "Saving Money on Computer Contract Negotiations." *Modern Office and Data Management,* Vol. 18, no. 4 (May 1979).

HYMAN, JOAN PREVETE. "How to Negotiate a Computer Contract You Can Live With." *Bank Systems and Equipment,* Vol. 15, no. 10 (October 1978).

HYNES, CECIL V. "Taking a Look at the Request for Proposals." *Defense Management Journal,* Vol. 13, no. 4 (October 1977).

KIRCHNER, JAKE. "DP Contract Litigation Viewed as Booming Area." *Computerworld,* November 6, 1978.

"Newsletter Offers Tips on Software Contracts." *Computerworld,* July 16, 1979.

PHILIPPAKIS, A. S., and PETER J. MILLER. "Requesting Quotations on a Minicomputer." *The Office,* Vol. 85, no. 2 (February 1977).

REPS, DAVID. "Sort DP Proposals with This Input/Ouput Cost Matrix." *Hospital Financial Management,* Vol. 31, no. 1 (January 1977).

SCANNEL, TIM. "Be Specific, Guide to Contracts Advise." *Computerworld,* December 5, 1977.

———. "Users Alerted to Vendors? Negotiating Tactics." *Computerworld,* January 30, 1978.

———. "User Should Anticipate Trouble in Vendor Contract." *Computerworld,* April 16, 1979.

SCHULTZ, BRAD. "Architecture-Specific RFPs Most Competitive?" *Computerworld,* September 18, 1978.

SHIDAL, JERRY G. "Preparing an Objective RFP." *Journal of Systems Management,* Vol. 30, no. 2 (February 1979).

TAYLOR, ALAN. "The Arbitration Clause: Whom Does It Benefit?" *Computerworld,* Vol. 12, no. 31 (July 1978).

TUFFIN, ROGER. "Buying a Computer—Advice for the Practitioner." *Accountancy,* Vol. 90, no. 1028 (April 1979).

WEIDMAN, DONALD R. "Writing Better RFP: Ten Hints for Obtaining More Successful Evaluation Studies." *Public Administrative Review,* Vol. 37, no. 6 (November–December 1977).

WHITTED, GARY. "Evaluating the Real Cost of EDP Proposals." *Hospital Financial Management,* Vol. 33, no. 1 (January 1979).

2

Hardware Evaluation and Selection

INTRODUCTION

The computer evaluation and selection process has become a complex one, requiring very detailed analyses; there are many technical and nontechnical options to be considered. This chapter discusses the considerations to be made during the configuration, selection, and procurement phases of the acquisition process.

The analysis and decision process of computer selection and acquisition can be categorized into eight phases, consisting of [1]

1. Exploration in which the requirements are compiled and quantitative benefits are determined
2. Analysis of the present data processing system
3. Detailed analysis of the proposed new system
4. Determination of the specific system configuration
5. Decision of method of selection
6. Determination of fixed and variable costs
7. Analysis of the results
8. Presentation of the recommendations to management

This chapter deals with phases 4 through 7 of the analysis and decision process, that is, the processes of computer configuration, selection, and procurement.

[1] I. Borovits, "Computer Selection and Acquisition," *Data Processing Journal*, Vol. 17, no. 2 (1975), pp. 98–100.

PROPOSAL EVALUATION TECHNIQUES

Preliminary Decisions

Prior to entering the configuration phase of computer acquisition, management should decide on two issues; type of selection and the use of outside assistance.
     The alternatives in the issue of type of selection are competitive selection or single-vendor selection. Competitive selection has the advantage over a single-vendor selection in that the former provides a better opportunity to match the acquired system with the proposed system requirements at a lower cost of procurement. The number of vendors solicited obviously impacts the evaluation time and effort. A frequently employed approach is first to survey the market and then to solicit responses from a small number of vendors (i.e., three to five). Single-vendor selection has the advantage of allowing for lower expenditures during the selection phase and the postprocurement conversion phase, assuming that the vendor was the source of the present system. Single-vendor selection is recommended only when the proposed system is small and functionally limited or when conversion costs are prohibitive.
     When procuring a large system, use of outside assistance is required for organizations having little experience with computer systems or little experience in dealing with vendors. There are a number of sources for outside assistance, for example, independent consultants, management consultant firms, and software houses.

Selection Criteria

The limitations to be imposed on the system to be selected, which are to be defined during the system study, are of two types: mandatory and desirable. The mandatory requirements are those items that are essential to the implementation of the organization's needs. The other type includes all the requirements that are desirable but not necessary. The criteria to be used for selection of the computer system should be clearly stated in the RFP. The selection criteria should include, at a minimum, the following items:

- Hardware capacity and performance
- Software performance
- Vendor support and viability
- Application software availability
- Costs (development, installation, and operation)
- Configuration flexibility and expansion capability
- Compatability with the present computer system
- Delivery date
- Documentation available

Due to its complexity, special attention should be given to the method of hardware and software capacity and performance evaluation. Two basic tools can be used for this evaluation: published reports and performance evaluation techniques.

Published evaluation reports[2] present characteristics of computer hardware, such as cycle time, memory access speed, word size, and I/0 transfer bandwidths. These data, however, are not sufficient for comparing computer performance and capacity, since there is no accommodation for differences in operating system efficiencies. Attempts have been made to quantify the number of operations per second under normal processing conditions. However the source of these data, known as mega operations per second (MOPS) or kilo operations per second (KOPS), is usually the vendors themselves. This, coupled with the lack of standard with respect to what conditions comprise a normal processing environment, suggests that an additional tool is required for capacity and performance evaluation.

Evaluation of computer systems can be also determined by the employment of computer performance evaluation (CPE) tools. The use of test programs for capacity and performance evaluation should be clearly delineated in the RFP to let vendors know that a reasonable facsimile of any proposed system must be available for testing. The CPE tools are discussed in Chapter Six.

Cost

The determination of costs is the first step in the analysis of the vendor proposal resulting from issuing the RFP. Costs can be structured into two categories: one-time and recurring. The following may be used as a checklist of the one-time costs:

1. Physical site preparation.
   Air conditioning (cooling, heating, and humidity control).
   Electrical power requirements (including all wiring).
   Fire protection equipment.
   Computer room furniture and fixtures, storage equipment, and floor changes.
   Provisions for computer room security.
2. Hardware-related considerations.
   Charges for removal and packing of installed equipment.
   Transportation and local cartage of new and old equipment.
   Installation charges for new equipment.
   Additional disk packs and tapes. Those initially required should be identified.

---

[2]For example, see *Auerback Reports,* issued by Auerbach Publishers, Philadelphia, Pa., and *Datapro 80* issued by Datapro Research Corp., Delran, N.J.

Investment tax credit. If equipment is purchased, the appropriate ITC should be considered and specifically requested in the contract. Some vendors pass along the ITC on rental equipment. Each vendor must specify what equipment qualifies and the appropriate ITC for each component. Assurance of obtaining qualified equipment at the time of order is a proper consideration for inclusion in the final contract negotiation.

Sales tax. For purchased equipment, this will be one-time charge. For rental system, it will be recurring.

3. Conversion costs. There may be a wide variance in the conversion costs among vendors. Depending on the compatability of the installed vendor's product line, there may be less effort in upgrading to his or her recommended configuration. Generally the installed vendor has an edge in this area. Other considerations that impact conversion costs are the amount and quality of available software and hardware conversion aids.

4. Education and training expenses for each vendor.

Training classes, travel, and expenses for management, operators, programmers, and user personnel.

In-house training including preparation of training materials and costs for machine time.

5. Data conversion costs.

Programmer time for special file conversion programs.

Machine time necessary for file conversion and. reconciliation.

Data-entry preparation time, manual file clean-up, keypunch or data transcription time, and machine rental of transcription devices used solely for conversion purposes.

6. Program conversion costs.

Programmer time.

Machine time, less applicable vendor test allowance, current system, outside machine time, and dual-systems installation.

Required documentation changes. Depending on the amount of existing documentation and the extent of changes required for conversion, this often overlooked cost could be substantial.

7. Purchase-lease software conversion aids.

Program acquisition expense.

Required machine and people time to install.

8. Personnel costs not considered eleswhere.

Overtime.

Hiring costs for additional people.

The following is a similar checklist for recurring costs:

1. Personnel related

Salaries and wages

Other payroll costs

Travel, education, and entertainment

2. Supplies and services
    Operating supplies (such as tapes, paper, and cards)
    Purchased services
3. Equipment related
    Depreciation
    Maintenance
    Hardware rental lease
    Software
4. Facilities related
    Building depreciation, rent
    Utilities
    Telephone and telex
    Taxes (all except payroll taxes) and insurance
5. Miscellaneous
    Corporate overhead allocations
    Indirect cost for space used
    Other expenses

Analysis and Evaluation

There are several methods for evaluating computer systems. These methods employ an analysis of the vendors' proposals, resulting in a ranking of the proposed computer systems from most desirable to least desirable. Following this ranking, a hardware performance and capability analysis should be performed on the most desirable computer system. If this system fails to perform adequately, it is rejected and a performance analysis is performed on the second most desirable system.

The most commonly used computer system evaluation methods are as follows.

Weighted scoring technique

A commonly used approach is the weighted scoring technique, [3] where an attempt is made to combine objectivity with consideration of apparently non-quantifiable factors. To overcome this problem, relative weights are preassigned to all items considered important. During the evaluation process, each competing system is subjectively rated with respect to each item (a score is assigned to each item for each vendor), and then the overall score for each proposed system is computed. The rating is on a subjective basis, with the lowest rating (for example, zero) corresponding to "no good" and the higher rating (for example, 1) corresponding to "entirely adequate." The score for each system is computed as follows:

[3]William F. Sharpe, *The Economics of Computers* (New York: Columbia University Press, 1969).

$$S = \sum_{i=1}^{n} W_i S_i$$

where: $\sum_{i=1}^{n} W_i = 1$
W_i = relative weight of item i
S_i = score assigned to item i
S = overall score of a system

The system earning the higher score is considered the more desirable. The prime advantage of this approach to selection is that it imposes completeness and requires a thorough understanding of the proposed systems. The prime shortcoming of this technique is that the relative values chosen are subjective values and there is no common denominator among the items being weighted. In other words, the relationship between an evaluation item and its relative value cannot be justified.

Cost-effectiveness ratio

The cost-effectiveness technique is simply a subcategory of the weighted scoring technique, except that with it, the total cost of a computer system is divided by the sum of its points.[4] The system having the lowest ratio is considered the most desirable. To employ this method properly, there are no points preassigned to cost.

Cost-value technique

This technique uses cost as the sole basic measure.[5] Under the cost-value technique, dollar values representing estimated cost-savings benefits are assigned to the desirable features of each proposed computer system. Mandatory features are not assigned dollar values. The summation of these assigned values is then subtracted from the total cost of the system. The resulting amount represents the cost of the system to meet the mandatory requirements. The system with the least mandatory requirements cost is the most desirable. The cost-value technique requires a complete understanding of the proposed system, which may be viewed as an advantage.

Requirement-costing technique

The requirement-costing technique differs from the cost-value technique in that in the former, estimated cost-savings benefits are assigned to a preselected set of desirable features, Those amounts corresponding to desirable features not part of a proposed system are then added to the total cost of that system. In addition, if a desirable feature is offered at an additional cost that is less than the estimated benefit, an amount equivalent to the additinal cost is added to the system cost. The system with the lowest resulting cost is considered the most desirable.

[4]E. O. Joslin, *Computer Selection* (Arlington, Va.: The Technology Press, 1977).
[5]Ibid.

Dynamic approach

The dynamic approach[6] employs the projected work load growth trend and the cost-effectiveness ratios of each vendor's proposed product line. This method assumes that it is feasible to install a system for as little as one year, provided that it will be replaced by a compatible system from the same manufacturer's product line and that a replacement will occur when dictated by the work load. Using the projected work load growth trend and measurement of system capacity, a schedule of replacement is developed. The cost of each system as determined by one of the methods previously discussed over its period of employment is then discounted with respect to an estimate of cost of capital and its scheduled future time of employment. The product line with the lowest discounted present cost is the most desirable. This method is equally valid for both rental and purchase.

To illustrate the use of this method, assume that three proposals from three vendors have been received, as exhibited in Table 2.1. Vendor A proposes two systems, and vendors B and C propose three systems each.

As part of the evaluation process, a benchmark is run on all systems proposed to determine their capacities. Then a relative performance, as compared with system A1 (as a multiple of A1) is computed for each of the systems. The results of these computations are presented in Table 2.2.

The next step in using the dynamic approach, is to compute the capacity per

TABLE 2.1 PROPOSALS SUBMITTED
AND THEIR COSTS—AN EXAMPLE

	Systems		
Vendor	1	2	3
A	$80	$120	—
B	90	110	$140
C	120	160	170

Note: Vendor A has submitted proposals for only two systems.

TABLE 2.2 CAPACITY OF
SYSTEMS RELATIVE TO SYSTEM A1

	System		
Vendor	1	2	3
A	1.0	1.5	—
B	1.2	1.8	2.3
C	1.6	2.2	2.5

[6]Phillip Ein-Dor, "A Dynamic Approach to Selecting Computers," *Datamation* (June 1973), p. 104.

dollar outlay by dividing the relative capacities by the costs of the systems. The results are shown in Table 2.3.

Then a forecast of the work load for a planning horizon of six years is prepared as well as the growth path for each proposed series of systems. The forecast of the work load and the systems growth paths are then compared, as illustrated in Figure 2.1. The systems whose capacities exceed the forecast work load are the candidates for selection.

The system, among these candidates, with the lowest cost becomes the logical choice. In our example, the optimal choice is vendor B's proposal, which not only exceeds the capacity requirements but also has the lowest cost. The same procedure may be used if the equipment is to be leased or rented. The only difference is that we will have to use the discounted cash flow based on the anticipated cost capital.

Although cost and capacity are the only criteria used here, they are by no means the only criteria for selection. Other criteria, as mentioned before, may be just as important. However, as the amount of dollars involved is usually large, and capacity is a paramount factor in peak load conditions, cost and capacity are definitely two of the most important criteria in equipment selection.

TABLE 2.3 CAPACITY PER
DOLLAR OUTLAY

	System		
Vendor	1	2	3
A	1.25	1.25	—
B	1.33	1.63	1.65
C	1.33	1.38	1.47

Present value analysis

The objective is to determine which system will cost the least and benefit the organization the most[7]. The net present value of the proposed system should be determined by discounting all cash flows associated with it, using the organization's cost of capital as the discount rate. The benefits projected by the new proposed system are the net cash inflows. The process employed under the net present value analysis is expressed by the equation:

$$NPV = \frac{S_n - (S_n - BV_n)T}{(1+K)^n} - P + \sum_{t=1}^{n} \frac{(R_t - C_t)(1-T) + D_t T}{(1+K)^t}$$

where: NPV = the net present value
R_t = the added gross revenue generated from the system
C_t = the added cost of operating the system

[7]R. L. Roenfelt and R. A. Fleck, "How Much Does a Computer Really Cost?" *Computer Decisions*, Vol. 8, no. 2 (November 1976), p. 77.

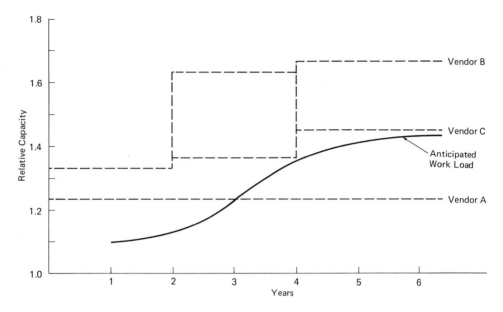

Figure 2.1 Anticipated Work Load and Growth Path for Each of the Proposed Systems

T = the company's tax rate
D_t = the depreciation
t = the accounting period
n = the number of accounting periods over which the system will be useful
S_n = the salvage value
BV_n = the book value
P = the initial purchase cost
K = the company's cost of capital

The system with the highest net present value is the most desirable.

WORK LOAD DEFINITION

One of the most important functions of the system specification is to describe the type and the amount of work load to be run on the new system. Once the work load is defined, performance measurement tools may be used to determine the degree to which the proposed system meets these expectations. It is, therefore, essential that the work load will be representative for the evaluation process to be significant. A good work load description should serve three important functions:

1. It should help the vendor to determine the correct hardware configuration and software to satisfy the requirements.
2. It should facilitate the verification of the proposed system as to its ability to handle the work load.
3. It should permit realistic costing of the proposed system.

Generally, the work load of a specific system does not fluctuate over time, and, therefore, the work load has some statistical properties that make it possible to characterize the work load by distribution of demands made on individual system resources. Once a unit of work is defined, the work load is expressed as a function of these units.

The projected work load can be used as the basis for the proposed system during the evaluation experiments. Once a good work load is defined, a benchmark (to be discussed shortly) may be used as one of the tools in the evaluation of the proposed systems.

The work load to be processed by the system is expected to increase over time. Therefore, the work load may consist of a number of levels, present level and projected growth. Using a probability theory, a sensitivity analysis may be performed.

BENCHMARK

Introduction

Several methods for evaluation of computer systems have been discussed. Among all the existing methods, benchmark is the most commonly used, the most applicable, and the most preferred. A good definition of a benchmark has been given by Joslin:

> A "Benchmark Mix Validation Demonstration" consists of a user witnessed running of a group (mix) of representative programs on a vendor's bid computer system to validate the vendor's claimed thruput time regarding the abilities of the hardware and software to handle the workload of procuring activity in the order and languages in which the actual programs are likely to be processed.[8]

Thus, the benchmark is a set of programs run together as representation of the expected work load. Originally, the term meant a single program run to test the computer system. But today, with multiprogramming and multiprocessing, running of a single program will tell us very little. The benchmark is a quantitative method of evaluation, and if it is prepared carefully and analyzed correctly, the results may be significant.

The Purpose of the Benchmark

The first purpose of the benchmark is to eliminate the possibility of an "undersell." Even the knowledge that part of the evaluation process will include a benchmark requires vendors to be more careful in preparing their proposals. Another objective of the benchmark is to test the configuration to see if it is capable of executing the expected work load.

[8]E. O. Joslin, "Guidelines for Benchmarking," in E. O. Joslin, ed., *Analysis and Selection of Computer Systems (Readings)* (Arlington, Va.: College Readings, 1974), p. 157.

The Representative Benchmark

Jobs should be selected from the real work load. These jobs should be "typical" (a subjective term) of the environment in which the new system is to be installed. Using the known characteristics of these programs, a benchmark is constructed with a distribution function similar to the distribution function characterizing the real work load. This is done by clustering the work load into groups; then a distribution function may be defined. The representative benchmark is constructed with the same clusters in the same proportions. Some programs have to be reproduced to achieve the correct mix. Some clusters cannot be represented, and new programs may be developed to fit a place in the distribution. There may be situations in which synthetic programs have to be used to create or increase the percentage of one or more of the characteristics.

Vendor Modifications

The representative benchmark is given to the vendor for conversion so it can run on the vendor's proposed system. Some changes may have to be made in the programs to allow for language implementation and hardware differences, but these changes should be kept to a minimum. All changes must be approved by the customer.

Exact Environment

As mentioned previously, the benchmark should run on the same hardware and software configuration that is proposed by the vendor. Normally no substitutions should be accepted. Since, in many cases, vendors do not construct the system with exact configurations, it is important to modify the results of the benchmark to guarantee correct evaluation.

Constructing the Benchmark

The benchmark cannot test every item; therefore, the representative benchmark should represent the work load and the qualitative and quantitative characteristics. Qualitative representation may include (1) use of certain methods of file organization, (2) use of certain sorting and merging techniques, (3) inclusion of jobs with large input-output, and (4) use of data base techniques. Quantitative representation of expected loads on the system may include (1) number of input records of all types (cards, magnetic tape, optical reading, etc.), (2) number of output records (such as lines to be printed, records to be written on magnetic media, etc.), and (3) CPU time.

The importance of the benchmark method is obvious, but a consistent method of constructing a benchmark is yet to be developed. The difficulties in constructing a benchmark are summarized by Joslin:

In selecting programs that are representative, it is essential to obtain programs that are representative of the types of processing, . . . the equipment and storage usage, the language used and any necessary order of sequence.[9]

Ahituv, Borovits, and Neumann[10] have proposed the use of an integer programming technique to help in selecting the job mix for running a benchmark. The model suggested is

$$\min X_1 + X_2 + \cdots + X_n$$

$$\text{Subject to:} \quad A_{11} X_1 + \cdots + A_{1n} X_n \geqslant B_1$$

$$\begin{array}{cc} \cdot & \cdot \\ \cdot & \cdot \\ \cdot & \cdot \end{array}$$

$$A_{m1} X_1 + \cdots + A_{mn} X_n \geqslant B_m$$

$$X_j \geqslant 0 \quad X_j \text{ integers}$$

where: X_j = the number of runs of program j in the process of running the benchmark test

B_i = the load variables; for example, B_1 = load of lines to be printed and B_2 = the amount of disk readings/writings

m = number of representative load variables

n = number of programs from which the programs to construct the benchmark are selected

A_{ij} = for each program j, there is a load A_{ij} of a certain type i
$(i = 1, \ldots, m \quad j = 1, \ldots, n)$

The interpretation of the decision variables, X_j, is as follows:

run program 1 X_1 times
run program 2 X_2 times

$$\begin{array}{c} \cdot \\ \cdot \\ \cdot \end{array}$$

run program n X_n times

Using this approach to construct a benchmark, the quantitative representation of the required load and the qualitative representation of the required characteristics are obtained. Also in using this model, the number of programs participating in the benchmark is minimized. Therefore, economical allocation of users' resources, as well as those of the vendors, is obtained.

If the user wants to decrease the cost of the benchmark, it is possible to add the cost of running each program to the objective function by multiplying the vector X by the prices pertinent to each of the programs and then to require

[9]E. O. Joslin, "Techniques of Selection EDP Equipment," *Journal of Data Management,* Vol. 8, no. 2 (February 1970), p. 29.

[10]N. Ahituv, I. Borovits, and S. Neumann, "Selecting a Job Mix for Running a Benchmark by Using an Integer Programming Model," *Computers and Operations Research,* Vol. 5, no. 1 (1978), pp. 73–79.

minimization of the total cost. In this case, the objective function will have the following form:

$$\min C_1 X_1 + C_2 X_2 + \cdots + C_n X_n$$

where C_i is the cost of running program i. This cost may include the cost of preparing the program, conversion costs, and so on.

METHODS FOR PROCURING COMPUTER SYSTEMS

Equipment-related costs are based on the manner in which the computer system is procured. The most common procurement plans are rent, purchase, and lease.

Rental

Under the rental agreement, the user is liable for a prepaid fixed minimum payment. The agreement can be terminated by a minimum of number of days (usually 90 days) prior notice. Under this agreement, the risk of ownership remains with the vendor. The renter has no obligation for such expenses as insurance and maintenance; however, the renter is responsible for paying any taxes that might be levied on the rental contract by the state or local government. Extra shift use, over and above the standard monthly base hours, also represent an additional cost to the user. The investment tax credit can be passed on to the renter.

Advantages of renting

- Requires least amount of commitment and has greatest degree of flexibility to change equipment and/or modification
- Is useful in a dynamic environment where the future cannot reasonably be determined
- Is easier to finance, with full tax credit available
- Does not pose problem of obsolescence
- Assures better vendor service, since computer is still vendor owned

Disadvantages of renting

- Is most expensive option available
- Is more difficult to find vendors or third parties willing to enter into such arrangements
- Provides little security to data processing operations (equipment might be removed)
- Does not provide the prestige that accompanies ownership

Lease

Leasing, in the context of computer use, usually means an operating lease, with ownership of the computer system retained by the vendor. The lessee pays a predetermined monthly price for the use of the computer for mutually agreed period of time. The length of the lease is very important in its effect on the rate. Since the leases that are proposed by the vendors are usually short term, the following discussion will concern itself with short-term leases.

Advantages of leasing

- Is less expensive than rental
- Requires a shorter commitment than that for purchase
- Has little risk of obsolescence
- Involves level and predetermined payments
- Reduces risk of being oversold by a vendor
- Does not require working capital
- Assures better servicing by a vendor who owns the equipment
- Reduces risk in relying on residual values

Disadvantages of leasing

- Is not always the least expensive way to acquire computer access
- Has expensible cash flow; firm cannot take advantage of borrowing or use of capital
- May lead data processing management to select a small machine since it will be replaced in the future

Purchase

When a computer system is purchased, ownership of it is acquired and its use is unlimited. Maintenance and service of the computer are contracted for separately with the vendor. With respect to taxes, the user may depreciate the purchased computer system as is done with any other item of capital equipment. Any operation of the system beyond the break-even point can be constituted as pure profit to the owner, if the value of expense is disregarded.

Advantages of purchasing

- Has lower cost over long term in comparison with rental or leases
- Provides residual value to the owner
- Involves no extra shift in rental or lease charges; thus cash overflow is controlled

• Represents solid investment
• Represents flexible acquisition cost
• Can be capitalized and amortized over time
• Can take full investment tax credit (ITC)
• Fulfills pride of ownership needs

Disadvantages of purchasing

• Usually involves the greatest (longest) commitment
• Requires a solid understanding of your company's future data processing needs
• Involves certain amount of risk in residual values (for resale purposes)
• Limits expansion flexibility somewhat
• Lacks purchaser leverage to apply pressure for better vendor service or other support

Summary of the Economic Factors

The principal cost elements of the alternate methods are as follows:

1. Rental
    Rental payments
    Overtime payments for use in excess of a stated amount (usually time)
    Passthrough of the investment tax

2. Leasing
    Monthly lease payments (and no overtime)
    Maintenance (which may or may not be separately stated)
    Full ITC (investment tax credit)

3. Purchase
    Initial purchase cost
    Cost of money
    Maintenance (except for warranty period)
    Insurance
    Residual value
    Full ITC
    Depreciation tax advantage

4. Installment purchase
    Same as purchase except for interest cost paid to manufacturer

All other burdens of ownership, such as property tax, sales tax, and the like are generally comparable.

Analysis of the Purchase Option of Computers

Ahituv and Borovits[11] suggest that in the process of computer selection, the economic analysis should deal basically with three alternatives of computer systems acquisition: purchase, rent, and leasing. One option that is usually omitted is the purchase option.

The purchase option is given by the vendor to the customer who rents the equipment but who may wish to purchase it at a later date. If the customer decides to purchase the system, a certain percentage of the rental payments that have already been paid will be deducted from the purchase price.

Possible reasons for considering this option might be (1) changes in the economic life of the equipment, (2) change in the monthly rental price, (3) a change in the current purchase price, or (4) a change in the interest rate. Under any of these conditions, the customer may continue the rental contract or exercise the purchase option.

The purchase option

The customer has an option to purchase the computer system after a period in which the computer was rented. The purchase price consists of the current price, less the rent paid up to the present time, multiplied by a certain percentage that is determined for each component of the system. This can be illustrated as follows:

Let

R = monthly rental price
C = purchase price
d = accumulation percentage toward purchase price

Then C'; the amount of money the customer has to pay if exercising the purchase option after m rental months, is:[12]

$$C' = C - (R \cdot m \cdot d)$$

An Example. When the purchase-to-rent ratio is 1:48, we may use the following data for illustration: $R = \$1$, $C = \$48$, $D = 60\%$, and $m = 20$. Then the purchase price using this option will be

$$C' = 48 - (1)\,(20)\,(0.6) = \$36$$

Usually two constraints are imposed by the vendors: (1) the total accumulated months cannot exceed m months, or (2) the total price reduction cannot

---

[11]N. Ahituv and I. Borovits, "Analysis of the Purchase Option of Computers," *The Computer Journal,* Vol. 21, no. 2 (1978).

[12]If the rental price is not constant for the whole relevant period, the correct formula should be

$$C' = C - d \sum_{i=1}^{m} R_i$$

where R_i is the rental price paid at month i.

exceed P percent of the price of the equipment at the time of exercising the purchase option.

The two constraints given are interdependent and may be presented as follows:

$$C' = C - (m \cdot d \cdot R) \geqslant P \cdot C \quad \text{or}$$
$$C (1-P) \geqslant m \cdot R \cdot d \quad \text{or}$$
$$\frac{C (1-P)}{R \cdot d} \geqslant m$$

In other words, the customer is permitted to use the purchase option within m months or $C (1-P)/(R \cdot d)$ months, whichever is smaller.

To compute the cost of exercising the purchase option after m months, the following equation may be used:

$$\begin{aligned} C_0(m) &= C + C_R(m) - d \cdot C_R(m) \\ &= C + C_R(m) \cdot (1-d) \\ &= C + R \cdot M \cdot (1-d) \end{aligned}$$

where $C_R(m) = R \cdot m$ represents the total rental cost paid.

Substituting M, the economic life of the computer, indicates the maximum number of months for which the purchase option is economical:

$$C_R(M) \geqslant C + R \cdot m \cdot (1-d)$$
$$R \cdot M \geqslant C + R \cdot m \cdot (1-d)$$

which yields

$$\frac{(R \cdot M) - C}{R (1-d)} \geqslant m$$

Using the data from the previous example, for $M = 60$,

$$m \leqslant \frac{(1)(60 - 48)}{(1)(1 - 0.6)} = 30 \text{ months}$$

which means that it is economically correct to exercise this option up to 30 months of rent.

From the preceding equation we can see that when the interest rate equals zero, the purchase option is not economical if the expected life of the equipment is less than or equal to the purchase to rent ratio. In other words, exercising the purchase option is economical only when the purchase alternative was economical initially.

If the interest rate, I is incorporated into our calculations, the cost of exercising the purchase option in month m is

$$C_0(m, I) = \sum_{j=0}^{m-1} \frac{R}{(1+I)^i} + \frac{C - d \cdot m \cdot R}{(1+I)^M}$$

where

$$C_R(m,I) = \sum_{j=0}^{m-1} \frac{R}{(1+I)^j}$$

is the total discounted rental cash flow.

The break-even point for m can now be obtained, as was done before.

Ahituv and Borovits[13] suggest that the feasibility of exercising the purchase option increases with the increase in the accumulation percentage and it definitely increases with the increase in the interest rate. They also suggest that the later the date of exercising the purchase option, the less economical this option is. The value of the purchase option is not affected by the value of the economic life cycle of the equipment. However, the net present value of the rent option increases as the life cycle increases. Exercising the puchase option becomes less economical as the purchase cost of the equipment increases.

The Financial Analysis

The financial analysis of the various options is similar to the analysis that is done for any other investment by the organization. It is important, however, to understand the effects that the analysis may have on budgets, income statement expenses, cash flow, balance sheet, and cumulative discounted cash flow. The concept of present value used is based on the mathematics of compound interest. The evaluation of a capital investment is determining the value of these future cash flows. When evaluating investments, income taxes must always be considered. The income tax rate is applied to total expenses, which include depreciation (a deductible expense for tax calculation purposes). When replacing a computer system or a component, there may be immediate savings in income taxes if the old equipment being scrapped has a book value. This immediate reduction in income taxes is offset by the fact that future tax savings are given up. When a tax loss is taken from scrapping the equipment, the advantage is only one of timing. The advantage is an immediate tax reduction in place of one in the future. If the old computer is sold, the basic calculations are exactly the same as when the equipment is scrapped. In both cases, the after-tax cash flows should be computed.

When purchasing a new computer system or a new component, the organization is allowed to reduce its income tax for the year in which the purchase was made by some amount; this is called an investment tax credit. The amount to be deducted is a percentage, regulated by the Internal Revenue Service, of the total investment. Therefore, when evaluating the method of finance, it is necessary to reduce the cost of the project by the amount of the expected investment tax credit.

To illustrate these effects and the analysis procedure, an example is presented.

---

[13]Ahituv and Borovits, "Analysis of the Purchase Option of Computers," p. 108.

An Example. The data used (for simplification, the numbers are based on the common purchase-to-rent ratio) for the sample case are as follows:

- Monthly rent, $1.00
- Purchase price, $48.00
- Maintenance cost, $.10 per month
- Warranty, 12 months

TABLE 2.4 ESTIMATED CASH FLOW IF COMPUTER IS PURCHASED

	Year					
	1	2	3	4	5	6
Cash outflow before taxes						
Principal	7.90	8.90	10.03	11.31	12.74	0.00
Interest (TAX)	5.68	4.68	3.55	2.27	0.84	0.00
Total installment	13.58	13.58	13.58	13.58	13.58	0.00
Maintenance (TAX)	0.00	1.27	1.27	1.27	1.27	1.27
Insurance (TAX)	0.02	0.02	0.02	0.02	0.02	0.02
Resale (TAX)	0.00	0.00	0.00	0.00	0.00	0.00
Total cash flow	13.58	14.87	14.87	14.87	14.87	1.29
Cumulative TC	13.58	28.45	43.32	58.19	73.06	74.35
Tax calculations						
Deductible expenses						
Tax depreciation	9.60	9.60	9.60	9.60	9.60	0.00
Deductible expense	5.70	5.97	4.84	3.56	2.13	1.29
Total expenses	15.30	15.57	14.44	13.16	11.73	1.29
Tax deduction	7.90	8.04	7.45	6.79	6.05	0.66
ITC (TC)	4.80	0.00	0.00	0.00	0.00	0.00
Tax effect	12.70	8.04	7.45	6.79	6.05	0.66
Cash outflow after Taxes						
Total cash flow	13.58	14.87	14.87	14.87	14.87	1.29
Less: Tax effect	12.70	8.04	7.45	6.79	6.05	0.66
Cash flow after taxes	0.88	6.83	7.42	8.08	8.82	0.63
Cumulative CFAT	0.88	7.71	15.13	23.21	32.03	32.66
Present value						
cash flow after taxes	0.83	5.67	5.49	5.33	5.12	0.32
cumulative CFAT	0.83	6.50	11.99	17.32	22.44	22.76

TAX – Can be deducted for tax purposes.

ITC – Investment tax credit.

TC – Tax credit.

CFAT – Cash flow after taxes

• Insurance, .05 percent of the purchase value per year
• Resale value, $0.00
• Investment tax credit, 10 percent
• Sales tax, 6 percent applied to purchase, rent, and maintenance costs
• Personal property tax, rate = 0 percent; final book value, 46.00 percent
• Estimated economic life, 6 years
• Depreciation method, straight line
• Interest rate, 12 percent per year
• Income tax, federal, 48.00 percent; state, 7.00 percent (.5164 tax rate)

Table 2.4 illustrates the estimated cash flow if the computer is acquired using financed purchase. To compute the equal payments for financed purchase, the following formulas were used:

$$\text{equal payment } (EP) = \frac{(P)(i)}{1 - 1 / (1 + i)^N}$$

TABLE 2.5   ESTIMATED CASH FLOW IF COMPUTER IS RENTED

	Year					
	1	2	3	4	5	6
Cash outflow before taxes						
Rent sales tax (TAX)	12.72	12.72	12.72	12.72	12.72	12.72
Total cash outflow	12.72	12.72	12.72	12.72	12.72	12.72
Cumulative TC	12.72	25.44	38.16	50.88	63.60	76.32
Tax calculations						
Deductible expenses						
(sum TAX)	12.72	12.72	12.72	12.72	12.72	12.72
Total expenses	12.72	12.72	12.72	12.72	12.72	12.72
Tax deduction	6.57	6.57	6.57	6.57	6.57	6.57
Tax effect	6.57	6.57	6.57	6.57	6.57	6.57
Cash Outflow after taxes						
Total cash outflow	12.72	12.72	12.72	12.72	12.72	12.72
Less: Tax effect	6.57	6.57	6.57	6.57	6.57	6.57
Cash flow after taxes	6.15	6.15	6.15	6.15	6.15	6.15
Cumulative CFAT	6.15	12.30	18.45	24.61	30.76	36.91
Present value						
cash flow after taxes	5.78	5.10	4.55	4.06	3.57	3.14
Cumulative CFAT	5.78	10.88	15.53	19.49	23.06	26.20

TAX – Can be deducted for tax purposes.

ITC – Investment tax credit.

TC – Tax credit.

CFAT – Cash flow after taxes.

where: P = purchase cost
i = interest rate
N = number of equal payments desired

To compute the principal portion and the interest portion in the equal payment for every period, the following equation may be used:

$$P_n = EP - \left(P - \sum_{j=0}^{n-1} P_j \right)(i)$$

where: n = the period for which the calculations are made
P_n = the principal portion for period n (P_0 = 0)

Then the interest portion for period n is equal to $EP - P_n$.

Table 2.5 illustrates the estimated cash flow if the computer is rented. in both cases the data presented are in budget, income statement, profit and loss, cash flow after taxes, and balance sheet forms.

The analysis of the cash purchase should be done in the same manner as the one for the financed purchase. Therefore, the format of Table 2.4 should be used. The analysis of the lease option is similar to the one presented for the rent option, and therefore, the format of Table 2.5 should be used.

Once these calculations are completed, a break-even point may be obtained. Then, based on the expected economic life of the system (hardware and software), a decision is made as to which method of procurement should be used.

COMPUTER SELECTION BASED ON CAPACITY MEASURES[14]

Introduction

Previous studies on the selection and procurement methods of computer systems have ignored the aspect of a component's or system's measured performance. Computation of the present value of the cash flows relevant to acquisition of a component or of an entire system were usually based on the financial outlays as quoted by manufacturers. However, system or component capacity is a paramount factor that must be taken into consideration in present value computations. Often one system is preferable to a much cheaper alternative because of the former's superior capacity. If a user firm expects to face increased demands or extreme load conditions, it cannot ignore the capacity factor in the computer selection process. The computations should be based on actual performance of the system to be selected. Such measures can be obtained by benchmark tests or other techniques rather than by relying on the performance as specified by the vendors. This discussion presents two distinct approaches to the selection problem that incorporate the capacity factor.

[14]This discussion is taken with permission from The Fourteenth International Hawaii Conference on System Sciences, *Proceedings*, Vol. 1 (1981), pp. 373–380.

To assist in comparing different methods of procuring computer systems, we will use the present value technique, based on the price of capital of the customer. Constant price of capital over all periods is assumed. A slight modification in the present value formula will ensure its validity even if the price of capital varies during the time period relevant to the computation. A weighting mechanism ensures that this procedure includes an appropriate weight for each component.

Computer System Selection

Proposed approaches

The computer selection process proposed is comprised of the following main steps:

1. Determination of hardware components required
2. Assignment of weights to each hardware component
3. Computation of present value of cash outlays on components while taking into account the capacities of the systems considered, according to two possible approaches; (a) present value per unit of capacity (without adopting a specific definition of the term "capacity unit") and (b) present value of systems of equal capacity

With these steps, it is possible to compare alternatives and select the preferred system. The prospective customer

1. Identifies the required components
2. Determines the capacity requirements for each component
3. Assigns a weight (between zero and 1) to each component, based on percent of total expected hardware cost, arbitrary measures, or some other criterion (sum of weights equals 1)
4. Issues requests for proposals to different vendors
5. Receives proposals from different vendors, stating the number of units required of each component, based on the actual (not rated) capacity of a unit and total required capacity
   This is formulated as follows, letting

B_i = required capacity of component
A_{ji} = measured capacity of one unit of component i in system j
E_{ji} = number of units of component i in system j

B_{ji} and A_{ji} are exogenous variables; E_{ji} is the decision variable (E_{ji} can assume only integer values). To find these, the following system of inequalities must be solved:

$$A_{ji} \cdot E_{ji} \geqslant B_i \tag{1a}$$

$$A_{ji} \cdot E_{ji} < B_i + A_{ji} \tag{1b}$$

subject to E_{ji}, assuming only integer values for all j and i.

6. Selects the "best" of all proposals.

   Two approaches are suggested here. Both approaches include capacity and weighting considerations.

The capacity factor

The capacities of proposed systems differ. This can be verified by a number of techniques, such as the benchmark method. Excess capacity will become especially important under peak load conditions or as demand increases over time. Present value computation must take this into account to prevent distorted evaluations.

Assume, for example, that a line printer is to be acquired and that the prospective customer expects to use it for a period of six years. The customer has decided on the desired method of procurement (i.e., buy, rent, or lease). In the following discussion, whenever this is not stated, it will also be assumed that the best method of procurement has already been determined.

Let us further assume that the present values of outlays (according to the preferred method of financing) on two alternative printers, X and Y, are $5,000 and $6,000, respectively, and that their relative measured capacities are 1,000 and 2,000 lines per minute. If the selection criterion was minimum present value of cash outlays, printer X should be selected; however, printer Y offers double the performance for price increment of only 20 percent. This demonstrates the importance of incorporating capacity in present value computation. The assigned weight of these printers relative to other components of the system may further alter the selection.

First Approach: Present Value per Unit of Performance

The present value of outlays according to the best method of procuring each component is related to the measured output of the component unit. Using the previous example, the present value of unit capacity (one line of print) costs $5 for alternative X and $3 for alternative Y. The relative results would be the same if any number of lines were taken as the unit of output. For instance, if the unit were defined as 5 lines of print, X would be rated as producing 200 units with a present value of $25 per unit and Y as producing 400 units with a present value of $15 per unit.

The definition of a "unit of output" for each system component is difficult to develop. To overcome this problem, one system is chosen as the "base system." The present value of outlays per unit of capacity for this system is computed, whatever the definition of a unit of capacity, and is equated to one. The corresponding present values per unit of capacity for the other systems (whose units of capacity are identically defined) are then computed relative to the value of the base system. If the relative present value per unit of capacity for system Y is called 1 (1 unit of present value), then the corresponding value for system X will be $1\frac{2}{3}$ units ($^{25}/_{15}$ or $^5/_3$). Thus, a uniform measure of relative present value is obtained, independent of the specific definition of capacity units.

The present value of outlays per unit of capacity should be computed for each relevant system component following the method exhibited by the printer example.

The formula

The total present value of outlays related to units of performance for a system is given by:

$$TPV_t = \sum_{i=1}^{F} PV_{ti} \cdot S_i \tag{2}$$

where

$$\sum_{i=1}^{F} S_i = 1$$

The parameters are:

TPV_t = the present value of outlays per unit of capacity for the *whole* system over t years of expected use
PV_{ti} = the present value of outlays per unit of capacity for acquiring a unit of component i with t years of expected use
F = the number of system components
S_i = the assigned weight of component i

The total present value of system outlays is thus the sum of the present values computed per relative capacity unit of all components multiplied by their assigned weights. From formula 2, the value of TPV_t for the base system is F over time t, since PV_{ti} of the base system is, by definition, 1 for all i and t.[15]

In selecting the best system for an expected period of use t out of H alternative systems, the first approach leads to the following algorithm:

1. Compute TPV_{th} for $h = 1, 2, \ldots, H$ using formula 2 for each system proposed.
2. find min TPV_{th}.
   $$H$$

The system h for which TPV_{th} is minimal is selected.

An Example. The selection of a system from two proposed alternatives is illustrated. For simplicity's sake, assume that the system is represented by two components: (a) a line printer (weight = .2) and (b) a CPU plus memory (weight

---

[15]PV_{ti} always refers to one unit of a component, since it measures present value of outlays per unit of capacity. Often there is more than one unit of a specific component in the system, but this does not change the relative present value. If, for example, there are n such units, both capacity and absolute present values are multiplied by n, so that in computing relative present values, the number of units, n, cancels out.

= .8); required capabilities are 3500 LPM and 30 Kbytes (see Table 2.9 for common components of computer systems and their defined units of performance), respectively. The user intends to keep the system for six years, so all computations will refer to this period.

Two proposals were received from different vendors as described in Table 2.6.

TABLE 2.6   SYSTEM SELECTION—DETAILS OF ALTERNATIVES

System	Component (1)	Measured Performance per Unit of Component (2)	Present Value for Rental (3)	Present Value for Purchase (4)	Number of Component Units Required* (5)
A	CPU + MEMORY	40	$4,400	$4,500	1
	PRINTER	2000	6,500	6,000	2
B	CPU + MEMORY	50	5,500	5,000	1
	PRINTER	1500	8,500	7,500	3

*The entries in column 5 are illustrative only; they are ignored in the computation of formula 2 for the reasons stated in the footnotes.

Columns 3 and 4 exhibit the present values of the outlays for the components. The number of components (column 5) was computed using formulas 1a and 1b.

Table 2.7 presents the computed relative present values of the two proposals.

TABLE 2.7   SYSTEM SELECTION—THE FIRST APPROACH

System	Component (1)	Best Method of Procurement (2)	Present Value per Unit of Capacity		Assigned Weights (5)	Total Relative Present Value* (6)
			$ Cash (3)	Relative (4)		
A	CPU + MEMORY	Rental	110	1	0.8	1.00
	PRINTER	Purchase	3	1	0.2	
B	CPU + MEMORY	Purchase	100	10/11	0.8	1.06
	PRINTER	Purchase	5	1 2/3	0.2	

*Column 6 = Σ (4) · (5)

The best financing method (column 2) is determined by comparing columns 3 and 4 in Table 2.6 and then selecting the procurement method with the lowest present value of cash outlays. Capacities for the computation in column 2 are taken from column 2 in Table 2.6 in terms of the units defined in Table 2.9. The ratio of present value for the component method as selected in column 2 to the capacity give present values per unit of capacity. Alternative A is assumed to be the base system. By definition, the relative present values per unit of capacity for each of its component are 1. The relative present values per unit of capacity for each component of the alternative system B are then computed as the ratio of the respective values in column 3 and the corresponding values for the component in the base system A. Column 5 shows the assigned weight of the components; column 6 shows the total relative present value. System A should be selected as it represents the lowest relative value.

Second Approach: Equal Capacity for All Components

The second suggested approach starts by bringing all system components to a common denominator in terms of minimum equal capacities. To illustrate the technique, the example of the line printer will be used again.

Two proposals, A and B, have the following characteristics:

	A	B
Unit measured capacity (LPM)	300	400
Unit price ($)	1000	1500
Units required for minimum equal capacity (in this case, 1200 LPM)	4	3
Total price for this number of units ($)	4000	4500

Thus there are two alternatives with equal capacities and different prices. The computation is performed for every system component, leading to a set of proposals of minimum equal capacities.

Computational steps

For each type of component, the number of units required to bring each alternative component proposed to a minimum equal capacity is determined by means of the following algorithm:

Let

C_h = capacity of a unit of a component in system h.
D_h = number of units of this component required in system h.
H = number of alternative systems proposed.
R = set of prime factors. When the algorithm is initialized, the set is empty.

Find the minimum common denominator M of all C_h ($h = 1, 2, \ldots, H$) by means of the following steps:

1. Let $h = 0$.
2. Let $h = h + 1$.
3. If $h > H$, go to step 9.
4. Decompose C_h into prime factors.
5. Find all the groups containing identical prime factors.

6. Perform step 5 for set R.
7. For each group created in step 5, find a group created in step 6 containing identical numbers. If such a group exists, go to step 8; otherwise, add its members to R and go to step 2.
8. If the number of members of the group created in step 6 is not less than the number for the group created in step 5, go to step 2; otherwise add to set R n group members, n being the difference between the two numbers and go to step 2.
9. Obtain M as the product of the prime factors in R.

Compute

$$D_h = M/C_h, \quad h = 1, 2, \ldots, H \tag{3}$$

where D_h is the number of units of a component in system h that are needed to bring the system's total capacity to a minimum common denominator.

In the printer example cited, the algorithm would yield 1200 as the minimum common capacity for 300 LPM and 400 LPM, and formula 3 would result:
For system A,

$$D_A = \frac{1200}{300} = 4 \text{ units}$$

For system B, $\qquad\qquad\qquad\qquad\qquad\qquad\qquad\qquad\qquad$ (3)

$$D_B = \frac{1200}{400} = 3 \text{ units}$$

In some cases, capacity M computed for a given component by the algorithm does not fulfill the user's capacity requirements B (computed by formulas 1a and 1b), namely, M is less than B. The least multiple of M that is larger than or equal to B must be taken as the minimum required equal capacity.

For example, assume that the minimum capacity requirements for the line printer is 3000 LPM. The least multiple of 1200 needed to satisfy the constraint $B < M$ is 3600; therefore three printer units will be required. If this procedure is repeated for all components over all the alternatives, a set of comparable systems satisfying the user's minimum capacity requirements is obtained as the starting point for the computations presented in the following section.

The formula

To compare present values of alternative systems, the following formula is applied to each equal capacity alternative:

$$TPV_t = \sum_{i=1}^{F} a_{ti} \cdot D_i \cdot PV_{ti} \cdot S_i \tag{4}$$

where $\sum_{i=1}^{F} S_i = 1$.

The parameters are

TPV_t = the value of cash outlays for acquisition of an equal-capacity system for t years
of expected use.
F = the number of system components.
a_{ti} = the average weight of component i in the total present value of proposed system
(formula 5). It represents the average weight of component i in the system.

Over all systems proposed,

$$a_{ti} = \frac{1}{H} \sum_{h=1}^{H} \frac{SPV_{tih}}{RPV_{th}} \tag{5}$$

The parameters are

SPV_{tih} = the present value of outlays on component i in system h for t years
RPV_{th} = the total present value of outlays on system h for t years
H = the number of alternative systems proposed
D_i = the number of units of component i required to achieve minimum
equal capacity
PV_{ti} = the present value of cash outlays for one unit of component i for t years,
according to the best procurement method
S_i = the assigned weight of component i

If a_{ti} were omitted when calculating formula 4, the values obtained might reflect an unrealistic weight for $d_i\, PV_{ti}$.

After computing TPV_{th} for each of the H alternatives ($h = 1, 2, \ldots, H$), the alternative with the minimum TPV_{th} is selected as preferable.

An Example. The example just used will be evaluated using the second approach. The two proposed systems, A and B, are those exhibited in Table 2.6. The minimum common capacity for the capacity of the CPU + MEMORY component is 200. To achieve this capacity, 5 and 4 units must be acquired for systems A and B, respectively. Similarly, 3 and 4 units of the PRINTER component must be required for systems A and B, respectively.

The present values of outlays for the acquisition of the two equal-capacity systems are exhibited in Table 2.8.

Column 3 in Table 2.8 exhibits the present values of outlays based on the best procurement method (taken from Table 2.6). Column 6 shows the average weight of each component in the *total* system, computed from formula (5); for example, the CPU + MEMORY component,

$$(4,400/10,400 + 5,000/12,500)/2 = 0.4115$$

Column 7 shows the assigned weight for each component. The total weighted present values for systems A and B are shown in column 9.

System A should be selected because it entails the minimum total present value of outlays.

TABLE 2.8 SYSTEM SELECTION—DETAILS OF ALTERNATIVES

System	Description of Component (1)	Best Method of Procurement (2)	Present Value for One Unit of Component (3)	Number of Units Required (4)	Total Present Value for Component Units Required (5)=(3)·(4)	Weighting Factor a_{ti} (6)	Assigned Weight (7)	Weighted Present Value for Components (8)=(5)·(6)·(7)	Total Weighted Present Value for System Acquistion (9)
A	CPU+MEMORY	Rental	$4,400	5	$22,000	0.4115	0.8	$7242	$9,361
	PRINTER	Purchase	6,600	3	18,000	0.5885	0.2	2119	
			$10,400						
B	CPU+MEMORY	Purchase	5,000	4	20,000	0.4115	0.8	6548	10,115
	PRINTER	Purchase	7,500	4	30,000	0.5885	0.2	3531	
			$12,500						

63

TABLE 2.9   PARTIAL LIST OF COMMON
HARDWARD COMPONENTS AND CAPACITY
UNITS

Component	Unit of Capacity (output)
CPU + MEMORY	Kilobytes
Mass storage unit	Megabytes
Magnetic tape unit	Kilobytes
Card reader	Cards/minute
Card punch	Columns/Seconds
Card reader/punch	Cards/minute
Line printer	Lines/minutes
Paper tape reader	Characters/second
Paper tape punch	Character/second
Optical reader	Documents/minute
Magnetic mark reader	Documents/minute

Summary

Competing computer systems have different capacities. When evaluated, any alternative system must satisfy the user's minimum capacity requirements. Excess capacity may be desirable in the long run to cover either future growth or unexpected peak loads. In the evaluation process, the prospective buyer faces two main problems:

1. Selecting the best system from among those proposed, taking into account their different measured capacities
2. Selecting the best procurement method for each component of the system chosen

The two approaches described in this discussion include considerations of capacity in the computation of present values of outlays for system acquisition.

The first approach computes present value of cash outlays for each system component according to the best method of procurement, relative to a unit of capacity and an assigned weight. Under this approach, the computation is independent of the definition of a "unit of capacity."

The second approach reduces all the alternatives proposed to a minimum common capacity base by finding the number of component units needed to obtain equal capacities for all systems proposed.

Both approaches are based on present value computations of cash outlays including capacity factors and assigned weights, offering the user a meaningful instrument for rational selection of a computer system.

SELECTED READINGS

BRANDON, D. H. "Computer Acquisition Method Analysis." *Datamation,* Vol. 18, no. 9 (1972).

BOROVITS, I., AND P. EIN-DOR. "The Purchase-to-Rent Ratio: Inferences Concerning a Pricing Policy." *Management Datamatics,* Vol. 5, no. 3 (1976).

CORTADA, J. W. *EDP Costs and Charges.* Englewood Cliffs, N.J.: Prentice-Hall, 1980.

JOSLIN, E. O. *Computer Selection: An Augmented Edition.* Fairfax Station, Va.: The Author, 1977.

TIMMRECK, E. M. "Computer Selection Methodology." *Computing Surveys,* Vol. 5, no. 4 (December 1973), pp. 199–222.

3

Software Evaluation and Selection

SOFTWARE: PURCHASE OR DEVELOP

Introduction

The computer industry is affecting many companies in the way they conduct business, sell products, control production, and perform accounting and many other functions. This is done by using application programs, as they are called, which are part of the computer software.

Software is defined as "a set of computer programs, procedures, rules, and associated documentation concerned with the operation of computers."[1] Software enables people to control the operations of computers. There are different types of software; however, most programs written by computer users are called application programs. The other types are called systems programs and utilities. The technique of writing software, called programming, is slowly becoming an important consideration of business managers.

Once the need for a computer program has been discovered, a decision needs to be made about how to acquire the product. Different options are available, depending on whether or not the organization owns a computer. If the firm does, a decision must be made as to who will own the software. The decision to purchase a software product or to develop it internally involves many different considerations about the current status of the organization's data processing and the decision-making ability. The following discussion presents the issues to be

---

[1]John, E. McNamara, *Technical Aspects of Data Communication* (Bedford, Mass.: Digital Press, 1977), p. 373.

considered in the decision process and provides tools of evaluating the different alternatives available.

Types of Software

Computer software, as has already been stated, can be broken down into three categories. The first is systems programs, also called the operating systems. This software is used to manage the resources of the computer to maximize their utilization or to provide a particular level of service to the users. These include scheduling routines, memory allocation schemes, language compilers, and other functions that must be performed to keep the system running.

Another category of software products is called utilities. These can be independent programs or part of the operating system. Utilities perform some of the routine work of a computer such as keeping track of user libraries, sorting and merging, copying of files, accounting of resource usage, and so on.

The third group, application programs, is the software that is written for the user's needs. These programs can be leased, purchased, or developed by the organization needing them. Unlike operating systems, which are usually obtained from the computer manufacturer at the time of installation and are rarely written by the individual user, applications software is often a result of in-house programming efforts. Utilities may be of either type and can be classified as such.

Applications software can be written specifically for the user firm and its individual needs, or it can be a general-purpose program that is commercially available to fulfill the needs of many users. There is an important distinction to consider here, and that deals with how accurately the capabilities of the program match the needs and requirements of the user. If the program is a general-purpose one, it may meet basic requirements but not provide the specific detail necessary. On the other hand, a tailor-made program should provide all the options and details originally requested when the system was being designed. The only way to acquire a general-purpose package program to meet these details is by in-house modifications or by outside vendor support in making changes.

Types of Changes

There are three basic classes of changes: corrective, adaptive, and perfective.

A corrective change involves the fixing of a preexisting error. This may be an error in the original specifications or in the code itself. This is part of the process called "debugging," where a code is examined and tested to ensure that it performs the tasks it was designed for. These changes are usually the responsibility of the individuals who originally wrote the program. This issue will be discussed later in more detail to examine the affect on the decision to purchase or develop the software.

The second type of change is called adaptive change. This involves modifying the software to accommodate any changes in the environment in which the application is run. Examples of this type of change could be to modify a program to add another option, calculate additional ratios, or restructure files to hold more data. These changes usually come about as a result of increased use of a program and the need to have it meet changing demands. The responsibility for making these modifications almost always rests with the user of the software product. The changes can be made in house or contracted to an outside software house.

Perfective changes deal with improving or augmenting a software product to increase performance capabilities. It is similar to adaptive change insofar as who has the responsibility for implementation of the change. For the purpose of this discussion, perfective and adaptive changes are grouped together and are simply called modifications or enhancements. This is to contrast them to corrective changes.

Another classification that must be considered deals with the size of the organization that is performing the software analysis and the size of the computer installation. The software for small computers is often written by users rather than by software vendors. The most significant vendor for large mainframe computers is usually the manufacturer. For the purpose of this discussion, it is the larger computer systems that will be considered. The organizations possessing these large machines are the most likely to have an in-house programming staff and will be required to make a decision between purchasing software and developing it themselves.

Sources for Software Packages

The sources of effective software packages are as varied as the applications themselves. They fall into the following basic categories:

1. Manufacturer of computer system
2. Other users of the same computer system whose programs are distributed by the manufacturers
3. Software supplies recruited by the manufacturer or "qualified" by the manufacturer
4. Turnkey suppliers who prepare specialized software for the system they market
5. Independent suppliers who offer application or utility programs for one popular model of machine
6. Other users who offer their programs through directories
7. Journeyman programmers
8. Academic institutions and other nonprofit organizations

As can be seen, there are many different sources for the purchaser to consider. Decisions should be based on the requirements believed to be important. As with any other product, the buyer should shop carefully before buying software. A recognized name may be important in the decision but should not cause the buyer to rule out unknown vendors who have a quality product. The entire process for selection is an involved topic and will be discussed later in this chapter.

The Need for New Software

Before looking any farther into the various factors involved in software selection, it should be determined how the user becomes aware of his or her need for a software application. Basically, there are three ways in which a potential user needs can be identified. The first is from an internal study by the organization to review its current structure and processes for handling information. An analysis is conducted and the need for a specific application is discovered and defined.

Another method is based on the recommendation of an outsider, such as a business associate, or various trade publications. Often, other users can be good sources for identifying potential areas for computer applications.

The third, and most common, method is through a vendor sales presentation. Usually, hardware manufacturers, eager to install new systems, try to present and convince potential users that there is a need for a new application software. Their sales representatives are well informed about the various types of computer applications available, and they can identify areas of concern and help to predict future needs and requirements. The major disadvantage of vendor presentations is the fact that vendors are trying to sell a product. Their goal is to complete a sale, and this can often interfere with their ability to be objective.

This is contrasted to a request from an organization that has performed its own internal study before calling on a sales representative. The company may have already identified the need and no longer have to be sold on the advantages of the new application software. The sales representative can then begin to concentrate on the more technical aspects of the application. The user firm will benefit most from the presentation since it will be gathering useful information that will aid in making a rational choice among the various alternatives.

Alternatives for Acquiring Software

It should be mentioned that the decision to purchase or to develop software is a more narrow topic than simply asking how to acquire software. If the potential user firm has no data processing facilities, it must buy services (application software and time) from a service bureau. This alternative may prove to be the most attractive solution for an organization operating a computer at near capacity.

It is also possible to lease software for in-house use. Whenever this option is undertaken, the application is usually specific and no programming changes are necessary to accommodate the user. Usually, the source code is not supplied to the user, and therefore no changes can be made.

Other alternatives for acquisition of software include purchasing a commercially available product, contracting for a tailor-made application, or performing the programming task in house. Each of these alternatives has advantages and disadvantages that need to be considered:

- *Cost:* Can the organization justify the expenditure from a cost-benefit perspective?

- *Availability:* How soon after the decision has been made will the software be ready for use? How easy will it be to become operational?
- *Maintenance:* Who will be responsible for maintaining the system making corrective changes)?
- *Specificity of Application:* Will the software meet specific needs or will it be too general?
- *Modifications:* How adaptable is the software? Can it be modified and upgraded easily (adaptive and perfective changes)?
- *Documentation:* How well is the software documented? Is the code readable? Can it be easily understood so that changes can be made?
- *Utilization of Resources:* How fully utilized are the current analysis and programmers? Is there ample computer time for development without affecting daily operations?

Each of these criteria should be considered in the decision process.

The option to purchase a packaged software product from a vendor is usually considered first, since, in many cases, buying the software costs less than developing it in-house. This stems from the fact that the vendor is selling the product to many users and can spread the costs over that number of users. Another advantage is that the product is immediately available. Since the software has been written and is being marketed commercially, the vendor will usually have knowledge of the required interfaces for the software to run on a specific computer system. It should be easily implemented and be running with minimal lagtime.

Maintenance of the purchased package is also an important factor. The vendor can sell the product with or without support in making corrective changes. Often, the vendor charges for this service, at a fee of 5 to 10 percent of the original purchase price. This is actually an important advantage, since maintenance of in-house developed software can be over 30 percent of the original development cost.[2]

Modifications are also very common in purchased software since the purchased package may not actually meet the specific requirements of the user. The vendor also can offer assistance in these adaptive changes, but almost always at cost. Here is where the importance of buying software from a reputable vendor comes in. It is uncommon for a buyer of proprietary software to go back to the vendor for assistance in making modifications only to find that the vendor has gone out of business. This is especially risky when documentation associated with the program is either poor or nonexistent. Even the code itself may be very difficult to understand and in-house programmers have the awkward task of trying to make sense of someone else's software.

Another factor that could influence an organization to buy a software package is availability of resources. If there are no analysts to design the system or no

---

[2]Jan Snyders, "Slashing Software Maintenance Costs," *Computer Decisions* (July 1979).

adequate programming staff to write it, the application software should probably be purchased, since it would cost less than hiring the additional staff necessary to do the job in house. In addition, if the utilization of the computer system is high, the system resources may not be available to do the programming in house.

These arguments for and against purchased software products should be compared with the benefits and costs of developing the software in house. Estimating the cost of in-house development is discussed in Chapter Five. Suffice it to say that all costs associated with the analysis, design, programming, testing, and implementation must be considered. In addition computer time and other resource usage must be also taken into consideration.

The decision to develop the software in house has both advantages and disadvantages. First, the product will not be available for use for some time. All the analysis and programming must be performed, which takes time. And if the application software is needed quickly, in-house development may not be the correct approach.

Maintenance and modification is the responsibility of the programming staff. Any changes needed are performed in house. In addition, documentation should accompany the writing of the code, so in the event where changes are required, it will be easier for another programmer to make the changes.

One major advantage of this option deals with how specific the application software will be. Since the analysis will be in house, the system can be designed so that it will meet the specific requirements of the users. There should be no fear that too generalized a program will be written (or one too specific). This control is another benefit of in-house development. Security is another, since no outside individuals need to be involved.

A key factor in the decision involves how fully utilized the current resources are. There must be enough analysts and programmers to perform the task, and equipment utilization needs to be relatively low to support the development. If the system resources are being fully utilized, with little programming time available, it is unlikely that any new projects could be undertaken without causing other tasks to suffer.

The third alternative is to contract the software project to an outside software company. This has some of the advantages of in-house development and purchase, but also some of the disadvantages.

For instance, the cost of this option would be similar to in-house development, and even more. The same requirement for system analysis would be necessary to determine exactly what the software needs to do. Once this has been determined the programmers can begin to work on the coding. This again is a drawback because the system will not be available for sometime in the future.

These contracts range from cost reimbursement to fixed price. Such contracts usually include tailored variations in incentives and awards related to fee or profit determination. There are five methods for procurement of contracted software: cost plus fixed fee, cost plus award fee, cost plus incentive fee, fixed price plus incentive, and firm price. Projects that do not yet have approved specifications usually have cost reimbursement contracts. Procurements of software based upon complete and approved specifications may have fixed price contracts. Large projects usually involve changing in the requirements, and these changes often occur as the software development proceeds concurrently. To allow the customer and the contractors more flexibility in incorporating required changes, a cost reimbursement contract is recommended. Procurements for off-the-shelf software are often appropriate for fixed price contracts, provided that the conditions to qualify the software are clearly understood.

Maintenance must also be considered. It may be possible to contract for this, but it is more likely that it will be performed in house. Modifications, too, will be done in house, and therefore, the contract for the software should include a clause about documentation. Without sufficient documentation, any modifying to be done would be very difficult.

A positive aspect of this option is that the application software, once completed, will meet the specific needs of the users as stated in the analysis document. This is important because the user firm is getting exactly what it needs.

Decision: Purchase or Develop

Once all the alternatives have been examined, a decision must be made. Some quantitative techniques do exist for evaluating alternatives based on applying weights to the relative importance of each of the criteria used. One technique requires the potential buyer to rank on a scale, say, 1 to 10, each of the alternatives according to each criteria.

For example, we may use three criteria of cost, documentation, and availability. The three alternatives to be considered are purchase, in-house development, and contracting to an outside software company (tailor made).

The first step in the analysis is to determine the relative importance (weights) of the set of criteria that has been chosen as the basis for the evaluation. Then scores are assigned for each alternative/criterion combination. The scores are multiplied by the weights and the results are summed for each alternative. The alternative with the highest score would best meet the requirements of the user. Table 3.1 shows how this technique is used.

In this example the contract option is the least attractive and will therefore

TABLE 3.1 PURCHASE, DEVELOP, AND CONTRACT

Criteria	Weights	Alternatives					
		Purchase		Develop		Contract	
		Score	Weighted Score	Score	Weighted Score	Score	Weighted Score
Cost	.5	10	5.0	7	3.5	5	2.5
Documentation	.3	4	1.2	10	3.0	9	2.7
Availability	.2	10	2.0	6	1.2	6	1.2
Total	1.0		8.2		7.7		6.4

TABLE 3.2 RISK ANALYSIS OF TWO ALTERNATIVES

| | Alternatives | | | |
| | Purchase | | Develop | |
Risks	Probability	Impact	Probability	Impact
Overutilization	M	H	H	M
Poor maintenance Support	H	M	M	M

be discarded. Since the scores for purchase and development are close, further analysis should be done. This can be done by using a second technique, probability of success and risk analysis.

Continuing with our example, two factors will be considered: utilization of resources and maintenance. The risks are overutilization of resources and poor maintenance support. Each risk will be given a high, medium, or low probability of occurrence and a similar score for the impact it will have on the organization. Table 3.2 displays an example of such an analysis.

From Table 3.2, it is obvious that the purchase option has a medium probability of overutilization, which is a high risk. In-house development has a high probability of overutilization. Poor maintenance support is a medium impact risk with a high probability of occurrence from the purchase alternative and a medium probability from the development option.

The objective of the analysis is to discard those options that have a high probability of occurrence of a high impact factor. Since the purchase alternative in this example has a high probability of overusing the system resources, and it is a high-impact factor, this alternative should be discarded. The favorable alternative would then be to purchase the software from a vendor.

Summary

The decision to purchase computer software or to develop it in house is one that cannot be made easily. Only after careful analysis of the alternatives can a good choice be made. Requirements vary with every installation, and no two lists of criteria are the same. The best advice is to be a good software shopper and carefully evaluate all the alternatives.

EVALUATING AND SELECTING SOFTWARE

Introduction

The rising costs of in-house software development are forcing potential users into the packaged software market. The following discussion reviews the process of software selection and acquisition. The selection process is very complex, and presently it may be considered more an art than a science. Acquiring a software package is an investment, just as any other, and must be evaluated in the light of the benefits it will provide relative to its cost. This process consists of five phases: (1) initiation, survey, and analysis based on the requirements (2) benchmarking of the candidate packages; (3) selection; (4) contract negotiation; and (5) installation and acceptance testing of the selected system.

The Evaluation Process

The number of factors to be considered in the evaluation process is usually very large and therefore may be exceedingly costly. To minimize the cost of the process, compromises must be made. Once it is decided to acquire a software package instead of developing it in house, the evaluation and selection process should include the following steps.

Survey

The most difficult step in the evaluation and acquisition of a new software is probably the recognition of need. Therefore, before beginning the process, user interest in or need for the new application or system must be established. The data processing department must have a clear understanding of the organization's objectives as well as the user's objectives and needs. Once this is done, the data processing department should identify its own objectives and requirements for the software and assure that a similar system does not exist within the organization.

Select all available vendors offering software packages that satisfy the requirements. Numerous sources exist for a software system: systems provided by the hardware vendors, systems provided by a software house, systems provided by service bureaus, and other sources such as other users of similar applications.

Obtain published reports that analyze the packages under consideration. Evaluation of a large number of systems is expensive. Therefore, it is important to eliminate candidates as rapidly as possible so that the total evaluation is applied to a small number of systems. Using published reports can help in the initial screening that determines the potential vendors to be considered, taking into consideration the hardware, software, and standards compatability. Resolve any questions concerning the packages with the vendors.

Submit an RFP for the software package to all potential vendors. As mentioned in Chapter One, an important part of the RFP is the statement of work, which should include all mandatory tasks to be performed by the vendor. These tasks include the following:

1. The vendor should provide a detailed project plan for all work to be done:
   a. *The schedule* includes all activities, milestones, and completion dates.
   b. *The Organization control plan* includes personnel assignments and reporting and working relationships for all phases.
   c. *The organization interface plan* describes liaison needs in terms of persons responsible as well as methods for monitoring and controlling the interface.

    d. *The reporting and review plan* describes methods to be used as well as frequency of dissemination of project information.

    e. *The installation plan* describes the approach and schedule for installation of the proposed system.

    f. *The conversion plan* describes the method for switching over to the new system.

    g. *Documentation* outlines all documentation for users, operation, maintenance, and modifications.

    h. *The acceptance plan* describes the method for acceptance test.

    i. *The training plan* describes the methods, materials, and schedule for training user's personnel in the use and maintenance of the proposed system.

2. The vendor should develop and provide for review the detailed logical system design for the proposed system. The design and associated documentation will include description of the inputs, processing, outputs, data elements, relationship of all programs, and relationships of all data elements and all programs. The vendor should also provide for a complete manual backup capability in the event of a computer system malfunction so that the operations are minimally disrupted. Also provided are measures to ensure the security and integrity of the data.

3. The vendor should develop and provide for review the detailed physical designs for the proposed system. The design and associated documentation will describe the relationship of the logical design to hardware and system software of the computer system.

4. The vendor should develop and install software and documentation for the proposed system. The system will operate on the user's computer and will be compatible with existing related systems. Documentation will include at least

    a. Source code and other required information and program documentation necessary to permit maintenance and changes by the user's personnel.

    b. User and operations procedures for use and operation of the system. Documentation must be easy to use and understand and easy to update. Procedures must contain all manual procedures necessary for operation of the system as well as security controls.

    c. Training materials to assist in training user's personnel in the use, operation, and maintenance of the system.

5. The vendor should develop a training program that will include at least the following:

    a. Formal presentation of the system to higher level of management personnel as well as to the personnel who will use, operate, and maintain the system

    b. Detailed presentation of all user and operation procedures

    c. Live demonstration and formal training in all aspects of the operation of the system for user's personnel

    d. Hands-on training with the user's employees operating and using the system

6. The vendor should provide technical support for operational use of the proposed system during the first three months of operation. Technical support will include aid in the use, operation, and maintenance of the system. The vendor will remedy any problems that occur during this period that arise due to materials supplied by the vendor.

7. The vendor should provide ongoing maintenance support for all application software.

The preliminary evaluation report

As a result of the preliminary survey, the vendor should prepare a preliminary report including

1. Definition of package requirements
2. Reasons for recommending a software package over in-house system development
3. Reasons for recommending one vendor software package over others
4. Summary of each software package including costs, specifications, and features

Evaluation

In the software evaluation process, it is important to determine if the proposed software complies with mandatory capabilities. The essence of a mandatory capability is that it totally excludes those software systems that do not have this capability. The selection of systems for consideration is the first part of the evaluation process. In addition to assessing the features and functional capabilities of the systems under consideration, other factors, such as training, maintenance, installation aids, documentation, flexibility, implementation, and operation of the software system within the organization must be considered. To make it possible to consider these factors, both the vendors and the packages need to be evaluated. It is also helpful to obtain information from users who have installed the systems that are under consideration. This can be done by developing a user questionnaire and package vendor questionnaire.[3]

User Evaluation. As it was mentioned, information that can be gathered from users may be very helpful in evaluating both the vendors and the packages. A user questionnaire may include the following:

---

[3]Dorothy G. Dologite, "Evaluating Packaged Software—Avoiding the Landmines," *Data Management* (January 1982), p. 23.

User questionnaire[4]

1. Operation
   a. Is the system easy to use?
   b. What is the level of technical knowledge required to use and maintain the system?
   c. Has there been any operator turnover? Why?
2. Reliability
   a. How long has the system been in use?
   b. During this time, how many updates, error corrections, and enhancements have there been? Was documentation supplied?
   c. How many bugs have you had during this time?
   d. What parts of the system are particularly error-prone? What other parts of the system become unusable? For how long?
   e. What errors can a user make which will bring down the system? What is required and how long does it take for recovery?
   f. Is a diagnostic package available on site to verify that the system is funtioning properly?
   g. Are vendor backup facilities available?
3. Maintenance
   a. How reliable and accessible is the vendor?
   b. How frequently are hardware and software maintenance required?
   c. Are service technicians competent in solving problems?
   d. What is the average time between maintenance call and response?
   e. Are backup procedures adequate? How long does backup take? Is there anything error-prone about the procedure?
4. Performance
   a. What are the daily transaction volumes? How long does daily processing take?
   b. What is the size of your files?
   c. How many terminals concurrently process transactions?
   d. How many users can be on the system before response time becomes sluggish? How serious is the degradation?
   e. How have multiple-user degradation problems been solved?
   f. Is your print capacity adequate?
   g. Are there any terminal lockouts when the printer is running?
5. Flexibility
   a. What package modifications have you had done? Who did them?
   b. If changes are not done on site, where are they done?

[4]Reprinted with permission from Dologite, "Evaluating Packaged Software," pp. 25–26.

   c. How long did changes in each area take?

   d. What custom programs have been added? Who did them? How long did it take? Interface problems?

   e. How has the system been expanded or upgraded? How successful was the conversion? Time, cost, and personnel involved?

   f. How is any kind of change implemented?

6. Installation

   a. Was the system installed as planned?

   b. How long did the installation take? What did it cost?

   c. Was vendor installation training adequate?

   d. Was the vendor installation support competent and complete?

   e. Was the system cut over smoothly?

   f. What anomalies marred the installation, if any?

   g. What environmental changes were required to install the system?

7. Costs

   a. What unanticipated charges were incurred during installation and training? afterward?

   b. Is your service agreement cost effective?

   c. What have new vendor package enhancements cost?

   d. What, if any, charges have been incurred to update or correct software?

   e. What does customized software work cost?

   f. In what areas have you found the system to be most cost effective? Least cost effective?

8. Security

   a. Are user and file security levels adequate?

   b. Can unauthorized transactions or programs be run?

   c. Are accounting audit controls satisfactory? Do they satisfy your accountant?

9. Documentation

   a. Is documentation accurate?

   b. Is it adequate?

   c. Is it kept up to date?

10. Miscellaneous

   a. Why did you buy the system?

   b. Would you buy it today if you were in the market for a system?

   c. What changes would you make?

   d. What changes do you think realistically could have been implemented?

   e. What did you learn from other users of the system?

Vendor Evaluation. An important issue in the evaluation process is to determine the vendor's reputation and reliability. This part of the evaluation is not a simple task. However, by posing the right questions using the software package vendor questionnaire,[5] it is possible to predict the vendor's reliability. Such a questionnaire may include the following:

Software package vendor questionnaire[6]

1. Application Package Use
   a. Name of package.
   b. Date of first use.
   c. Number of installations using same package.
   d. Name, address, and phone number of local user reference.
   e. User group, if any, contact name, address, and phone number.
   f. Number of installations where package was modified.
   g. Can a demonstration of package be made at a user site?
   h. Are there restrictions on the purposes for which the product may be used?
   i. What is the delay between order placement and delivery of the package?
2. Documentation
   a. Is package documentation, consisting of the following, supplied?
      System flow diagrams
      System description
      Program listing
      File layouts and capacities
      Operator instructions
      User manual
      Report and screen output examples
      Start-up procedures
      Operating procedures
      Restart procedures
   b. Can documentation be obtained now (attached) for examination?
3. Package Modification
   a. To what extent can the package (software and documentation) be modified to meet user requirements? Who does the changes? Where are they done? How long does it take?
   b. Will modification cancel the warranty?
   c. Describe any package enhancements planned or in process.
   d. Will future package enhancements (software and documentation) be made available?

[5]Ibid., p. 20.
[6]Reprinted with permission from Dologite, "Evaluating Packaged Software," pp. 22–23.

4. Costs
    a. What pricing arrangements are available?
    b. If the package is rented, what are the license terms and renewal provisions?
    c. Document what is included in the purchase price or license fee.
    d. What are any other special charges, taxes, or financial burdens associated with the purchase/licensing of the package?
    e. What, if any, costs are associated with an unconditional warranty period?
    f. What is the cost of maintenance after the warranty period?
    g. What, if any, costs are associated with multiple installations of the package?
    h. What do additional copies of documentation cost?
    i. What, if any, are all other charges associated with installing and using the package, including shipping, vendor personnel lodging, expenses, training, documentation, and so forth?
    j. What is the cost of package modifications? Enhancements?
    k. Are updates and error correction provided at no cost?
    l. Can the package be resold or rented to someone else?

5. Operations
    a. Is a copy of the source code for the package provided? If not, is it held in an escrow account? With whom?
    b. What facility requirements (computer make, model, central memory size, operating system, compiler language, input/output devices, special environment, etc.) are needed to run the package?
    c. Is the package portable to other operating environments?
    d. What is the technical level of personnel needed to operate and maintain the package?
    e. How many versions or releases of the package are there? Are error corrections and enhancements release dependent?
    f. What are the documented responses times for the main transaction entries?
    g. Describe any off-line control procedures required.
    h. What summary reports or other package features can be ignored or deleted without affecting the overall package functionally?

6. Installation and Maintenance
    a. Describe the steps required to install the package and the time, personnel, and facilities required in each step.
    b. Describe assistance provided at installation time.
    c. Can staff training be provided on site?
    d. Who provides for file initiation/conversion and system interfacing requirements?

      e. Does the successful execution of an agreed-upon acceptance test initiate the unconditional warranty period?

      f. Does an initial unconditional warranty period provide for a specified level of package performance for a given period at the installed premises?

      g. How long is the initial unconditional warranty period?

      h. Is there a guarantee in writing about the level and quality of maintenance service provided?

      i. Will ongoing updates and error correction with appropriate documentation be supplied?

      j. Who implements updates and error correction? How and where?

7. Security

      a. What kind of security is provided to prevent unauthorized use of the package?

      b. Are all transactions journalized?

8. Other Warranties

      a. Does the vendor have absolute right to rent or sell the subject package? If not, can a third-party contract be examined?

      b. Can the vendor provide indemnification from copyright, patent, or proprietary right infringement on others?

9. Business Description

      a. Name, address, and phone of vendor.

      b. Name of sales and technical representatives.

      c. Support office closest to proposed user installation.

      d. Names of support personnel at closest office—can they be interviewed?

      e. Number of people in vendor company by job function.

      f. Can a current financial statement be obtained now (attached) for examination? a Dun & Bradstreet rating?

      g. Has the company or any of its principals ever been involved in a bankruptcy or computer-related litigation?

      h. What other software packages are sold and number of installations of each?

      i. Can vendor install package at a remote location?

10. Contracts

      a. Is a standard contract used? Can it be obtained now (attached) for examination?

      b. Are contract terms negotiable?

      c. What objections, if any, are there to attaching a copy of this questionnaire with responses to a contract?

After responses to the vendor questionnaire have been received, it might be useful to obtain a vendor sales and technical presentation. To complete the information gathering, obtain the opinions of the presentation participants.

After all data are collected, conduct a benchmark test of the package on the data processing equipment to evaluate the software package as well as to determine if the hardware is sufficient in terms of resources, such as memory, disk storage, and so on. The primary items to be covered by the benchmark are presented in the checklist that follows. One form for each application tested would be filed. If needed, sections should be expanded to accommodate the needs of the potential user firm.

Benchmark Test Checklist[7]

Application: ————————————   Vendor: ————————————

1. Functionality
   Input transactions (data entry)
   Description
   a.   Response time
   b.   Response time
   c.   Response time
   Ad hoc inquiry utility/design
   a.
   b.
   c.
   File maintenance
   a.
   b.
   c.
   Report utility/design
   a.
   b.
   c.
   Output screen utility/design
   a.
   b.
   c.
   End-of-period routines
   Audit trial controls
   Test data performance
2. Ease of use
   Operator instructions
   Dialogue
      User friendly
      Logical

[7]Reprinted with permission from Dologite, "Evaluating Packaged Software," p. 24.

      Consistent
      HELP routines
      Easy EXIT routines
      ERROR correction routines do not deadlock processing
    Screen formats
      Consistent
      Clear and uncluttered
    Hardware
      Keyboard familiarity
      Video display quality
      Printer handling
      Disk handling
      Noise level
      Heat level

3. Backup procedures

The evaluation report

After completing all phases in the evaluation process, an evaluation report should be prepared. This report should include the following:

1. Costs
   a. Cost of acquiring the system
   b. Training costs
   c. Modifications costs
   d. Implementation costs
   e. Maintenance and support costs
2. Tangible and intangible benefits and savings
3. Payback period
4. Recommendations and comments
5. Expected throughput and performance including volumes, timeliness, and accuracy of output

Implementation Plan

Once the evaluation is completed and the software package is selected, an implementation and installation plan should be prepared. This plan should include at least the following items:

1. Schedule, using Gantt or critical path chart showing all target dates, scope of project, and sign-off procedure for each function
2. A schedule of training sessions
3. A plan for modifications (if any are required)
4. The amount of support that the organization is obligated to provide to the vendor

    a. Coordination and liaison effort

    b. Analyst and technical support

    c. Data-entering and clerical support

    d. Computer test time, tapes, disks, supplies, and office space

5. Definition of each user group's responsibility

This plan should be reviewed with the vendor and the users. A good practice is to include the implementation plan in the contract.

The Contract

Once a contract is signed, it is usually very difficult to obtain additional services from the vendor. The user has an advantage during the negotiations, and that is the best time for obtaining concessions from the vendor. Therefore, it is important to plan the contract negotiations and make sure that all points are covered. A negotiating team of experts in different areas should be formed. The negotiations should be conducted by one person to prevent making conflicting commitments and concessions. No decision is final until approved by that person. It is crucial for the user firm to protect itself with a detailed written agreement between it and the vendor. All promises and commitments by the vendor should be in writing. It may be very useful to include the RFP, the vendor questionnaire, the proposal, and the implementation plan as part of the contract. Avoid as much as possible restrictions on the user of the software package. Before the negotiation process starts, arrange for a contract presentation by the vendor, and then ascertain the opinions of the presentation participants. Do not forget to review the contract with the organization's legal department. And always remember, the vendors have more experience in negotiating such contracts.

Before signing the contract check the vendor contract for the following clauses:

1. Definition of package requirements and performance specifications.
2. Specifications and agreed-to package modifications.
3. Purchase or lease price and features included.
4. Sign-off procedure (include payments terms, the date of operation, and acceptance for operation as determined by the user).
5. Warranties, waivers, and penalties (liability limitation, errors, compatibility, and compensation for late delivery and support).
6. Arbitration.
7. Free trial and method of termination of contract.
8. Availability of package source coding.
9. Vendor support, maintenance, and training provided.
10. Acceptance tests.
11. Adherence of package to company standards.

12. Number of documentation manuals provided.

13. User, operations, and training manuals provided.

14. Program and file loading and testing provided.

15. Frequency and content of package upgrades.

16. Ownership of the software. If the software is custom developed, it should state in the contract that this software is the sole property of the user. If the service is provided by a service bureau, it should state that the data as well as the software are the sole property of the user.

Installation and Implementation

In this phase the specific user and analyst personnel for package coordination and vendor liaison are designated. The coordinator should use the preliminary report, evaluation report, implementation plan, and contract as project control tools. The customer should do the following:

1. Assure that the delivered version of documentation matches the programs.

2. Compile and catalog all programs. Keep all programs on a test library and transfer to the master library after they are tested and operational.

3. Modify the control language, if needed, to meet the organization's hardware and operating system requirements.

4. Test the original programs delivered before making any changes, modifications, and corrections.

5. Review the results of the test with the vendor and make corrections, if needed.

6. Review the package flow for maximum job stream efficiency; make adjustment if needed.

7. Modify programs to meet user requirements as needed.

8. Update the user documentation based on the tests and modifications.

9. Construct a test data set that meets all anticipated conditions.

10. Test the modified package using the test data set.

11. Review the results of the test with the vendor and make corrections if needed.

12. Update the computer operating documentation to conform to the organization's standards.

13. Begin file initiation and conversion and perform parallel system tests.

14. Review the results of the tests with management, operations, technical support, and users. Make corrections as needed.

15. Install the full system when operational.

16. Obtain sign-off for all those concerned.

Train user personnel

The installation of a new package/application results in the need to train the users. Although the vendors of software packages often supply training programs, it is the responsibility of the data processing department to supplement with in-house education tailored to the use of this package in the organization. Therefore, before installing the new software package, training programs should be initiated for data-entry, computer operation, scheduling, control, file backup and retention, and output distribution procedures. The training program is prepared for the installation and implementation period as well as for the ongoing operation of the system.

The Costs

A large amount of time and effort are consumed by the selection and evaluation process, and, therefore, we must take into account the firm's financial commitments. Acquisition of a software package results in costs for selection, maintenance, operation, and training. Selection and installation are usually one-time costs, whereas the maintenance, operation, and training costs are experienced throughout the life of the software package. Table 3.3 provides a breakdown of some of these cost items. These cost items represent the commitments that the organization must consider when a new software package is to be acquired. Actual implementation and operation of the new software generate, in most cases, expenses many times greater than the original cost.

Rating of the Candidate Systems

The major problem in rating candidate systems is to quantify or measure their various characteristics. The effectiveness of the evaluation is dependent on the decisions on what and how measurement is made. Therefore, it is very important to define carefully the set of criteria for measuring each characteristic. To overcome this problem, it is possible to set up a scale by which each criterion can be measured. An example for such a scale may be as follows:

10	8	6	4	2	0
Excellent	Good	Satisfactory	Adequate	Poor	Unacceptable

Thus, with some effort, it is possible to provide a tool by which the various features of the proposed software systems can consistently be measured.

Selection criteria

Nearly all objectives for software products fall into one or more of the following 11 categories.[8] To evaluate each of the criteria, a set of questions should be answered, based on the user questionnaire, the vendor questionnaire, and the benchmark test results.

[8]Craig Johannsen, "Software Selection Criteria Outlined," *Computerworld* (February 4, 1980), p. 33.

TABLE 3.3 A BREAKDOWN OF COSTS ITEMS

	Initial Analysis	Benchmark	Acquisition	Installation	Education	Documentation	Maintenance
Personnel time	X	X		X	X		X
Computer costs	X	X		X	X		
Travel costs	X				X		
Education costs	X	X					X
Vendor charges		X			X		X
Support costs		X		X	X		
Presentation					X		
Teaching facilities							
Legal fees			X			X	
Standard features			X			X	
Special features			X				
Interface to other packages			X				
Future enhancement			X				
Price per copy						X	
Shipping costs						X	
Annual cost							X
Taxes				X			
Supply (tapes, disks, ect.)							

Functionality. Do the input transactions, files, and reports contain the necessary data elements? Are all necessary computations and processing steps performed the way you want them performed? Are the types of ad hoc inquiries the ones you would like to make possible?

Capacity. Will the product be able to handle your requirements for size of files, number of data elements, number of table entries, volume of transactions, volume of reports, and number of occurrences of certain data elements?

Flexibility. Can transaction and report formats be changed easily? Can screen layouts be changed easily? How easy is it to add new computations or processing steps? Can the programs be adapted to new applications?

Usability. Does the level of technical knowledge required to use this product properly match the level of knowledge of those who will be using it? How readable, informative, and easy to interpret are the reports and screen displays produced? Is training available from the vendor? Will the users be enthusiastic about the product?

Reliability. Does the product have clean, modular design? Has it been actually used long enough to make sure that most of its bugs have been cleaned up? How much of the system will become unusable when a part of it fails? Does the product rely on any failure-prone hardware or noisy communication links? Does the product incorporate any features for the detection and self-correction of errors? Can a user make errors that will bring down the system? What are the recovery capabilities?

Security. Does the product incorporate standard types of controls? Does the product permit adequate backup procedures? Does it assist in any way to prevent intruders from extracting sensitive data from files or transaction input streams? Does it help prevent employees from entering unauthorized transactions or running programs without authorization? Does the product provide adequate detection and diagnosis of data-entry and other types of errors? Are transactions journalized? Is a standard procedure provided that can be used to verify that the system is functioning properly?

Performance. At what rate will the product typically use machine cycles? At what rate will it be requesting disk accesses? How much main memory will it require? If it will be run on a virtual system, how much paging activity will result? How many users can be on the system before it begins to bog down?

Maintainability. Are source programs available? Often they are not. If the vendor is doing the maintenance, how reliable and accessible is the company? Some vendors operate out of post office boxes. What level and quality of maintenance will the vendor supply? Is this guaranteed in writing? Will changes to the system cancel the warranty? Can the product easily be used in another operating environment? That is, is it portable? If your staff will be doing the maintenance, are the programs written in a language with which your staff is familiar? Do they use techniques with which staffers may not be familiar? Are sets of test data available with adequate documentation of how to use them and of what results to expect? Obtain the opinions of past and present users.

Ownership.   What kind of rights to the product are you buying? Can you resell or rent the product to someone else? If the vendor is making this product especially for you, will it also be marketed to others? If so, will the vendor pay you a royalty on each sale? Are there restrictions on the purposes for which the product may be used? Are there restrictions on copying the product or its documentation? Will you be able to obtain full ownership rights and copies of the source programs if the vendor goes out of business?

Minimizing Operating and Maintenance Costs.   How much does the vendor charge for maintaining and upgrading the product? How frequently will maintenance probably be required? What is the cost per transaction of using this product? What will the storage cost be? Will purchase of this product require acquisition of additional hardware or personnel? How much will they cost on a continuing basis? What will be the usable life span of this product?

Minimizing Purchase and Installation Costs.   What initial costs are there besides the basic costs of the product? Will you have to pay shipping costs and transportation and lodging costs of the vendor personnel who will install the system and train your staff? Will there be considerable delay between placement of the order and actual delivery of the product in ready-to-use state? How much will this cost? What will conversion costs be?

Once the criteria are established, a comparison can be made of the proposed software packages. Weighted scores are then computed for each proposed package. Table 3.4 presents an example of this technique using the criteria discussed previously.

TABLE 3.4 WEIGHTED SCORES FOR CANDIDATE PACKAGES

Selection Criteria	Weight	Package 1		Package 2	
		Score	Weighted Score	Score	Weighted Score
Functionality	0.10	5	0.5	7	0.7
Capacity	0.10	6	0.6	8	0.8
Flexibility	0.10	6	0.6	6	0.6
Usability	0.20	8	1.6	4	0.8
Reliability	0.05	8	0.4	8	0.4
Security	0.05	6	0.3	8	0.4
Performance	0.20	4	0.8	10	2.0
Maintainability	0.05	6	0.3	2	0.1
Ownership	0.05	4	0.2	6	0.3
Operating and maintenance costs	0.05	10	0.5	8	0.4
Purchase and installation costs	0.05	8	0.4	8	0.4
Total Weighted Score	1.00		6.2		6.9

4

Organizing the Data Processing Activity

INTRODUCTION

The organizational location and structure of the data processing department are discussed in this chapter, taking into account the numerous issues that are involved in managing this department. The main objective of the data processing department is to supply computerized information services to the organization.[1] This objective is achieved by performing three functions: (1) system development (analysis, design, programming, testing, implementation, and documentation of new applications); (2) system maintenance (corrections, modifications, maintenance, and enhancement of existing systems); and (3) production (daily operation of the data processing equipment, data entry, scheduling, jobs setup, production control, supplies procurement, magnetic tapes and disks media library). To perform these three functions, there is a need for two additional functions: (1) administration (coordination, budgetary planning and control, costing, personnel, clerical services, etc.) and (2) technical support (system programming, data-base administration, communications control, hardware control, performance measurement, etc.). The data processing department is usually divided into two major parts: development and production.

The data processing department provides the following services: (1) it operates computer systems that may involve communication systems, data bases, and software; (2) it consists of a large number of employees with different professions

---

[1]N. Ahituv and M. Hadass, "Organizational Structure of a Complex Data Processing Department," *Information and Management,* Vol. 1, no. 2 (1978), p. 53.

as described later in this chapter; (3) it supplies information services to users with different requirements and applications; (4) it processes data as defined by the various applications; and (5) it operates data bases and manages them.

Principles of Organization Structure

The principles of organization structure include the following concerns:

1. Objectives of the data processing activity and its component elements should be clearly defined, agreed upon, and known.
2. The data processing organization structure is not a permanent one. It should remain flexible and be reviewed periodically.
3. The structure of the data processing function should take into consideration the personalities and the people involved.
4. Reasons for reorganizing of the data processing department must be known and clearly defined.
5. All data processing activities and functions should be grouped according to homogeneity of objectives and purposes.
6. The number of levels of authority should be kept to a minimum.
7. Controls and procedures are, in many situations, more imortant than job descriptions.
8. The data processing organization is only as good as the people within it.

ORGANIZATIONAL LOCATION OF THE DATA PROCESSING ACTIVITY

The location of the data processing function within the organization is an important factor that may determine the success or failure of the information systems. There are three basic approaches: location within the user boundaries, location within the central service department, and location independent of the user boundaries. The following paragraphs describe the three alternatives and their advantages and disadvantages.

Operational Location

When the data processing activity is located within the user's organization (see Figure 4.1), users that do not have an independent data processing unit may acquire services from one or more of the other data processing activities or may acquire services from outside vendors. This approach is suitable for a very large, decentralized organization where there is a very little interaction between the information systems and the data bases. Some of the data processing applications are probably dedicated systems.

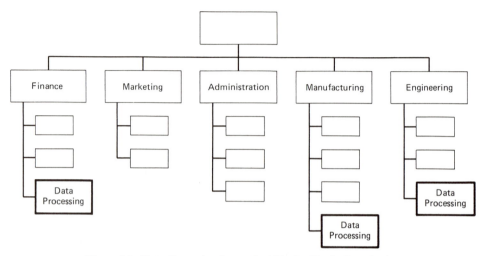

Figure 4.1 Data Processing Located within the User's Organization

Advantages

- Users have direct control of the data processing resources, especially for day-to-day operation.
- Users are usually more sensitive to the economic use of data processing resources, since the cost comes out of their budget.

Disadvantages

- Costs of mulitple data processing groups are higher since each has its own staff, equipment, and other resources.
- Integration and coordination of data processing activities are difficult to achieve.
- Implementation of overall organization standards and practices is difficult to accomplish.
- Control is difficult to exercise and it requires development of special measures and tools.

Location in a Service Department

When the data processing activity is located within the central service organization, as in the administration function (see Figure 4.2), it is separated from the users. In this approach the data processing function services all users and centralizes all data processing resources, such as equipment and personnel. It is possible that there will be more than one physical location if it is desirable as a result of geographical constraints or a need for different applications. This approach is suitable for small- to medium-sized organizations or organizations in which there

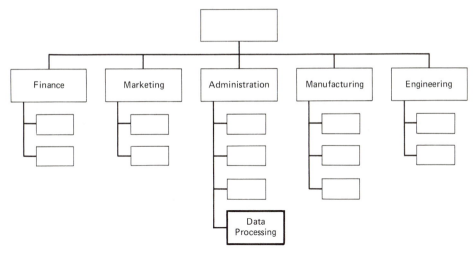

Figure 4.2   Data Processing as Part of the Central Support Department

is a high degree of integrated data-base usage. Under this approach, if different activities or locations have the same kind of data processing, true economies of scale may be achieved.

Advantages

- All users are treated equally by the data processing department.
- Stronger computing power is available, and better utilization of resources is obtained.
- It is easier to integrate systems and applications development as well as all data processing activities, including data bases.
- Control by top management is simplified and easier.
- Economies of scale of data processing resources are achieved.
- Additional requirements by a single user can easily be accommodated, usually without the need to add resources.

Disadvantages

- A centralized staff may not be familiar with all users' needs and may result in longer time of designing and development of new applications.
- It may lead to waste and unimportant demands by users if a charge-back system does not exist.
- Establishing priorities among users is difficult.
- Because of the large number of users and their unknown plans, it is very difficult to have resources planning.

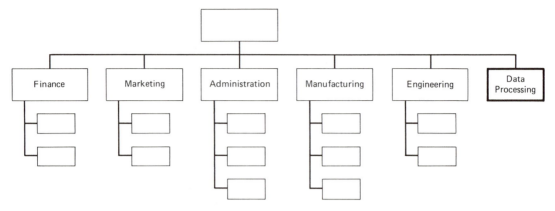

Figure 4.3   Data Processing in an Independent Location

Independent Location

In this approach the data processing function is independent and is placed at the organizational level, directly under the head of the whole organization (see Figure 4.3). The data processing department has the same importance, independence, and management attention as do all other principal functions in the organization. In internal organizational structure, it is very similar to the one described in the location within the service group. This approach is suitable for organizations where data processing is an integral part of the operations, as for airlines and banks.

Advantages

- See those of the previous approach, in which the data processing activity is located within the service department.
- Because of its location, it enjoys the same importance, independence, and management attention as any other principal function in the organization.

Disadvantages

- See those of the previous approach.

CENTRALIZATION VERSUS DECENTRALIZATION

The question of whether to centralize or decentralize data processing activities is one with no definite answer, the reason being that it depends very much on the structure of the organization for which the data processing function provides services. It should be noted that there is a distinct difference between physical dispersion and managerial decentralization. The latter implies mainly the delegation of formal authority. Decentralization is the tendency to delegate formal authority to lower organizational units; centralization is the tendency to withhold such authority. In practice, these two approaches are usually not alternatives: data processing is either more centralized or more decentralized.

In discussing this question, it might be useful to review the characteristics of centralization and decentralization.

Centralization

In this structure all data processing resources are located in one major data center. These resources, which include personnel and data processing equipment, are managed as one entity. The primary characteristics of centralization are

- Development and implementation of new applications are done in uniform manner. This approach provides better control for standardization.
- Control of new applications is maintained, thus preventing duplication of new application systems development and saving in resources is achieved.
- Economies of scale are possible. Large systems and pooling of personnel may result in reduced cost per task.
- Managment is facilitated, since all resources are located closely.
- Planning and control is easier.
- Large data processing installations attract highly qualified people because such installations offer better career opportunities. Therefore, better design and programming productivity is possible.
- Management and control of data bases are easier, thus preventing duplication in both data preparation and storage.
- Security measures and control may be implemented more easily.

Decentralization

Although the term "decentralization" may imply a weakening of the center of the organization, this does not have to be the case. Decentralization can strengthen the central function by clarification and correct procedures. The primary characteristics of decentralization are

- Flexibility is greater.
- Greater motivation at the local levels is combined with greater knowledge of the local needs.
- Better response time both in service and development of new applications can be achieved.
- Economies of scale are lost.
- Each unit will attempt to opitmize its performance, sometimes at the expense of other parts of the organization.
- Lack of uniformity may exist.

• Implementation of security measures is more difficult, since the resources are located in various locations.
• It might be easier to manage small groups.

Centralization and decentralization combined

Combining the structures of centralization and decentralization may take advantage of the best of the two approaches. If we consider centralization and decentralization as two extreme approaches, then five organizational combinations of data processing resources can be identified.[2]

1. Centralized hardware with decentralized system development and programming
2. Centralized hardware and programming with decentralized systems development
3. Decentralized hardware with decentralized development and progamming
4. Centralized hardware, systems and programming with directly linked satellite installations
5. Centralized hardware, systems, and programming with autonomous satellite installations

The decision of which approach to select, and to what degree it should be implemented, depends on a number of considerations, including cost of equipment and personnel, cost of communications, the need for local availability of applications, the need for control of all data processing activities, reliability, and work load in the central site.

DATA PROCESSING FUNCTIONS

System Development

Each new system or application must be analyzed, designed, coded, tested, installed, maintained, and evaluated periodically. The following are brief descriptions of each function. A detailed discussion of the first six can be found in Chapter Five.

Systems Analysis. The first step in developing a new application system is the analysis of the present system, the perceived requirements, and the alternative solutions. The primary objective of this function is to determine the best alternative for the user's requirements as they were defined during this process. This activity is also responsible for conducting the cost-benefit analysis of the proposed solution.

[2]P. Ein-Dor and E. Segev, *Managing Management Information Systems* (Lexington, Mass.: Lexington Books, 1978), p. 85.

Systems Design.   The primary aim of this function is to produce the detailed design and specifications of the new application system. This task should also include the data elements definition and the data-base design as well as the documentation definition.

Applications Programming.   The task of this function is to translate the detailed design into coding and to perform testing of the programs according to the specifications that were developed by the system design function. Documentation of the programs is the responsibility of this function.

System Testing.   This function is responsible for the testing of the new application system in accordance with defined requirements and specifications. This task includes designing the testing procedures, selecting the test data, performing the test using the test data, and just before the actual installation, using the live data and volumes.

System Installation.   This task includes planning the installation procedures, acceptance of the system and its documentation, training the users and data processing personnel, and integrating the new system with the existing systems and data bases.

System Maintenance.   This function is responsible for making minor modifications and corrections. This function is essentially a combination of the five functions discussed previously.

System Performance Measurement and Evaluation.   This function is responsible for conducting periodic measurements studies of the system, so that improvements can be made. A detailed discussion of this topic is presented in Chapter Six.

Operations

The production function of data processing is very similar to that existing in the manufacturing environment. Computer operations provide processing support for jobs requiring various resources of data processing equipment. This is done by operating the computer system, mounting tapes and disks, and performing program-directed operations. The operational functions may be divided into three categories; scheduling and control, equipment operation, and production support.

Scheduling and Control.   This function typically consists of scheduling, interfacing, auditing, maintaining user contacts, providing job setups, and maintaining the work flow.

The scheduling function involves priority and resource allocation decisions. The objective of the scheduling function is to improve the efficiency and effectiveness of the computer installation by using decision-making procedures. To perform the scheduling function, both availability of resources and processing requirements have to be identified. In developing a scheduling system, a measure of performance is selected to determine the effectiveness of the scheduling system.

The measure may be of one or more types, such as utilization of available resources, throughput, response time, and so on.

The control function is responsible for supporting the flow of work within
the computer installation. It is also responsible for quality control of input, processing, output, storage of data and other material used during the processing of
work, and contact with the users.

Equipment Operation. The functional responsibilities of this operation are
to provide the resources and procedures required for processing the work, such as
operators, backup, and maintenance.

Production Support. This function is responsible for all the needs required
for operation, such as maintenance of the tapes and disks library, performance
measurement and evaluation, maintenance of supplies, and security implementation of the central site.

Technical Support

A large and complex data processing activity requires technical support in various
fields, such as data processing standards, technical assistance, system programming, data-base administration, communication and teleprocessing, and performance evaluation.

Data Processing Standards. This function is responsible for developing, approving, publishing, maintaining, and enforcing procedures for data processing
standards for all functions of the data processing activity.

Technical Assistance. This function provides technical support to the data
processing activity as well as to the users. Technical support includes consulting,
maintenance of the technical library, maintenance of a library of a system and
programs documentation, and publication of newsletters to inform all involved of
any changes in or additions to the data processing resources.

System Programming. This function is responsible for the maintenance of
the general software systems, such as the operating system, data-base mangement, and so on.

Data-Base Administration. This function is responsible for planning, selecting, designing, installing and maintaining the organization's data bases.

Teleprocessing Facilities Administration. This function is responsible for the
design and acquisition of all equipment needed for installing data communications
facilities as well as the management of these facilities.

System Performance Evaluation and Configuration. This function is responsible for measuring and evaluating system performance and utilization. Using
various techniques, such as operations research models and simulation, this function may propose modifications, changes, and solutions to existing problems.

Management and Administration

Management and administration of the data processing function include a number of tasks that support the activities performed by this department: supervision, planning, security, reporting, personnel management, financial management, and administrative support.

Supervision and Project Management. Supervision and management refers to the organization, direction, measurement, and control of all data processing resources, such as people, equipment, software, and all other resources that are part of the data processing activity.

Planning. Planning refers to the estimation, projection, and scheduling of future activities. Planning is usually done for the short, medium, and long range and is updated constantly. Data processing management is responsible for preparing plans that take into consideration the organization's goals and objectives.

Security. The security task is responsible for ensuring adequate protection for the data processing facilities, such as backup, physical security, controls, and protection from error, fraud, and vandalism.

Reporting. An important component of management is the reporting function. Reporting in data processing may include reports on projects progress, plans, and systems performance and utilization.

Personnel Management. Personnel management is one of the most important management responsibilities. It involves recruiting, selection, placement, training, testing, compensation, and benefits. Personnel management may also be defined in terms of planning, organizing, motivating, and controlling human efforts for the accomplishment of the data processing organization goals.

Financial Management. This function is responsible for maintaining the financial records, budgeting, pricing, billing, purchasing, and all other financial tasks of the data processing activity.

Administrative Support. This function provides the general adminstrative support services required by the data processing activity.

PATTERNS OF DATA PROCESSING ORGANIZATION

Basic Organizational Structure

Figure 4.4 illustrates the organizational structure of a typical data processing activity. In this form data processing is divided into three major groups: system development, production, and technical support. This is the basic organization structure of a data processing department, and it is usually the appropriate structure for small-to medium-sized data processing departments. This partitioning may be refined to more than the three basic units depending on the size and the

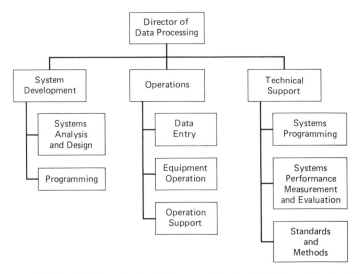

Figure 4.4 Typical Organizational Structure for the Data Processing Function

complexity of the data processing department. In the following sections we discuss the traditional approaches of data processing organizational structure.

Applications Organization

In this system, the data processing activity is organized according to the organization structure. Each unit specializes in systems for a specific set of users, such as marketing, finance, and manufacturing. Figure 4.5 illustrates this type of organizational structure. Each of these units is further divided into system analysis, design, and programming, which are responsible for both development and maintenance of application systems. The members of each unit have specialized knowledge of their users' counterparts. The primary advantage of this structure lies in the specialization it creates. Its primary disadvantage is the problems it creates when integration of data bases is needed.

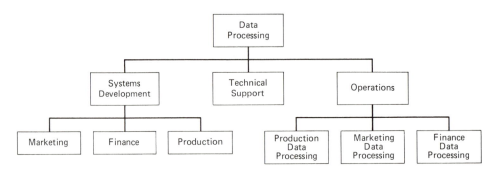

Figure 4.5 Applications Organization

Functional Organization

In the functional organization plan, the data processing activity is divided according to the functions performed. There is a system analysis unit, a system design unit, a programming unit, and so on. A project is transferred from one unit to another according to its progress, until it is completed. The advantages of this organization type include the specialization of people within their profession and the standardization of enforcement. The development process, however, may take longer since knowledge of the specific application also needs to be transferred. This structure is illustrated in Figure 4.6.

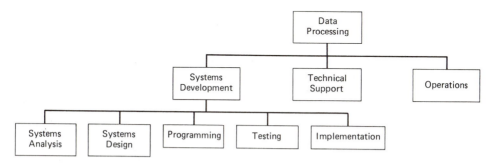

Figure 4.6   Functional Organization

Matrix Organization

This type of organization is based on the functional organization plan, but it includes project managers/coordinators for each project or groups of related projects. The project manager is responsible for controlling the project development process. This type of organization eliminates some of the disadvantages of the applicational and functional structures. An example of the matrix organization structure is given in Figure 4.7.

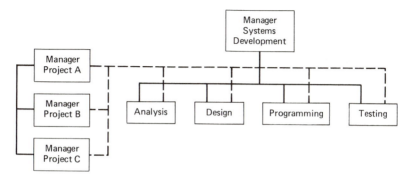

Figure 4.7   Matrix Organization

Complex Data Processing Department Organization

Ahituv and Hadass[3] have proposed an organizational structure for large data processing departments that combines the three approaches discussed previously. This organizational structure is illustrated in Figure 4.8. The data processing department consists of five major units:

1. A managerial unit, which is responsible for all management tasks, such as administration, clerical services, and so on

2. A economic unit, which is responsible for the financial aspects of the data processing activity, such as budget, cost accounting, and pricing.

3. A production unit, which is responsible for all production work, such as equipment operation, data entry, input/output control, tapes and disks library, and so on.

4. An information services unit, which is in charge of application development, maintenance, and modifications for a specific user or for a group of related users. Each unit employs systems analysts, designers, and maintenance programmers, while application programmers are borrowed from the programmers' pool. Standards and procedures are coordinated by the chief system analyst.

5. An internal resources unit, which is responsible for all internal resources, including computer systems utilization measurement and evaluation, capac-

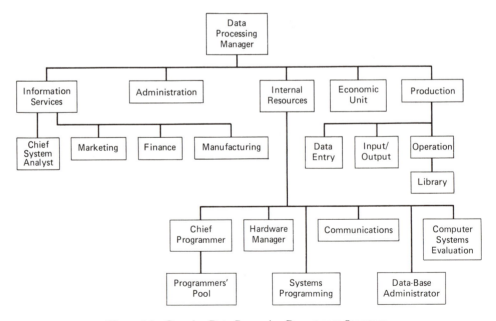

Figure 4.8   Complex Data Processing Department Structure

[3]Ahituv and Hadass, "Organizational Structure," p. 53.

ity planning, development and implementation of operating systems and other major software systems (e.g., data-base management), communications, managing the data base, security measures implementation and control, and the programmers' pool.

This organization is based on the following principles:

1. Development of user-oriented applications is done by personnel who specialize in the user's area.
2. Users do not have to deal with numbers of people; for each user there is one person who coordinates the user's need.
3. Production is centrally managed.
4. Personnel are divided into two categories: professionals, who provide technical support and are managed by highly skilled professionals, and administrative staff, who support the management of the data processing department.

DATA PROCESSING POSITIONS

Definition of Job Families

Job families are categories of jobs that have similar responsibilities and skills and require similar qualifications and knowledge. It is important to note that these descriptions are general and may vary from one organization to another. The following list may be used as a guide in preparing job descriptions for any data processing environment.

Management

Director of Data Processing (or MIS). This individual plans and directs all data processing of the organization. The director of data processing is responsible for long-range planning, budgeting, and operations.

Business Manager (Associate Director). This individual is responsible for preparation and review of data processing budget, controls pricing and billing of computer services, and negotiates contracts with vendors. The business manager reports to the director of data processing.

Systems analysis and design

Manager of Systems Analysis. This individual is responsible for the development of data processing and the design of the data processing solutions. The manager of systems analysis plans and supervises the work of systems analysts and designers, prepares designs and/or specifications for the programs, estimates resources (personnel, cost, and time) requirements for systems projects, and plans and directs recruiting, training, and development of systems personnel. The manager of systems analysis reports to the director of data processing.

Senior Systems Analyst. This individual is in charge of the analysis effort on major projects. Together with users, the senior systems analyst defines data processing projects, formulates statements of problems, defines objectives, and designs solutions; translates requirements into systems design; establishes and administers a project planning, control, and reporting system; and analyzes project status and informs mangement of deviations from plan. The senior systems anaylst reports to the manager of system anaylsis.

Systems Analyst. This individual works with the senior analyst on large projects. The systems analyst works alone on small projects, works closely with personnel in problem areas to gather information and define systems objectives and documents all findings and results. The systems analyst reports to the manager of systems analysis.

Methods and Procedures Analyst. This individual is responsible for development of improved methods and ways of organizing work. The methods and procedures analyst designs procedures for improvement and participates in the design of data processing systems to ensure that procedures are designed correctly. The methods and procedures analyst reports to the manager of systems analysis and design.

Operations Research Analyst. This individual applies management science techniques, such as mathematical modeling and simulation, in solution of difficult systems design. The operations research analyst reports to the manager of systems analysis and design.

Programming

Manager of Applications Programming. This individual is responsible for the development and maintenance of programs. The manager of applications programming plans, directs, and evaluates the work of programming personnel; is responsible for establishing and enforcing standards; and usually works from program specifications and designs prepared by the system analysis function. The manager of applications programming reports to the director of data processing.

Senior Applications Programmer. This individual performs detailed designs, coding, testing, documentation, and implementation of programs. The senior applications programmer is responsible for changes and maintenance of existing programs. He or she reports to the manager of programming.

Applications Programmer. This individual usually works on only one or a small number of applications and is capable of working independently. The applications programmer reports to the manager of programming.

Operations

Manager of Computer Operations. This individual is responsible for the operation of computers and all other data processing equipment, including scheduling, assignments of operators, and monitoring of operations efficiency. The manager of computer operations establishes and enforces standards to ensure the quality of production. He or she reports to the director of data processing.

Shift Supervisor. This individual is responsible for all data processing operations during the work shift, including computer, support, and peripheral equipment; assigns operators as needed; and ensures that rules and procedures are followed. The shift supervisor is responsible for maintenance of equipment and for all backup procedures. He or she reports to the manager of operations.

Senior Computer Operator. This individual is responsible for the operation of a large-scale computer for the duration of the shift or for the operation of one computer system in a multisystem site. The senior computer operator monitors the console and reacts according to instructions. He or she reports to the shift supervisor.

Computer Operator. This individual assists in operation of computers and may operate the central console when needed, usually mounts magnetic tapes and disks, services printers and card readers, and operates stand-alone computer support equipment. The computer operator reports to the shift supervisor.

Magnetic Media Librarian. This individual is responsible for maintaining the library of magnetic tapes, disks, and any other magnetic media. The magnetic media librarian reports to the manager of operations.

Supervisor of Production and I/O Control. This individual is responsible for setting up and scheduling of jobs for production. He or she reports to the manager of computer operations.

Senior Production Control Clerk. This individual is responsible for the data control function during a shift or for the data control function of a single site in multisite organization. He or she reports to the supervisor of production.

Production Control Clerk. This individual prepares jobs for processing, enters the appropriate commands, and gathers output for postprocessing. The production control clerk reports to the supervisor of production.

Data-Entry Supervisor. This individual is responsible for the staff that performs key entering and verification, plans and directs work load, and is responsible for all data entry equipment. The data-entry supervisor reports to the manager of operations.

Data-Entry Operator. This individual operates one or more data-entry devices. He or she reports to the data-entry supervisor.

Supply Clerk. This individual is responsible for maintaining an inventory of supplies used in data processing installation, including issuance of orders when replenishment is required. The supply clerk reports to the manager of operations.

Systems programming and technical support

Manager of Systems Programming and Technical Support. This individual is responsible for creating and/or maintaining the operating system software, including selection and installation. Also, he or she is responsible for the data-base management and the telecommunications systems, helps in projecting hardware and software requirements, and directs the technical support function of the data processing department. The manager of systems programming and technical support reports to the director of data processing.

Senior Systems Programmer. This individual is a specialist in one or more components of the operating system software and is responsible for problem determination and repair. The senior systems programmer reports to the manager of systems programming.

Systems Programmer. This individual specializes in one of the operating system components or subsystem such as compiler and is capable of modifying utilities or installing changes in the operating system. The systems programmer reports to the manager of systems programming.

Manager of Data-Base Administration. This individual designs and controls the use of the organization's data resources. He or she is responsible for file organizations for shared data, creation of data dictionaries and standards for the use of data, and ensuring data integrity and security. This individual reports to the manager of systems programming.

Data-Base Administrator. This individual helps to determine applications information requirements, coordinates data collection and external storage needs, and helps in organizing the data. The data-base administrator reports to the manager of data-base administration.

Manager of Data Communications/Telecommunications. This individual is responsible for the design of data communications networks and installation and operation of the data links. He or she reports to the manager of systems programming.

Data Communications Analyst. This individual specializes in network design, traffic analysis, and data communications software. He or she performs simulation and modeling, defines standards for data transfers and evaluates and selects communication equipment and telecommunications access methods and protocols. The data communications analyst reports to the manager of data communications.

Technical Librarian. This individual is responsible for organizing and maintaining the library of technical literature and documentation and reviews documentation for conformance to standards. The technical librarian reports to the manager of systems programming.

Documentation Support Specialist. This individual provides services as required, such as technical editing, graphics, and publication. He or she may also participate in systems specification and design. The documentation support specialist reports to the manager of systems programming.

Administration

Data Processing Budget and Costing. This function coordinates the preparation of the data processing budget and establishes costing and charging methods and procedures. It reports to the associate director of data processing.

Data Processing Planning.   This function is responsible for preparing long- and short-range plans, including new applications, systems development, and software and hardware acquisition. It also assists in preparing training programs and organization changes. It is responsible to the associate director of data processing.

Training and Education.   This function is charged with the planning and administration of training and educating the data processing staff to enhance their skills. It arranges education programs for users and management, and it arranges, if necessary, for outside education. It reports to the associate director of data processing.

Computer Security Specialist.   This individual is responsible for the protection of data and computer resources. He or she reports to the associate director of data processing.

Fitting Jobs to the Environment

The jobs just outlined are present in almost every data processing environment. However, the exact definition of a specific data processing activity may vary from one organization to another depending on the particular environment. In preparing job descriptions and definitions the following factors should be taken into consideration: the size of the data processing department, the extent of systems development being done by the data processing department, type of work performed, and the work load. Analyzing these four factors will help in determining the number of people required, the structure of the organization needed for effective management, the possibility of combining duties, and so on.

Preparing Job Descriptions

Job descriptions are formal definitions of duties and responsibilities for each position in the data processing environment. The advantages of implementing job descriptions are the following:

- It defines the location of the job within the organizational unit to which it belongs.
- It is the basis for determining the relative importance, difficulty, and qualifications needed, so reporting, evaluation, and salary determination can be made.
- It may be used as a training device. The employees will know what they should do, to whom should they report, how they will be evaluated, and so on.
- It defines career paths.
- It provides a basis for planning and budgeting.

The basic structure of job description should include at the least the following items:

- *Job title.* Short functional description of the job assignment, for example the manager of system analysis and design.
- *Salary group.* Salary level within the organization that is assigned to this job.
- *Reports to.* Job title to which the position reports, for example, reports to the manager of systems development.
- *Job titles.* Titles of those who are supervised by this position, for example, systems analyst, system designer, management science anaylst, and so on.
- *Number of persons supervised directly by this position.*
- *Narrative description.* Short description of the work to be done by this position.
- *Responsibilities.* List of all the responsibilities of this job position.
- *External contacts.* A short list of job titles outside the data processing department contacted by this position.
- *Qualifying experience.* Description of the qualifications, training, and education required for this position.
- *Evaluation criteria.* A short description of how this job position is evaluated.

SELECTED READINGS

AHITUV, N., AND M. HADASS. "Organizational Structure of a Complex Data Processing Department." *Information and Management,* Vol. 1, no. 2 (1978), pp. 53–57.

DAVIS, J. J. "Economic Effects on DP Departments." *Data Management,* Vol. 14, no. 10 (October 1976), pp. 41–43.

GILDERSLEEVE, T. R. "Organizing the Data Processing Function." *Datamation,* November 1974, pp. 46–50.

GREEN, R. J. "The Data Processing Manager's Status." *Datamation,* June 1974, pp. 66–67.

HENEMAN, HERBERT G., III, DONALD P. SCHWAB, JOHN A. FOSSUM, AND LEE DYER. *Personnel/Human Resource Management.* Homewood, Ill.: Richard D. Irwin, 1980.

INTERNATIONAL BUSINESS MACHINES. "Organizing the Data Processing Activity." In *Installation Management Series.* White Plains, N.Y.: IBM, 1973.

SCHRODERBEK, P. O., AND J. D. BABCOCK. "The Proper Placement of Computers." *Business Horizons,* October 1969, pp. 247–258.

TANSIK, DAVID A., RICHARD B. CHASE, AND NICHOLAS J. AQUILANO. *Management: A Life Cycle Approach.* Homewood, Ill.: Richard D. Irwin, 1980.

WHISLER, T. *The Impact of Computers on Organizations.* New York: Prager, 1970.

5

Managing the Data Processing Activity

MANAGING PROGRAMMING PROJECTS

Introduction

Computer technology has been developing at quite a rapid pace, and the hardware that exists today is so efficient that prices have been driven down. Software development, on the other hand, has not kept up with this rapid pace of advancement. The traditional method of designing software actually involved no particular formal methodology and it was typically up to the designer to go about it however he or she saw fit, frequently just coding from scratch. When new ideas emerged or problems crept up, more codes were added to the already existing program to add the new idea or to work around the problem. The final outcome was often a very large program that was very complicated, logically confusing, and largely inefficient.

With software projects growing in size and complexity, software developers had to develop some better programming habits in analyzing the problems before even attempting to start coding. Thus, software experts recently have sought to develop a more systematic and formal approach in the design, development, and implementation of their software. What they have developed is a very structured approach that starts at a very high conceptual level that is systematically and logically decomposed into smaller and smaller, more detailed, levels. The designer, in essence, begins with a very general concept and proceeds to analyze and detail this design in a step-by-step fashion.

This chapter presents a general discussion of the generally used approach to software development, including a brief, but thorough, outline of the concepts, procedures, and characteristics involved.

The ideas presented here are not set in concrete; there is no recipe for software development. All the ideas are for the consideration of the reader to aid in stimulating structured conceptual approaches to project management. Certain concepts are relevant to almost any job, such as structured analysis and design, while others are only truly applicable to specific situations, for example, chief programmer team.

The Software Development Life Cycle

To increase the success rate of managing the processes and tasks associated with the development of a computerized system, the concepts of project life cycle, configuration management, phased system life cycle, or the stages a system passes through as it matures was introduced to the modern-day working environment in the late 1970s. This approach subdivides the project tasks into manageable sections or phases. This subdivision provides the necessary understanding required to produce the desired end result and identifies milestones, ultimate control, and discrete deliverables.

This approach was developed out of a need to manage. To manage one must understand the mechanics of the entire system. The understanding of what is to be accomplished becomes clearer as the job is broken down into smaller, self-contained pieces of work.

The objective of the system life-cycle approach is to create, deliver, and sustain an operable and supportable system. The advantages of this approach include the minimization of the risk of excluding important tasks, a reduction of project planning time, the definition of the phases used to develop good communications among all involved parties, the identification of the project responsibility at all times, the establishment of the project accountability, and the identification of the tasks that need to be delegated to other organizations. The phased approach presented here, subdivides the project in five areas:

- Requirement analysis
- Process specifications
- Architectural design
- Detailed design
- Implementation

Any number of phases is viable; the important idea is that identification enables management to see and exert control over the project.

For each of these phases, we present methodologies and related tools that will aid in achieving the goals of the particular phase under consideration. The methods presented here should give a good, solid base to develop the software development life cycle. However, the methods presented are by no means going to cure all your software development problems. In developing your own methodology, you must mold techniques that fit your own organization. Be flexible; if the environment changes, the method can be reshaped to accommodate those changes. The most important thing about your own software development life cycle is that it work and that it work effectively. To progress from one phase to another, the current phase must first be successfully completed. When a successful completion is impossible, the project leader has the option of regressing to a previous phase or terminating the project.

Requirement analysis phase

The method presented here to aid in the requirement analysis phase was developed by Tom DeMarco[1] and is known as structured analysis. Structured analysis is a systematic method of transforming user requirements for a computer system into structured specification of what the system should do.

Two tools are used throughout the structured analysis process. The first tool is called a data flow diagram. This tool helps to partition the requirements and document that partitioning before specification. The second tool (which will not be discussed in depth) is the data dictionary, which aids in documenting and evaluating the process interfaces produced by the data flow diagrams. There is a third tool, structured English, which is commonly associated with structured analysis. This tool will be discussed later, as part of the specification phase.

To illustrate just where structured analysis fits into the modern project life cycle, let us examine Figure 5.1, which represents a data flow diagram of the software development life cycle.

In the data flow diagram, each circle represents a process and the lines indicate the data entering or leaving a process. The purpose of the diagram is to illustrate how data flow from one process to another. The first item shown in the diagram is a survey of the user requirements, which is really a minianalysis phase. Although it is much less thorough than structured analysis, this phase is used to define what is to be built, to produce a budget, and to schedule information. The inputs to this phase are data gathered from dialog with users; the output is a feasibility document.

The second item is called simply structured analysis, but it really includes both structured analysis and process specification. These two phases will be described after pointing out what are the input and output from this phase. As input, the structured analysis phase receives both the feasibility document and the user requirements. This phase produces the budget, schedule, and physical requirements of the new system; the primary output is the structure specification of the system.

The next phase in the project life cycle is the structured design phase, which consists of two components, the architectural design and the detail design, both of which are discussed later. The inputs are the structured specification and configu-

---

[1]Tom DeMarco, *Structured Analysis and Systems Specification* (Englewood Cliffs, N.J.: Prentice-Hall, 1978).

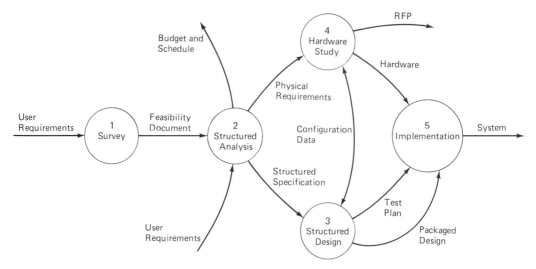

Figure 5.1   Data Flow Diagram of the Software Life Cycle

ration data from the hardware study; the outputs are the system test plans and a final system design.

Phase 4, the hardware study, actually is done concurrently with the structured design phase. This study analyzes the hardware needs of the system and determines what the final system hardware configuration will be.

Finally, the implementation phase will take the hardware, test plans, and system design and output a completed system. This phase will also be discussed later.

Now let us examine the structure analysis phase by discussing the data flow diagram presented in Figure 5.2.

Initially, we study the current environment. First, we determine the context to be studied and which people will be affected by the new system. Next, an early guess is made as to the scope of the project: Who will the users be and how much of their work will be subject to change? Now we begin to work with the users to learn and document the current operations. Here we build up data flow diagrams of the current operation from the user's viewpoint; we employ the user's terms, partitioning, department and individuals' names, form numbers, and whatever else might make the diagrams easier for the user to follow. The study is complete when the user accepts the data flow diagrams as an accurate representation of his or her current mode of operation. The diagrams are then published internally and we move on to the next stage.

Now we derive the logical equivalent of the data flow diagrams. This is primarily a clean-up task that involves replacing all physical items that were included in the data flow diagrams for the user's benefit with the logical equivalent of those items. This leaves us with data flow diagrams that illustrate the current logical system.

The next step is to make a model of the new logical system. We do this by

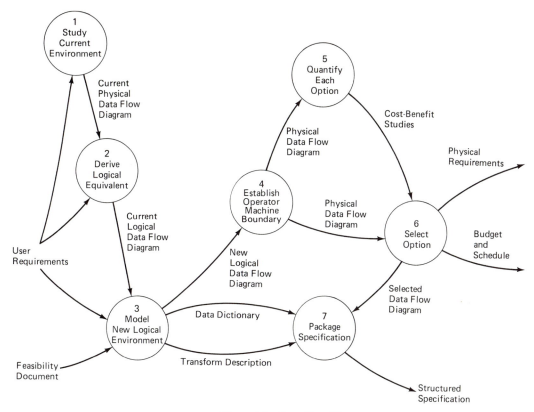

Figure 5.2 Data Flow Diagram

incorporating the ideas in the feasibility document and the user requirements. The goal here is to build a paper model of the new system using data flow diagram and the data dictionary and actually specifying each process. But, remember, you are still looking only at a logical model of the system, so you only describe what is to be done, not how to do it.

We now establish the user-machine boundary by partitioning the activities between user and machine. Here we want to produce several alternatives with varying degrees of automation. This process produces several new physical data flow diagrams.

Next we perform a cost-benefit analysis on each of the previously produced alternatives from which we select the best.

Then, finally, we organize and enhance the components of the structured specification.

The structured specification has several qualities that make it superior to the large documents commonly found. First, it is graphic, which makes the system easier to understand. Next, the system is designed modularly, and small modules are easier to design, understand, and maintain. The structured specification is rigorous, maintainable, precise, concise, and highly readable.

Adoption of structured analysis in your organization is much like introducing a new idea. First, we try it on a small, noncritical project. We involve people who want to make it work. We document the effects of using the method, but do not go overboard. Before global introduction, we introduce an expert in structured analysis who can be referred to for all questions.

Structured analysis will tend to add work at the beginning of the software development life cycle. But in the long run, a better analysis will lead to less backtracking and faster design and implementation, not to mention a paper model of the system that the user has already seen and approved.

To begin work in this phase, a description of the desired end process/ product, a budgetary and time limit specification, the proper authorization that allows the commencement of work, and the associated business risks need to be obtained.

From this phase a statement of the scope of work and a user requirements report are generated. The statement of the scope of work describes in detail the amount of effort that will be required to produce the desired end system. The user requirements report explicitly details the user's needs and contains an initial glossary of data terms that will be used in the proposed system, the major conclusion made by the analyst/user team, the specific business requirements, the system specifications, and the amount of resources expended for this phase.

Process specifications phase

Process specification involves writing descriptions of each process identified in the structured analysis phase. In reality the process specification phase is part of the structured analysis, (it is discussed separately for simplicity), and the process specifications are included in the final structured analysis. Recall that in a data flow diagram, a process is denoted by a circle, and within each circle is a short phrase indicating what the process does. A complete data flow diagram will fully partition a system and document all the process interfaces, but it does not specify what is done within each process. It is the process specification techniques that are of help here.

There are two primary goals of process specification. The first is to describe fully, for each process (every process has its own specification), the transformation of the data flow from input to output. In developing the specifications, the second goal is to avoid, wherever possible, doing the same type of work in different processes; the specifications should be orthogonal.

The classical approach to writing process specifications has primarily been through text descriptions. The major difficulty with this method relates to problems in the English language (or any other language). English is replete with implications, ambiguities, and so forth, which always prevent the creation of specifications that have only a single unique interpretation. So what we need are methods for specifying systems that remove all possible ambiguities and thus are not subject to interpretation. DeMarco[2] advocates the use of three methods: structured English, decision tables, and decision trees.

[2]Ibid., pp. 37–46.

Structured English is a subset of English that eliminates undefined qualifiers (adjectives and adverbs), compound sentence structures, all modes but the imperative, all but a limited set of conditional and logic statements, most punctuation (semicolons, dashes, exclamation points, question marks, and ellipses), and out-of-line descriptions (specifically, footnotes). What we have left is a specification language with a limited vocabulary and a somewhat formal syntax. Structured English consists primarily of imperative English language verbs, terms defined in the data dictionary, and reserved words for logic formulation. There are three main types of structured English statements.

The first type is the simple declarative sentence, which performs a single action and continues; its flow chart representation is given in Figure 5.3(a). The second statement is the closed-end decision construct that processes one of two statements based on a conditional check; the flow chart is given in Figure 5.3 (b). The third type of structured English statement is a closed-end repetition construct that provides looping ability (see Figure 5.3(c)). Any mixtures of these types of statements are valid as well.

The following examples are really identical structured English specifications. The first example is much more rigid and formal than the second; however, the second is perhaps more readable than the first. The idea is to write specifications in a form that the user wants to see. Structured English is very flexible and can be altered, within reason, in many different ways to be comprehensible to the users.

A. Policy for grading MAPS 535 students

FOR EACH student in the class;

1. Record student's name in role book.
2. IF project completed AND was submitted on time, record grade of "A." OTHERWISE record grade of "F."

B. Policy for grading MAPS 535 students

FOR EACH student in the class,

1. Write the student's name in the role book.
2. If the student completes his or her term project and the student turns it in on time, give the student an "A" in the course. If this does not happen, give the student a grade of "F" in the course.

There are several advantages to the use of structured English. Structured English description techniques can be applied in almost all phases of project development. The descriptions can be stored in automated format. Structured English is a quick and natural way of writing specifications that are concise, precise, and readable and can be tailored to suit the user who must read the specifications. Also, when structured English specifications are coordinated with the data dictionary and data flow diagram, they help to check the system's consistency.

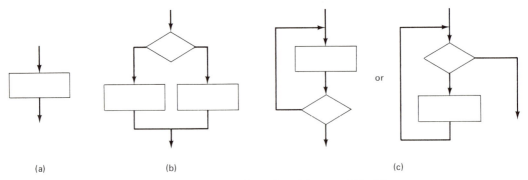

(a)   (b)   (c)

Figure 5.3 Examples of Structured English

Some disadvantages of using structured English also exist. It takes time to build the skills necessary to use structured English. Another disadvantage is that, given a specification that is syntactically correct, there is certainly no guarantee that it accurately specifies what it was intended to do. And, finally, the fact that it looks more formal than it really is will tend to scare off some users.

The following example, taken from DeMarco,[3] is used to illustrate decision tables and decision trees.

> If the flight is more than half-full and costs more than $350 per seat, we serve free cocktails unless it is a domestic flight. We charge for cocktails on all domestic flights . . . that is, for all the ones where we serve cocktails. (Cocktails are served on flights that are more than half-full.)

The problem with this statement is that it does not specify what to do if the flight is not domestic, if the flight is not half-full, or if each seat is not over $350. This flaw will be made apparent in both the decision table and the decision tree.

In a decision table we list all possible conditions that could occur and the actions taken given each case. The decision table for our example clearly points out the inconsistencies mentioned.

				Rules				
Conditions	1	2	3	4	5	6	7	8
1. Domestic	Y	N	Y	N	Y	N	Y	N
2. Over half-full	Y	Y	N	N	Y	Y	N	N
3. Over $350	Y	Y	Y	Y	N	N	N	N
Actions								
1. Cocktails served	Y	Y	N	?	Y	?	N	?
2. Free	N	Y			N			

The decision tree is simply a decision table in free format. Again this method easily points out the problems in the sample specifications (see Figure 5.4).

[3]Ibid., p. 215.

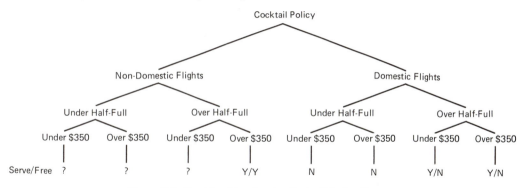

Figure 5.4   Decision Tree for the Cocktail Policy Example

When writing the specifications for the processes in structured analysis, one should not restrict oneself to a single method. Rather, one should use structured English, decision tables, and/or decision trees; whichever combination of methods is appropriate at the time.

To begin work in this phase, the user requirements report, the scope of work statement, a conceptual business and data model detailing the flow of information in the organization, and the data dictionary output are needed.

The documentation produced during this phase is primarily the process specifications, which are included in the structured specifications document produced throughout the analysis and specification phases. This report also contains a management summary, the schedule and budget plans, and cost-benefit and risk analysis statements for each alternative solution. In addition, a preliminary user manual may be produced at this point. The manual should describe, from a user's point of view, the flow data within the system and what is done to the data (again, we have not yet specified how the data manipulations are carried out).

Architectural design phase

At this point of the software development life cycle, we have a complete specification of what the new system is going to do. However, no thought has yet been given to how the new system is going to be implemented on the computer, so we must now begin to design a computer solution to the problem. Computer system design is a two-part process. Initially, the system must be divided into several small modules, where we state only what each module will do and the module's and output data; this is the architectural design phase. Then we design how each module is to perform its task; this is the detailed design phase.

The method of architectural design presented here is a rather informal method known as hierarchical functional design. This method is really just the combination of a method known as structured design and HIPO (Hierarchical Input Process Output) charts.

HIPO charts were originally developed by IBM[4] as a tool in the documenta-

[4]J. F. Stay, "HIPO and Integrated Program Design," *IBM Systems Journal,* Vol. 15, no. 2 (1976).

tion and maintenance of its software. It basically consisted of three parts; a visual table of contents (block diagram), an overview input processing output (IPO) diagram, and a detailed IPO diagram (see Figure 5.5). One of the major things that HIPO lacked, however, was the concept of the relationship between the data base and the overall system. To incorporate this idea of the data base, the HIPO/DB technique was developed, which was an extension of the original HIPO technique. It added two new features. First a data-base box was added to the IPO diagram, and second, the process block was further elaborated upon within to include a structured pseudolanguage to describe the function of the process block (see Figure 5.6).

Structured design is a set of techniques used to reduce the complexity of large programs by dividing them into a hierarchy of independent modules that are easily implemented and maintained. The partitioning of the system may or may not be the same as that achieved by the structure analysis phase. First, let us examine some reasons for partitioning the system into several modules. Simplicity is enhanced by dividing a system into several small pieces so that the pieces can be considered, implemented, tested, fixed, and changed with minimal consideration of their effect on the other elements of the system. It is easier to see how and why actions occur in a modular system. The goal of structured design is to subdivide the problem into simple, independent modules, where each module corresponds roughly to a procedure or function in a high-level language.

Structured design states three concepts to be considered when partitioning a system into modules. The first concept, known as modular strength, states that each module should perform only one function and do no unrelated processing. The next concept, known as functional strength, states that modules that accom-

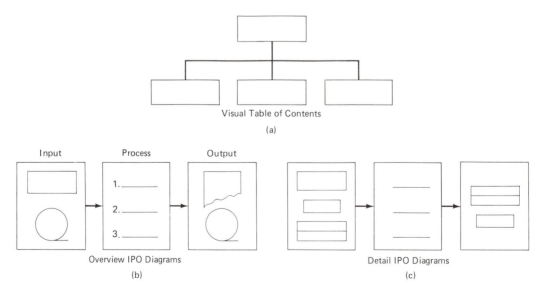

Visual Table of Contents

(a)

Input   Process   Output

Overview IPO Diagrams   Detail IPO Diagrams

(b)   (c)

Figure 5.5   Standard HIPO Package

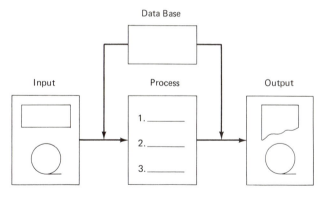

Figure 5.6 The HIPO/DB Package

plish a single logical task should be grouped together. For example, all various commands for an editor routine should perform a single logical task. The final consideration, module coupling and communication, includes several points. The fewer connections between modules the better; fewer connections mean less error propagation when modules are changed. Modules must certainly receive and transmit some data or they cannot function together as a system, but an attempt should be made to minimize the data coupling to include only parameters wherever possible, because global data and common data fields lead to endless error propagation and system debugging; the use of flags and artificial switches should also be avoided. The application of these three concepts when modularizing a system will yield a system that is understandable, easy to implement, and easy to maintain.

The most common complaint about breaking up a system into many small modules is the overhead incurred, in terms of execution time and memory overhead, by frequent routine calls. For execution overhead, some modules may execute only very few times, optional functions may never be called, codes for control switches are reduced or eliminated, and frequently used modules can be optimized. For memory overhead, single-function modules permit flexibility and precise grouping, possibly resulting in a lower memory requirement at any one time; optional modules may never be called, duplicate codes are reduced, and if any overlaying is necessary, it can be based on system characteristics and not on some arbitrary condition.

After structured design has been used as a guide for partitioning the system, the design must be documented. Documenting the system is done with HIPO charts. A hierarchy chart shows how each module is divided into submodules. An example of this is given in Figure 5.7.

One or more hierarchy charts will be used to show the hierarchy of the system's modular breakdown, which is defined through the structured design process.

The IPO chart expresses each function in the hierarchy in terms of its input and output and describes what the module does. An example is presented in Figure 5.5.

Each module in the system will have its own IPO chart, which completely

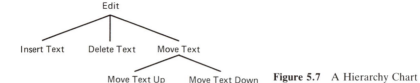

Figure 5.7 A Hierarchy Chart

specifies the module's interfaces with the rest of the system as well as defines what the modules does.

The hierarchy charts and the IPO charts serves as a complete description of the system's architectural design.

The hierarchical function design method regulates the interaction of the structured design and HIPO techniques. The system should be designed in a top-down manner; several passes should be made through the design process. Initially, the system's modular design should consist only of a few general modules; then on each pass through the system, the modular partitioning should become increasingly more detailed, until you reach a level consisting of only small, easy-to-manage modules. On each pass, the design should be documented using HIPO charts, and all the charts should be included in the final documentation. There should always be frequent review sessions with the users to make sure that the system that is being designed fits the users' needs.

There are many benefits to the hierarchical design process. User understanding and agreement on functional content are made easier. Missing or inconsistent information is identified early. Functions are discrete and thus more easily documented and modified. Module interfaces are simple. And, finally, the resultant design supports structured top-down coding.

To begin work in this phase, the user requirements and the structured specifications reports, the schedule and budget plans, and the data dictionary output are needed.

The primary documents produced during the architectural design are the HIPO charts, which describe the modular system. Audit and security specifications, detailed hardware and software requirements, and revised budget and schedule plans should also be documented. In addition, some high-level detail, such as file names, can be added to the user manual. And remember always to review all documents against the original specifications as well as with the users themselves.

Detailed design phase

The purpose of the detailed design phase is to give a detailed description of how each module, identified in the architectural design phase, is to perform its function. The classical method of doing this has been with the use of flow charts. Another method that is widely used today, and seems to be better than the flow charts is program development language (PDL).[5] PDL is a self-documenting pseu-

---

[5]Stephen H. Cain and Kent E. Gordon, "PDL—A Tool for Software Design," *National Computer Conference Proceedings*, Vol. 44 (1975), pp. 271–276.

docode approach of conveying the functional flow of a program as well as the flow of the modules themselves, by using English words written in a structured manner to describe the processing.

PDL has many advantages over classical flow charting methods. The most significant advantage of PDL is that the language is machine processable; that is, a PDL processor can analyze a detailed design of a system and find either obvious errors in logic or areas in which certain warnings may be appropriately issued. PDL produces a very people-oriented, readable, top-down design. When developing a design using PDL, you start with a very high level of detail, which is really nothing more than a restatement of what the process should do; then you proceed to iterate through the design adding more detail on each pass; the topmost level of this top-down design process is easily understood by all.

At the lowest level of detail, a complete PDL design contains all external and internal interface definitions, definitions of all error situations, identification of all procedures, identification of all procedure calls, definition of all global data, definition of all control blocks and most important, detailed specification of all processing algorithms of all procedures.

PDL is a structured language used to express how a module accomplishes its task. PDL uses the vocabulary of a natural language (English) and the syntax of a structured programming language. Structured English was developed from PDL; however, PDL is more a formal language than structured English.

The PDL language constructs, like that of any structured programming language, are designed to encourage and support the development of well-structured codes. To demonstrate the use of PDL, the six most common language constructs are discussed.

The assignment statement evaluates an arbitrarily complex expression and sets a variable to that value.

```
variable  :=  expression
TOTAL   :=  SUM1  +  SUM2
```

A procedure will change one or more variables that are returned as parameters of the procedure, or it will change some global data. A procedure must be "called" with its name and zero or more parameters (depending on the structure of the procedure itself).

```
CALL procedure name (parameter list)
CALL COMPUTE-GRADE (STUD-NUMBER,RESULT)
```

Functions always return a value. A function call appears anywhere within an expression; the function itself will be evaluated along with the rest of the expression.

```
variable  :=  function name (parameter list)
VOLUME   :=  HEIGHT*AREA(LENGTH,WIDTH)
```

The IF construct is used for conditional execution. Various IF conditions are checked and the statements following the first condition [which is True] are executed. If no conditions [result in True], the statements following the ELSE are executed; if no ELSE clause exists, then nothing is done.

```
IF condition
    one or more statements
ELSEIF condition
    one or more statements
ELSEIF
    one or more statements
ENDIF


IF EMP-NUMBER  =  3
    PAY  :=  PAY*1.1
ELSEIF EMP IS THE BOSS
    PAy  :=  PAY*2.0
ELSE
    PAY  :=  PAY*0.9
ENDIF
```

The DO construct is used to indicate repeated execution. The statements within the DO loop are executed repeatedly until the iteration criterion causes the process to terminate.

```
DO iteration criterion
    one or more statements
ENDDO


DOWHILE THERE ARE RECORDS TO PROCESS
    UPDATE RECORD
ENDDO


DO UNTIL THE "END" STATEMENT IS REACHED
    READ A RECORD
ENDDO


DO FOR ALL LEVEL 6 EMPLOYEES
    GIVE A 20% RAISE
ENDDO
```

The final PDL language construct to be examined is the DO CASE construct. This construct is used to select statements to execute based on some criterion. The selection criterion is evaluated to a particular value, and the statement next to that value is then executed; if none of the criteria is matched, then the statements next to the OTHER: are executed.

```
DO CASE OF selection criteria
      criteria 1: one or more statements
              .
              .
              .
      criteria N: one or more statements
      OTHER:  one or more statements
ENDDO

DO CASE OF TRANSACTION-TYPE
      ADD:     CREATE INITIAL RECORD
      DELETE: IF DELETION IS AUTHORIZED
                  DELETE RECORD
              ELSE
                  REPORT ERROR
              ENDIF
      OTHER:  REPORT ERROR
ENDDO
```

These examples have shown how some of the individual PDL statements function. A complete sorting module written in PDL is given next. Figure 5.8 shows the equivalent module using a flow chart.

```
SORT (LIST, SIZE OF LIST)      IF SIZE OF LIST > 1
            DO UNTIL TO ITEMS WERE INTERCHANGED
            DO FOR EACH PAIR OF ITEMS IN LIST
                IF FIRST ITEM OF PAIR > SECOND ITEM OF PAIR
                    INTERCHANGE THE TWO ITEMS
                ENDIF
            ENDDO
        ENDDO
        ENDIF
```

It is obvious that the PDL design is much more compact and readable than is the flow chart solution.

One of the factors mentioned erlier that made PDL a useful tool is that it is machine processable. The PDL processor receives as input several PDL segments (like the sorting routine) as well as text segments. A text segment may contain purely textual information such as commentary, data formats, assumptions, and constraints. The processor will analyze the PDL segments for validity and perform formatting on the segments as well. The output from the PDL processor will be a complete document containing a cover page, table of contents, the body of the design (PDL and text segments), a reference tree that shows how segment references are nested, and a cross-reference listing that contains the page and line number at which each segment is referenced.

There are many advantages to the use of PDL. As was seen in the earlier examples, PDL can be written at any level of detail. A rough outline of the entire problem solution can be quickly constructed. Criticisms, suggestions, and modifi-

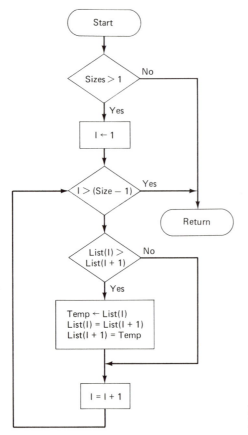

Figure 5.8 A Flow Chart of a Sorting Module

cations can be easily incorporated in the design. The PDL design process is an iterative process with increasing detail, where the top level is easily understood by all. A PDL design is a highly readable way of communicating ideas to other people. It is hard to wave your hands in PDL; if there is a gap in the logic, it will become immediately apparent. And, finally, PDL works equally well on large and small projects.

To begin work in this phase, the user requirements report, system specifications, architectural design, and data dictionary output are needed.

From this phase the program specifications, test system, updated data base and dialogue design documents, production procedures, conversion plan, implementation plan user/operator training programs and reference tools, and system documentation are generated. The test system includes the test data and testing procedures. The conversion plan will state how the data in an existing system are to be converted to the proposed one. The system documentation consists of drawings, manuals, and other support items that completely and accurately reflect the system being developed. The major document produced by the detailed design phase is the document output from the PDL processor. Lower levels of detail may also be added to the user manual; for example, the questions that the system will ask the user will be known, and some of the data types should also have been determined by this point. Finally, you should always review the system with the users and see if the goals specified in the analysis portion of the development are being met.

Implementation Phase

The implementation phase involves three processes: translating the detailed PDL description into programming language, testing each module individually, and then testing the integrated system.

In the following system structure, we can implement the system in a bottom-up or a top-down manner, An example is presented in Figure 5.9.

Using bottom-up implementation, the bottom modules are implemented first. Each of these modules is easily tested individually since it needs no other modules to function. Then the modules on the next level above are implemented, and again these modules are easily tested since all the modules they need to function are already implemented and tested. When the modules on a higher level are being tested, you are already performing the integrated system testing as well. The process of iterating up the tree is continued until the system driver is reached. At this point the entire system has been implemented, and system integration testing has been done.

The bottom-up approach is a good technique when a solution is very well defined and is not likely to change. However, the problem with this technique is that the user cannot see the actual system until the top-level driver is implemented. This is after the entire system is implemented and fully tested (i.e., at the end of the project). At this time, changes will be hard to design and expensive to implement.

The top-down implementation approach avoids the problem mentioned for the bottom-up approach; however, this method is more time consuming and more expensive. In the top-down implementation the top level of the system is implemented and tested first. The additional work that is needed here is that, since the top-level modules call routines that have not yet been written, program stubs, which pretend to perform the actual operations of a module, must be written for

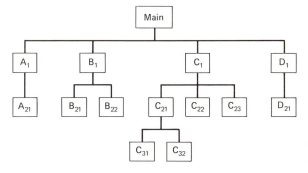

Figure 5.9 An Example of Implementation

lower-level modules and inserted into the system to test the individual, higher-level modules and the integrated system. This implementation method is also an iterative process, but in this case you implement from top-most modules to bottom-most modules.

Top-down implementation is a good approach because the user is able to see the top-level operation of the system in the implementation, and at this point modifications will be much easier to accomplish. The problem with this method is that system correctness is assumed, not proven, until the last stub has been replaced, and if a major problem is encountered with a low-level module, the problem could spread upward and necessitate altering the entire system.

From this phase, a fully operational application system, a project completion report, and a system evaluation report are generated. The project completion report details how the project meets its scheduled milestones and any problem encountered. This evaluation process will reveal weaknesses in the original projects estimates. By identifying the problems, one can strive to circumvent them. The system evaluation report details how closely the system performs the tasks outlined in the user requirement report. The primary document produced during this phase should be a very-well-documented, well-written code that can be easily maintained. In addition, any final details, such as I/O formats and actual examples of system usage, should be added to the user manual. And, finally, the product should be reviewed against the original goals, and the new system should be extensively tested.

Summary

Several different methods that can be used to improve the software development life cycle have been presented. These methods are not intended to solve all the problems associated with software development, but merely to serve as an improvement over many of the more commonly used techniques. In creating a software development life cycle for your organization, you will need to select the most appropriate combination of techniques for the surrounding environment and mold these techniques to fit what works most effectively in your organization.

Management Considerations in the Transition Period

Making changes is never easy. Whenever we are used to doing things in a certain way, we are resistant to new approaches, even if we know that there are probably many benefits in the change. Actually, we are downright scared. Such is the case in implementing the software development life-cycle approach. It is very hard to convince analysts and programmers who are used to conventional methods that the new method of design may be better than the methods they have been using. After all, they attribute their success to their ability to perform well in the existing software environment. And the proposed new method has not even been proven to be worthy of all the attention.

Thus, the transition period of changing the methodology of software design to something so different can certainly be a difficult one. Where the previous environment placed emphasisis on unstructured situations, the new environment emphasizes structured ones. Where the previous method based performance on individual efforts, the new one bases it on team efforts. Therefore, once it has been decided that some form of structured design is to be adopted, the organization should determine some sort of plan to follow to make the transition easier for the organization as a whole. In doing do, the organization should also be very careful to take into consideration several organizational aspects that must be incorporated into the plan.

First, there is the consideration of age versus youth. As has been mentioned earlier, the senior members of the software environment may be resistant to change. Yet it is their experience, wisdom, and sound judgment that are the most valuable if a structured environment is to work. We cannot emphasize enough the importance of educating these individuals to adapt to the new environment and, at the same time, reinforce the status they have deservedly attained.

Another consideration to be dealt with, in addition to the personnel already existing, is the personnel selection and evaluation in this new software environment. In an unstructured environment, a subjective approach by management has often been used to hire individuals, but it is questionable as to whether that approach will be effective in a structured environment. A person who may have been suitable in the past may not be for this new environment. For example, a person who is very independent may work well in the previous unstructured situation, researching problems independently, but in a structured environment, where one of the key factors is team effort, the same individual may not fit in as well.

And then there is the question of personnel evaluation. Previously, personnel could be evaluated on individual performance. But in an environment where group effort is emphasized, it is simpler to evaluate the performance of the group as a whole rather than its members individually. And if current evaluation methods were used to evaluate individual performance, this, in the sense, is a direct conflict with emphasizing the role of a team.

Measurement of progress is still another consideration. In the traditional software environment, one of the key measurements of progress on a project was how many routines of the program have been coded and tested. But in the new environment, that is what it wants to avoid. It is more important to have the design laid out, analyzed, studied, reanalyzed, and so on well before the coding and testing are done. Thus, a new standard of measurement is needed where measures of completeness of definition and design at each level of the system need to be determined.

Costing presents one of the biggest problems. As it stands, there is not even a clear-cut method of determining the cost required to develop software in the traditional method, let alone the new method. Some measurement of cost, however, will have to be determined.

There are several steps that management might take to make the transition period easier and smoother. Some of these steps may include[6]

[6]Lawrence Peters, "Managing the Transition to Structured Programming," *Datamation* (May 1975), p. 93.

1. Obtaining support for the transition from upper management; have its commitment.
2. Defining the features of structured design that are to be used.
3. Developing a training program to educate the people about structured design methodology.
4. Identifying the key individuals and obtaining their help and support.
5. Reorganizing the structure of the organization if it is necessary.
6. Establishing some sort of quality control to maintain and monitor this software environment.
7. Monitoring the costs associated with this environment.
8. Reviewing and revising, if necessary, current methods of evaluation.

Management Tools

The estimation of software development is necessarily based on certain assumptions regarding project management. This results from the fact that any attempt at controlling costs, and thus cost estimation, is based on a presumed methodology of project management that derived from the application of certain management tools. This section describes specific management tools that have been instituted to address some of the characteristics of software development that were described previously.

Project plan

The project plan as described by Metzger[7] provides one of the more important tools for managing development projects. Under difficult circumstances that characterize the management of the development project, proper and extensive planning is an absolute necessity.

It should be pointed out that a good effort in this direction will have the following characteristics:

1. The plan must be modular for the same reasons as those applicable to the development cycle and programs. Here, that means that, whereas each section must be able to stand alone while retaining its own identity, the plan must be divided so that there is a reasonable, logical flow from one section to another.
2. It must be in writing; otherwise, the entire exercise is pointless.
3. It aims to describe what the problem and job are, how these are to be approached, and which resources are necessary.
4. It deals with contingencies of two types and allows for the extra resources to meet these 'unplanned' obstacles.
   a. Specific, identifiable problems for which specific solutions are detailed

---

[7]Phillip W. Metzger, *Managing a Programming Project* (Englewood Cliffs, N.J.: Prentice-Hall, 1973), pp. 145–190.

   b. Unforeseeable problems for which specific solutions are not yet possible
      but must nevertheless be anticipated through realistic resource planning
      and allocations.

 5. It must be sufficiently readable and brief so that everyone concerned with
    the project will actually take the time to study it. Remember: People are
    only people and mountains of heavy reading will go untouched. What is
    necessary is enough discussion to define terms and guide the reader through
    the plan.

 6. It will have been contributed to by everyone with a continuing responsibility
    on the project including the user. If not, its reference will be reduced.

 7. It will include an index to complete its usefulness.

As part of this plan, continually updated PERT (program evaluation and
review techniques) charts provide a means for monitoring project slippage.
Hence, it is immediately clear where a one-day slippage in schedule results in the
project being one day late. As is said about how projects get to be late, "you get
there one day at a time."

Another part of this plan specifies the control and distribution of documentation. In large development projects, which are characterized by having more
than one level of project management, the interaction among various groups on
the project is key to the projects' success. Therefore, it is essential that all necessary documents be distributed to all parties concerned in a timely and easily
updated form. A method that proved to be successful is the use of microfiche.

Metzger[8] suggested that the project plan should be divided into sections and
that each should broadly follow the same outline:

Objective: Clear but brief statement of the section's purpose.
Discussion: In tutorial style, an outline of the type of information appropriate to
             the section. Enough discussion is included to give the reader an under-
             standing of the philosophy on which the section is based. By scanning
             the objective and discussion subsections, the reader will be able to gain
             a good understanding of the plan without being burdened with heavy
             detail.
Detail: The heart of the plan. Defines terms, tools, procedures, functions,
             responsibilities, and schedules.

The project plan should be outlined at the outset and progressively completed as soon as the relevant decisions are made. Certain documents; such as the
design specification; will be subject to modification throughout the project's life;
however, the plan should be essentially finished by the end of the structured
design.

 1. *Overview.* Identifies the customer, the job, and the project's objectives.
    Gives background on the job environment. Explains how the plan is orga-

_____
[8]Ibid., p. 147.

nized and states whatever assumptions underpin it. Establishes a gross schedule noting each major effort.

2. *Phase Plan.* Describes individual phases, including primary and secondary objectives of each. Establishes the basic definitions to be used in further sections of the plan. Gives calendar dates.

3. *Organization Plan.* Identifies all groups and specifies responsibilities of each. Details changing structures as the project moves from phase to phase, giving an organizational chart at all junctions. Outlines the work flow.

4. *Test Plan.* Describes separate discrete levels, detailing facilities, tools, procedures, responsibilities, criteria, and objectives for each. Demonstrates the coherence of the testing hierarchy. Explains the testing of the test tools themselves.

5. *Change Control Plan.* Defines the procedures for controlling changes to the program system. Specifies the documents to be used as baselines, relative to which events are to be controlled. Describes compositions and operation of the change control board.

6. *Documentation Plan.* Defines the procedures and resources necessary for publication. Outlines the set of documents to be used. No new forms are to be written unless a proven need exists.

7. *Training Plan.* Describes training responsibilities and types: internal, external, technical, and nontechnical. Identifies required resources, detailing schedules, instructors, materials, facilities, and special considerations.

8. *Review and Reporting Plan.* Describes the formal procedures and general reporting structure. Demonstrates consistency between financial and technical reports and between financial reports and the accounting system.

9. *Installation and Operating Plan.* Defines obligations and degree of participation. Gives schedules, conversion methods, and cutover criteria. Includes multiple-site considerations if applicable.

10. *Resources and Deliverable Plan.* Gathers into one place all resource estimates and deliverable items mentioned or implied elsewhere in the plan. Includes personnel and computer schedules, milestones charts, and the budget.

11. *Project Plan Index.* To be complete and render the entire plan more usable.

Risk analysis

Work done by Howard, Schick, and Lin[9] and others have established procedures for measuring risk preference. With these tools developers have a methodology for translating their "expert" opinions into specific risk premium charges for specific projects. Hence, we have another example of a management tool useful in reducing errors in cost estimation.

---

[9]Lawrence H. Putnam and Ray W. Wolverton, *Tutorial Quantitative Management: Software Cost Estimating* COMPSAC 77 (Long Beach, Calif.: IEEE Computer Society, 1977), p. 313.

Development team approach

The team approach to software development is a useful mechanism for project control. First, it provides a focal point of control for interaction with parties outside the group, be they customers or other groups on the same project. Second, it provides a support structure for the numerous inexperienced persons, and it provides a control mechanism for programming products produced by junior-level programmers. Third, it increases team efficiency by relieving developers, whose skills are in high demand, of administrative tasks.

Change control board

The change control board is another important tool for management control of software development projects. One of the most unsettling characteristics of software development is that the definition of the task is always changing via new specifications. By overseeing changes, the change control board provides a mechanism for controlling the inevitable changes.

The principal feature of this board is that it provides for a systematic approach to change that includes a modification of the contract fee and the original cost estimates. One of the important consequences is that the customer gets feedback on the impact of changes to both schedule and the total cost of the project. This gives the customer an opportunity to review each change for its cost and benefits so that a decision in keeping with his or her interests can be made. Having the customer take the responsibility for the changes also keeps the customer from faulting the developers later in the project if the product is not delivered on the original delivery date.

One final advantage of the change control board is that it provides a focal point for the distribution of changes carried out through documentation changes. Accordingly, the board, by having the responsibility for changes, provides a focal point for resolution of ambiguous specifications.

Chief programmer teams

Chief programmer teams have as their primary focus a senior programmer who is responsible for the detailed development of the programming system. While often supported by additional personnel, the three main members of the team are the chief programmer, a backup programmer, and a program librarian. An interesting feature of the chief programmer team is the separation of clerical activities from the creative programming activities. This allows the technical people in the team to use their time more productively while, at the same time, enabling reliable and up-to-date records to be more readily available for monitoring and documentation purposes. As a result, this form of organizational structure enables better utilization of personnel and reduces the number of people involved in a programming project, thereby suppressing numerous communication and coordination problems, and subsequently achieves a tighter and better control of the progress of the development project.

Matrix management

The matrix management approach is achieved by superimposing the temporary project assignment upon the functional groups of the organization. The new structure is one of overlapping, task-oriented groups composed of persons with complementary specializations. This approach is a flexible and adaptive way of achieving a series of project objectives that use the diverse knowledge and skills of participating specialists without relying on a one-way flow of work or a rigid functional allocation of authority. As a result, this form of organizational structure enables a rapid gathering of diverse resources in response to changing external demands so that the project will not be interrupted.

Project library

The project library, or the librarian concept, is a key management tool for controlling documentation, both changes and updates, and for institutionalizing good communication flows, internal and external to the organization. The project library serves these functions by collecting at a central point all information concerning the project in a highly organized and accessible fashion. Additionally, the library staff performs the important clerical tasks, thus relieving programmers, designers, and so on of much of their burdensome paperwork and freeing them for their specialized duties. The results should be documentation that is complete, accurate, available, and up to date, at a focal point to service inquiries from within or outside the project team.

ESTIMATING SOFTWARE DEVELOPMENT COSTS

The following paragraphs describe the problem of estimating the costs associated with software development. The past history of frequent failure in forecasting development costs accurately has been due in part to the complexity of the estimating task and the lack of tools to perform the task.

The Nature of the Software Development Task

Introduction

The frequent story of mismanaged development projects suggests that a lack of understanding of the nature of the software development task is a significant cause of projects to exceed their estimated costs. In the following discussion, four factors are noted that help to explain the reason for this common problem. First, the development process is sometimes poorly understood. Second, it is difficult to measure adequately characteristics of the development process. Third, it is difficult to draw meaningful conclusions from the gathered data. And, finally, the software development task is, by nature, difficult to control because much of the process still remains an art.

Understanding the development process

The development of software can be characterized as an unstable process with frequent changes and large risks. Thus, it is the consequences of this risk that frequently contribute to failure of cost estimates.

Risk stems from two sources. First, because no software project is identical to any previous project, there are always the difficulties inherent in doing something for the first time. Frequently, the proposed project is sufficiently similar to some previous project that the risk is limited. However, whenever a completely new application is attempted, the risk involved becomes greater. It is in these situations that errors in judgment are frequently made. Typically, a concern takes on a new development application with which management has had little experience. Then it is not until the job is half completed and behind schedule that the members on the project realize that this task is different from previous tasks in some fundamental way. Although this phenomenon can sometimes be predicted ahead of time, rarely does the concern decline initiating new projects. The tremendous demand for new software is frequently just too great for either the designer or user to permit this to be a significant stumbling block.

Risk also stems from the instability frequently found in a development project. At the beginning of a project, it is common that even the user will not understand the requirements. As a result, both user and designer slowly evolve to a better understanding of the task to be done as the project progresses. This translates to frequent changes in software specifications. However, unless the original estimates and the user requirements are updated as the changes are made, disaster is nearly inevitable. Interestingly, this kind of problem is much more common on small- to middle-sized projects than on larger ones. It appears that designers of large projects find that they can ill afford these kinds of mistakes because of the large dollar variances they can cause. However, on smaller projects where designers are frequently less skilled or perhaps in a weaker position to force this methodology upon the user, this problem often causes projects to deviate from original estimates.

Several other factors, in addition to exceptional risk, are sometimes poorly understood in the development process. One characteristic involves the distribution of effort that is applied during the course of the development. The shape of this distribution (Rayleigh curve) is such that when the project is about 90 percent complete, it is only 67 percent done in time. Thus, this distribution supports the common experience that the project seems to stall in the "almost done" stage. What is important here is that managers be aware of this characteristic and that they communicate this fact to impatient users. Thus, a better understanding of this fact would help to reduce some of the tensions and frustration frequently experienced between users and designers.

A third misunderstanding of software development involves the type of programming product. There are four major types of programming products. First is the simple program, which is developed by the author to perform a specific task. Then there is a "programming product," which costs at least three times as much because its development is more elaborate.[10] The product must be generalized to perform on a class of problems. It must be well tested to assure reliability, and it must be documented so that it can be tested, corrected, and executed by anybody. The next programming product is the "programming system"; the costs are also up by at least a factor of three from the simple program.[11] This is a reflection of multiple programs whose interactions are rigidly defined through extensive documentation. Testing is extensive and time consuming because of the potential for subtle bugs hidden in the interactions between programs. The fourth type of programming product is the "programming system product." It costs nine times as much as the simple program[12] and is the most common result of a software development effort. The distinction among these types of programming products is not so important for the designer, who is usually fully aware of the distinction, as it is for the user, whose experience with programming may only have involved the simple program.

A fourth misunderstood characteristic involves the effort-time trade-off. Thus, Brooks' law, which states "adding manpower to a late project just makes it later," is supported by empirical evidence.[13] Brooks argues that "the man-month as a unit for measuring the size of a job is a dangerous and deceptive myth."[14] Implied in the notion of a man-month is that these two resources (effort and time) are interchangeable and that development time can be reduced by adding more personnel. This is far from the truth; the development time increases as we add more personnel in tasks with complex interrelationships. Thus management must be careful when deciding how to speed up a late project or it may delay it still further.

A fifth misunderstood characteristic of software development involves discrepancies between the model depicting the sequence of events and the actual sequence of events during the development process.

This phenomenon is actually just another way at looking at risk. Thus, if one is not experienced with a project similar to the one proposed, the risk is greater and the development sequence will more likely be different from the original one. Consequently, projects do need to be assessed for their risk potential so that an associated risk premium can be added to the base development cost.

Measure the characteristics of software development

A second factor important in describing the nature of the software development task centers on the difficulty involved in quantifying the characteristics of the development process.

First, there is a problem resulting from the lack of standard terminology.

[10]Frederick P. Brooks, Jr., *The Mythical Man-Month* (Reading, Mass.: Addison-Wesley, 1978), p. 5.

[11]Ibid., p. 6.

[12]Ibid., p. 6.

[13]Ibid., p. 25.

[14]Ibid., p. 16.

Although some success has been achieved in quantifying such measures as productivity, difficulty or complexity, effort, and verifiability, further work is still required.

Productivity is usually measured in terms of coded lines per unit of time. The first problem lies with the definition of coded lines: machine language, source code, simulation language code. The most common definition is delivered executable lines of object code. However, even this refinement is inadequate because a programmer is more productive when writing in a high-level language than when writing in a machine language.

A second problem involves the extent to which support staff will be included in this standard. Because the number of executable object instructions is a good measure of the size of a program, one would like to know how long it will take to produce a system containing X number of instructions. But there is more to the development of a system than programming. Forty to 50 percent of the development costs go to overhead costs for management, control, test development, standards, documentation, simulation, training and education, liaison administration, and so on.[15] As a result these costs are usually incorporated into a productivity measure. Thus, for just these two reasons, it is evident that a productivity standard remains of limited use in quantifying the programming development task.

Complexity is another characteristic of software development that has yet to be standardized. As previously alluded to, the complexity of a development project can significantly impact its costs. Some methods have been developed for measuring complexity, but their application remains somewhat less than universal. These methods will be described further later.

Although effort measured in person-months is among the more accepted standard measures in software development, this measure lacks true precision in that its mapping is neither one to one nor transitive. Because effort and time do not trade off directly, as previously described, the same task can take different amounts of effort when performed by two different teams.

Another reason, in addition to the lack of standards, that explains why it has been difficult to measure characteristics of software development centers on management resistance to collect data on the development process.

There are two reasons for this resistance. First, management and designers in general frequently find that they are under significant time pressure. Thus, they respond that they are too busy to spend time collecting data on their development projects. However, with management's pressure for better cost control and with the availability of automated data collection packages, more data from development projects are being collected today than in the past.

The second reason for management's reluctance to collect data stems from a fear that the data will be used against them. This fear, although perhaps well founded given the poor cost-control track record on many development projects, should not be a determinant because, without data on previous projects, the task of estimating costs for proposed projects is quite impossible.

---

[15]Putnam, *Quantitative Management: Software Cost Estimating,* p. 260.

Evaluate the software development data

An important factor in describing the nature of the software development task centers on the inability of researchers to evaluate the data previously accumulated on software development projects. A major consequence of this fact is that it is hinders research efforts in developing management controls such as cost estimating models.

Primarily, data from previous projects are difficult to evaluate because of the inconsistency of the data. In collecting cost data, each development shop includes different overhead items so that productivity standards between organizations cannot be compared. Similarly, the size, difficulty, and development time of a project are frequently measured differently. Size may be in source lines of code, machine lines of code, or even machine words of code. Difficulty has no universal measure but is usually dealt with in the imprecise terms of easy, medium, and hard. Total development time may be deceptive because it does not account for overtime among programmers, a practice that is common especially among projects that are late.

Recognize that control is difficult to achieve

The fourth factor important in describing the nature of the software development task is the difficulty involved in controlling a development project. The four characteristics that contribute to programming being thought of as an art are (1) lack of a reliability measure, (2) lack of a verification measure, (3) lack of a resource efficiency measure, and (4) lack of a specific programming methodology.

The lack of reliability measure encompasses the notion that there is no good way to assure that a program or system is free of bugs. This makes the manufacturing of software inherently different from traditional forms of manufacturing where there exists means to measure the quality of the product.

Verification involves the notion of whether a program does what it is supposed to do. Because there is no good way to check the "correctness" of a program, there can be no control of this measure of quality either.

Another characteristic of the software development task that makes it difficult to control projects involves the efficient allocation of resources. This problem stems from the fact that as of now it is difficult to distinguish between overruns that are the result of inherent difficulty of the task and overruns that are the result of bad decisions of project managers. Even if a project is completed within budget and on time, there is no assurance that the resources were efficiently used. It is possible that the piece of software could have been developed for half the cost. Although this is unlikely in practice, the fact remains that the lack of standards within the industry contributes to the difficulty in managing projects and controlling costs.

At present, programming remains something of an art because there is no specific methodology. However, as automated tools for program development, such as design languages and automatic code generators, become more commonplace, the ability to control projects costs will improve.

Thus, as the previous discussion shows, the nature of software development task is distinctly different from the typical manufacturing task. Because this task is not always well understood and because it is difficult to measure and control, the estimate of software development costs is unusually difficult to achieve.

Software Cost Estimation

Estimation of the costs of software development is based on several factors that in recent years have become fairly well established. Approaches, even if somewhat philosophical, have also been identified. However, before discussing these two aspects of estimation methodology, a comment and a warning about estimation are appropriate.

Cost estimation involves an assessment of what resources over what period of time will be required for a specific project. Because the mapping of this distribution to actual dollars is by far the easier task, literature on cost estimation generally focuses on the derivation of this structured distribution. Therefore, the context in which this presentation views cost estimation is in the derivation of this resource allocation distribution.

The warning required about software cost estimation centers on the fact that estimating procedures produce minimum cost functions. This is the result of assumptions made about the management of the project. Estimating procedures assume that project management will be performed in the optimal way. However, as experience has shown, this is not the case, and bad decisions by management can cause projects costs to increase. An example of this is when management delays a project further by adding more personnel.

Factors of cost estimation

There are several factors important in software cost estimation. Two of these factors, already adequately addressed, need no further comment here; person-months as a measure involving both effort and development time and object instructions per unit of time as a measure of development productivity. A third factor, which will be addressed next in detail, is difficulty.

Difficulty is usually at a minimum measured in the relative terms of easy, medium, and hard. However, Putnam[16] describes difficulty as measures that are superior.

In attempting to deal with noncomparability among projects due to their differences in difficulty, Wolverton breaks down programming into six difficulty categories[17]. First, there are control routines that determine execution flow. Second, there are I/O routines that control the flow of data in and out of the machine. Third, there are pre-/post alogrithm processors. Fourth, there are algorithm programs. Fifth, there are data management routines that manage data transfers within the machine. Sixth, there are time-critical processors that contain highly optimized machine-dependent code. Although Wolverton does not quan-

---

[16]Ibid.

[17]Ibid., p. 166.

tify these terms, this categorization goes a long way to explain variances among historical cost data. Finally, with a more refined data base of historical costs, one is better able to forecast future costs.

Putnam describes a different measure of difficulty that is based on his macro estimation model and a notion that difficulty is a function of the complexity of interaction between modules.[18] Putnam reports that difficulty is linearly related to the number of application subprograms and either the number of files or the number of reports. In Putnam's model, difficulty is the ratio of two system parameters: life-cycle size in person-years and the development time squared. The usefulness of Putnam's model measure is that it provides a quantitative measure of an intuitive concept.

Traditional methods

Management needs effective and accurate methods of estimating software costs. This need arises both from the trend of increasing of software costs as a percentage of total project costs and because software technology, being relatively young, results in lack of management familiarity and expertise in this area.

Several approaches to estimation have traditionally been employed. However, all follow the basic pattern of estimating the size of each activity and its duration and then making adjustments for risk and complexity. Finally, the amount of person-months, computer resources, and overhead support are converted to dollars, which establishes the total cost. These traditional techniques are described in the following paragraphs. Combinations of the approaches are often used.

Top-Down Estimating.   The top-down macro approach uses historical cost data from other similar software projects. This can be done for individual parts of the task or for the total project. It is a good method for the preliminary estimate. However, it has a danger of hiding technical difficulties. This is especially true for projects that are outside the organization's experience base.

Similarities and Differences Estimating.   This technique takes the top-down estimating approach one step farther by analyzing the project for similarities and differences compared with past projects. Complexity factors are often applied to the differences. Activities lacking in past projects must be estimated by other means.

Ratio Estimating.   Ratio estimation includes establishing standards for various characteristics such as productivity and program size and then classifying the task in terms of type and in terms of complexity. The estimator makes a quantitative rather than a qualitative estimate of program task magnitude. The most common measure is the number of instructions. The project cost is obtained by multiplying by some ratio cost per instruction factor. The problem with this approach is that it requires a very extensive data base of past projects to produce believable statistical standards. Because a data base cannot be transferred from one organization to another due to differences in the definition of terms, this approach is not available except to more experienced organizations.

---

[18]Ibid., Lecture 1, p. 1; Lecture 2, p. 39

Standard Estimating. When specific tasks are performed repeatedly, a cost standard can be defined and used in future task cost estimate. However, software tasks are not as standardized and definable as, say, manual factory production line operations, where this approach works best.

Units of Work Method. The units of work method, which utilizes in military terminology and a work breakdown structure, involves dividing the development task into units small enough to be estimated by those doing the actual work. However, although this method is good for formal costing, it is impractical for really large projects, the reason being that the design would have to be completed before the units were known. When performing the estimation, there is a tendency to lose sight of the project as whole, much interface coordination is needed, and groups sometimes tend to "pad" their own cost estimates.

In practice, it is recommended that a combination of all methods be used. In industry each organization attempts, in one way or another, to forecast future development costs from a data base of past experience.

Use of the Software Life-Cycle Model

By now it should be evident that an approach using system concepts should be applied to solve the difficulty of software cost estimation. A systematic approach has been evolving as an outgrowth of the traditional methods. The first is using the software life cycle and will be discussed next. The other two, algorithmic approaches and cost data bases, will be described in the next sections.

The basis for the life-cycle model, which is also known as Putman's macro model,[19] is illustrated in Figure 5.10. Here the cost build-ups for each stage of the software life cycle are shown as they are phased in time. The total cost envelope is shown also over time. This envelope is very closely approximated by a Rayleigh curve. The Rayleigh personnel equation is given as:

$$Y = 2 K (a)(t)(e)^{-at^2}$$

where: Y = rate of personnel use in time
K = Total life-cycle personnel used
a = $1/2t_d^2$
t_d = development time
e = is the base of the natural system of logarithms = 2.71828

Other relationships are:

$D = K/t_d^3$ = a measure of program difficulty
$t_0 = (1/2a)^{1/2}$ = the time of peack personnel
$t_1 = (3/2a)^{1/2}$ = the reflection point where the decrease in personnel slows

Figure 5.11 shows how the Rayleigh curve is integrated into a cumulative S-shaped pesonnel curve. The management implications of the software life-cycle model are as follows.[20]

---

[19]Ibid., p. 277.
[20]Ibid., p. 35.

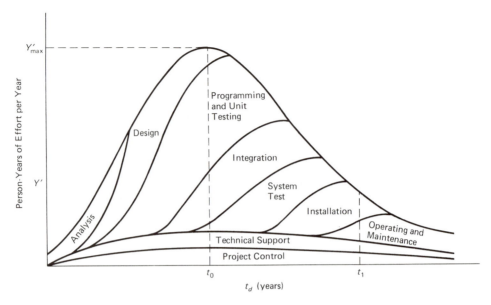

Figure 5.10   The Life-Cycle Model

The life-cycle size, development time, and difficulty are natural parameters of a system. The system is inherently stable and will be driven to these natural parameters. This will be a minimum-cost solution to the software design problem.

Management cannot shorten the development time of a system without increasing the difficulty. All changes take place in the negative time direction. Development time is the most sensitive parameter. It cannot be set arbitrarily by management.

Given a proper set of project parameters, a system can be designed to cost with only a small uncertainty.

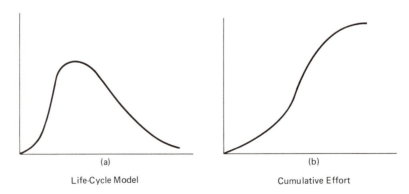

Figure 5.11   The S-Shaped Curve of the Life-Cycle Model

A method for estimating the system parameters by multiple linear regression analysis has been developed. The equation relationships are in terms of number of system files, number of system reports, and number of application subprograms. Given historical data, the multiple regression analysis will give equation coefficients. From these, the system parameters can be determined from estimations of the three variables given, which are generally not difficult to estimate.

Algorithmic approach[21]

The algorithmic approach to cost estimation is based on the assumption that costs vary proportionately with the number of instructions. The total number of instructions is divided into six categories of software for which the cost per instruction is estimated from historical data. The six categories (as described early) are

1. Control routines
2. Input/output routines
3. Pre- or postalgorithm processing
4. Algorithm (logical or mathematical) processing
5. Data management routine
6. Time-critical, optimized, machine-dependent code

Next, adjustments are made for complexity and/or risk factors before a final cost summation is made. Some organizations apply a programmer skill factor; however, empirical data have not shown the need for a skill factor. Each organization may develop its own costs per instruction for software projects categories as a function of degree of difficulty.

Cost data base

Based on the previous discussion of cost estimation, it is imperative to have accurate historical cost information in a well-organized data base. The algorithmic approach requires cost per instruction for key software instruction categories. In addition, sensitivity coefficients are needed for relative difficulty and familiarity.

It may also be desired to break down further the cost estimates into major software functions. A typical software project may include the following functions:

1. Software requirements analysis
2. Preliminary design
3. Detailed design
4. Coding and debugging
5. Development testing
6. Validation testing and operational demonstration

For each of these functions, a percentage of the total cost should be developed. These percentages could be applied after a total cost is obtained by the cost

[21]Ibid., p. 166.

per instruction algorithmic method. Cost estimates reports could thus be broken down both by cost per instruction category and by cost per software function.

Reasons for Failures

The well-defined project life cycle is not a panacea. In newspapers and trade journals, one will encounter stories of abandonment of projects, wasted resources, overrun schedules and budgets, and unsatisfactory and unused end products. The occurrence and degree of intensity of these problems are not related to a selected group of industries; the effects are felt universally.

The few projects that deliver the desired goods and meet budget and schedule goals are touted by project leaders and associated management. The many projects with a success level below that desired are concealed. The reasons quoted as causes for failure are numerous. Specific factors quite often cited are:

- Misallocation of resources
- Incomplete user requirements
- Lack of user commitment and/or support
- Lack of accurate and timely documentation

Misallocating of resources

The resources required to produce a computerized system include people, dollars, and time. Each resource exists in sufficient quantity until extraordinary demands are made for them.

Considering the many requests that a data processing organization receives for its services, the subdivision of these resources drastically reduces the amount available to a single project. The allocation of resources is usually based on the priority system. The resources for the most important projects are allocated first. The remaining resources are divided among the least significant projects. Project leaders that start a project with a fight for resources should be prepared for the challenge of trying to finish on schedule and within budget. The chances of the project being completed according to the estimates are slim.

Projects also fail to meet budget and schedule estimates because of the staff's past work experience. When the project with high priorities uses the most competent analysts and programmers, the remaining projects actually have a staff partially composed of part-timers, new hires, and employees waiting for retirement. The projects leader is forced to work with a staff that is not available for full-time employment. He must devote time to training the new hires and part-timers and try to increase the productivity of the older employees.

The problem of misallocation of resources can be minimized by employing better organization techniques. Management needs to keep abreast of the organization's commitment. Agreement to perform work should be based on the available resources, not on promises of acquiring more in the future. To minimize the schedule and budget overruns, better estimating procedures should be used. The best way to receive feedback on the performance of the current methods is to review the project performance report. The report will highlight the problems encountered. Based on the report, alterations in the current estimating procedures need to be made.

Incomplete user requirements

The prepared user requirements report is the key to all system development. It is this documentation that provides the baseline and guidance required by the data processing project team. When this report excludes details or makes false statements, the final system will not be what the user specified. This discrepancy can be a result of communication failure between the user and analyst, user and user, analyst and analyst, and analyst and programmer. Other causes for the inconsistencies are the analyst's misinterpretation of what the user wants, the promise of technology not yet in existence, and the end user not being sure of what is needed.

The effects of this problem can be minimized by the data processing organization developing an educational program. Analysts equipped with skills that can be applied in their work environment perform good work. This education should include a methodology for managing a project, the selected structured analysis and design techniques, how the user's organization fits into overall company plans, common phrases used by the users in their environment, the resources available to a project leader, and the ability to be more compassionate and understanding with people who are new to the data processing environment. Another way to improve communications is for the data processing organization to develop educational programs for the end user. These programs should clarify the common phrases used by analysts and programmers, state how data processing is providing support to reach the long-range business goals set by top management, and encourage them to question the analysts or programmer when they are confused or do not understand.

Lack of user commitment support

The lack of user commitment/support has the largest impact on the user requirements definition phase. This can be seen by examining the lack of concern for one's job or apathy. Apathy is common in today's working environment, no matter the industry or level of responsibility. When employees do not care, they exert little effort to help an analyst understand the problem outlined by the user. For employees who feel the automation of the current system will result in the loss of their jobs, they also provide little help to the analyst, trying to understand the environment and the problem.

Apathy can be minimized if the user's interest in his or her own job increases. Job insecurity can be eliminated by demonstrating to the end user how the new system will make the job more challenging, replace the old work with a new work load, and possibly provide a new channel for advancement.

Lack of accurate and timely documentation

The failure to make timely revisions to the internal and external documentation reflecting program/system additions or changes usually results in confusion. This confusion appears in the working environment when a newly hired programmer makes the statement, "Where is the documentation for the system I was hired to maintain?" And the reply is, "Here is what we have to date. Do the best you can." This situation usually is the result of the shortage of time and people resources. This limits the amount of effort devoted to documentation during the project life cycle. The shortage often is created because the project documentation task is left as the last one in the schedule. As the last task, the efforts are reduced when the pressure of overrunning the budget and schedule estimates rises.

One method to encourage a mirror image between the system and the documentation is to use the librarian approach, which would provide programmers with clerical help. The clerical employees would be given responsibility to maintain the internal and external documentation for every program written. The project leader can also rely on the programmers to document the source code as they write. But this approach will succeed only if the project leader is willing to "police" the programmers' output for comments. A third approach is to use one of the automated documentation tools. The purpose of these tools is to read the source code and produce structure and flow charts that reflect the real world.

An Integrated Model of Software Project Management

Throughout the previous discussion, we concentrated on the various techniques that can help us in managing a software project. However, we must emphasize that no project can be executed in a vacuum. Projects are carried out in organizations. As such, the organization environment, which includes the organization's structure, support, and resources, provides the basic foundation to support the techniques employed in managing a project. Therefore, to understand better the overall project management process, these three components—organization environment, techniques, and project together with their interrelationships—should be thoroughly investigated. As a result, we shall propose an integrated model using these three components as our basic building blocks. Figure 5.12(a) illustrates our goal: a well-managed project. In this case, the organization environment provides the strong foundation to support the techniques appropriately employed in a well-chosen project. As a result, the three components are in perfect harmony, and the project is in equilibrium with no destabilizing force acting upon it. In other words, appropriate mixtures and combinations of these three components with each complementing and supporting the other two are required to keep the project in balance.

Figure 5.12(b), on the other hand, indicates a situation in which the techniques are not appropriately employed in a well-chosen project. As a result, even if the organization provides a favorable environment, the project is unstable and is bound to fail.

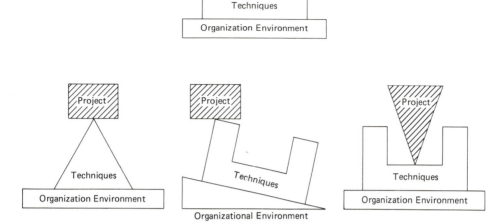

Figure 5.12 Possible Relationships among Project, Techniques, and the Organization

Oftentimes, we have a situation in which both the project is well chosen and the techniques employed are appropriate; however, the project still fails. This happens because the organization environment does not provide a solid foundation for the techniques employed. As a result, the techniques are "distorted" by the organization environment and cannot be utilized effectively to complement and support the project with which they would have worked perfectly otherwise. Figure 5.12(c) illustrates this situation.

Also, the organization environment and the techniques can be utilized poorly to support an inappropriate project. A project that should not have been undertaken at all fails simply because the supports are inadequate for the project. Figure 5.12(d) illustrates this situation.

It is interesting to note that these four situations are only a subset of the eight possible situations we can have according to our integrated model of software project management with three components—organization environment, techniques, and project. Figure 5.13 exhibits all eight possible situations.

MANAGING COMPUTER OPERATIONS

Introduction

The manager of the computer operations of the data processing department is responsible for many different areas, such as personnel, the environment of the computer center, and the hardware being utilized by his department. The predicament of the operations manager is the continuing and rapid escalation in the costs directly associated with the operations of the data processing equipment and the

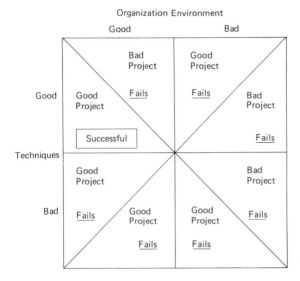

Figure 5.13 An Integrated Model of Software Project Management

production activities. The new developments that are taking place continuously in the computer industry may help the operations manager in reducing these costs. Some of the areas of interest to the operations manager are discussed throughout this book, for example, computer performance evaluation, organizational aspects, control and planning, and budgeting. The following discussion examines topics that are concerned with the operations function that are not covered elsewhere in this text.

Maintaining the Computer Center Environment

The data processing manager is responsible for the entire operation of the data center. One responsibility has to do with the environment of the computer center. This includes areas such as air conditioning, fire protection, security, and the constraints imposed on the computer center environment by the choice of computer hardware. When designing a computer center, there are four areas to be examined when selecting the proper equipment to be used for maintaining the operating environment for the data center.[22] These are

Computer Hardware Requirements. The computer manufacturer usually supplies the customer with all required data, such as recommended temperature and humidity for maximum uptime of the equipment. These data sheets usually indicate the ranges, maximum and minimum.

Cooling Load of the Computer Room. The computer manufacturer provides the customer with a simple cooling load calculation form that helps in identifying the capacity of the required cooling equipment. This load calculation form should be filled out by a specialist, combining the details of hardware with the heat

[22]James E. Hasset, "Hot and Cold Data Centers," *Datamation* (March 1981), p. 176.

equivalent of lights, people, outside air, and so on. In making these calculations, a reserve for future growth should be taken into consideration to prevent future problems.

Redundancy. Since air conditioning is vital for uninterrupted operations of the data processing equipment and the comfort of people working in the data center, a redundancy in cooling and heating equipment should be implemented. Usually, two units of air conditioning systems are installed.

Heating Needs of the Building. If the heat from the data center is to be used for heating of other parts of the building, this needs to be taken into consideration. It is recommended that the data center have its own unit.

How to conserve energy

A vital concern to many organizations these days is the conservation of energy, which if it is done properly, may reduce the costs of operation. There are many areas where energy can be conserved.[23]

Reduce Ventilation. Outside air that is brought into the data center must be cooled and dehumidified during warm weather and heated and humidified during cool weather. Cool air may reduce the cooling load, but the cost of humidifying it outweigh the cooling gain.

Use a Vapor Barrier to Minimize Infiltration and Exfiltration. It is very important to insulate the data center so that no loss of air-conditioned air occurs.

Minimize System Dehumidifying. Air-conditioning systems take out moisture while they are cooling air, so any moisture removed by the cooling process will have to be put back by the humidifier. Therefore, the amount of dehumidification should be limited whenever possible.

Operate Cooling Systems at Maximum Efficiency. Planned and preventive maintenance will keep the operating costs down as well as minimize downtime of the equipment.

Reduce the Cost of Humidifying. Humidification is required to replace moisture that is removed by the cooling process. Controlling this process may result in large savings.

Reduce the Cost of Reheating. There are times when the room temperature is satisfactory but moisture content is too high. To wring out the moisture, the air temperature is reduced. This air must be reheated during this "dehumidification-only" period.

Reduce the Cost of Providing Cooling. Proper operation and maintenance of the air-conditioning system will reduce the cost of providing cooling.

Use the Reject Heat for the Building Heating Needs. Using excess heated air for other parts of the building may result in large savings.

[23]Ibid., p. 176.

Troubleshooting

Occasionally problems will develop in normal operation of the computer center. Some of the more common problems that arise and the means of troubleshooting those problems are the following.[24]

The room will not hold temperature and humidity. This is usually the result of having too much outside air coming into the room.

The room temperature has been rising steadily with time. In most cases, it is because additional equipment has been purchased and installed, thus adding an increased sensible cooling load that the cooling equipment cannot satisfy. Not only must more cooling be supplied, but this means there is not enough cooling equipment to provide backup in the event of a failure.

Humidity is too low. The humidifiers may not have been maintained, resulting in malfunctioning floats, burned out heaters, and so on. This happens frequently because of the inactivity of the humidifier during the summer.

Humidity is too high. This happens when the humidistat malfunctions and keeps the humidifier on all the time.

Temperatures are constantly too low. Some rooms are controlled using wall-mounted thermostats. Look for heat-producing hardware that has been recently moved under the thermostat. The thermostat continuously calls for cooling and lowers the temperature of the entire room. Either change the thermostat location or move the hardware. Check the setting of the thermostat.

The room has hot spots and cold spots. Some air rebalancing is necessary to provide outlets for the heat-producing equipment.

The Operations of the Computer Center

Machine operations produce the EDP product. Computer center operations is the production line of the information system function, and there are strong similarities in the principles for efficient EDP operations and ordinary factory production. Senior managers can play a significant role in improving computer center operations, especially those aspects relating to personnel, housekeeping, performance measurement, and mechanics.

Computer operations generally consist of six major activities.[25] Understanding these activities and the work flow would help management in using the available potential resources of the data center.

1. Data preparation (conversion)—converting source documents (user supplied information) into machine-processable data.

2. Data control—organizing both input and output data into forms so that it gets where it is supposed to in the proper format at the proper time.

[24]Ibid., p. 177.

[25]ADL Systems, "Good Management of Computer Operations: 1. Whys and Why Nots of Facilities Management; 2. Computer Operations: A Little Attention Can Yield a 30% Productivity Increase," *Computers and Automation* (February 1973), p. 22.

3. Scheduling and staging—Schedule jobs and assembly of the needed data for processing, as well as disassemble them for distribution.

4. Machine operations—process the work, monitor its progress, deal with problems and maintenance.

5. Output control—Performing output processing and checking that the right data have been organized for dissemination.

6. Work delivery (post-processing)—prepare output and assure that the output is delivered to the right recipient at the right time in an orderly sequence.

Hardware costs are a substantial portion of the EDP operations budget (as discussed in chapter 7). Assuming that you have a balanced configuration matching your needs—an important but separate topic—it is then important to give attention to realizing the productive capability of this equipment. Therefore, a continuous review of the operations personnel might be beneficial.

The computer operations function is sufficiently critical that it should have a career path of its own, made attractive by the same status, policy, and incentive considerations given to other skill groups. This means establishing methods of recognition, reward, and motivation. Attitude plays a major role in obtaining sound performance in the operations area. Incentives, career path planning, programs that ensure stable staffing levels, training efforts, and broad review of personnel procedures and policies must be the starting point to realize such gains.

The following checklist outlines some of the most common problems encountered in computer operations.[26] If an organization reports some of these problems on a fairly regular basis, then it can be sure that it is time to look into the performance of its operations group.

Operations review checklist

1. There are regular delays in getting production-type work completed.
2. There is a high level of job reruns in the computer center.
3. There is a regular need to schedule extra machine time because of job overflow.
4. There is a regular flow of requests for additional hardware components or complaints about hardware inadequacies.
5. There appears to be a general lack of orderliness in physical plant, report flow, and internal procedures.
6. There is a relatively high rate of personnel turnover in the operations staff group.
7. There is no development program or route of advancement for operations personnel.
8. There is a relatively high, chronic level of keypunch or data-entry error.

[26]Ibid., p. 26.

9. There is a high level of reported hardware failure or hardware maintenance problems.

10. There are a limited number of internal performance measurement reports or procedures.

Most of these chronic problems are amendable to improvement because they are tangibles that are definable and easily measureable, with operations utilization and performance evaluation systems that are easily put into use.

Another step in determining areas of needed improvement is a tour of the computer room. It can tell the manager very quickly the level of management control that is being encouraged and exercised by his or her subordinates.

These are housekeeping items, to be sure, but they are a critical part of the operation of the computer center. If a visual inspection shows inattention to these details, you can be certain that it signifies lack of attention to larger, more significant details as well.

Written communications are vital to coordinate machine operations and provide management controls. All too often, EDP managers concentrate their systems analysis efforts on other departments while ignoring their own needs.

Recruiting and Retaining Computer Operations Personnel

The most critical resource in data processing is people. Without people, hardware cannot be operated and software cannot be developed or maintained. As a resource in short supply, people represent an economic problem to the data processing manager who must recruit and staff.[27] There is more detailed discussion of this topic in Chapter 10.

Hiring and retaining people will continue to challenge even the most successful manager of data processing. The problems in hiring and retaining personnel are becoming more serious as inflationary costs force salaries higher and higher. Naturally, one solution is allocating more dollars to pay top wages. However, dollars alone will not retain a professional: nor will dollars necessarily even be available. There are some alternatives and considerations that should not be overlooked in the search for both old and new methods to manage human resources.[28]

Basically, we manage people through motivation; however, motivation is produced by the responsibility in performance. There are five goals to utilize in the attempt to motivate a responsible employee. These goals are[29]

[27]Glenn T. Wilson, "Workforce Strategies: Hire, Win, Hire, Lose," *Data Management* (December 1981), p. 27–29, 32.

[28]Frank B. Thomas, "Hiring and Retaining Quality Computer Center Personnel," *Journal of Systems Management* (October 1979), p. 24.

[29]Ibid., p. 24.

1. Place the employee in the right job
2. Demand and measure the employee's performance
3. Inform the employee of his or her duties and responsibilities
4. Give the employee an opportunity to participate on a limited basis in some decision-making process
5. Reward the employee for good performance

Many computer centers have job descriptions, but do not have enough levels to motivate the people within a certain classification. Any person within the organization that cannot see a level above him or her to move into will not strive very hard to accomplish his or her job. Also, if an organization has all its employees in the same job classification level, then it will be that much more difficult to break the structure and to justify to upper management individuals who should be promoted.

By promoting people, a structure is created where people can easily equate it with the ability to move upward. Also, by promoting from the bottom, the manager can enhance the department's budget when the top person leaves because he or she can promote and drop the top classification.[30] This reduction in dollars spent by dropping the job classification line will assist the manager in justifying his or her promotions.

Employees want to know where they stand with their employers; thus, the evaluation should contain constructive criticism that is discussed face to face with the evaluator.[31] Unfortunately, many managers do not like to evaluate others and either fail to do the evaluation or "overdo" the evaluation. Basic strengths as well as weaknesses should be identified for each employee in the evaluation. Employees should be evaluated in the performance of the duties listed in their job descriptions, not by comparison with fellow employees, although this rule is sometimes hard to follow. The evaluations are a substantial help in ranking the candidates to be promoted. And a structured organization gives the manager the capability to promote.

Each person wants to be motivated, wants recognition, and is willing to take the risk of responsibility if the manager is willing to delegate. The best way to motivate is to delegate and be certain that the employee is held responsible for the tasks at hand. The ability to retain quality people depends to a great extent on the manager's ability. The use of detailed job descriptions, and if possible the breaking down of each job classification into three levels, will greatly enhance the manager's ability to motivate employees effectively by offering them job mobility within the operation.

Motivation for the employees will be greatly increased if an annual promotion schedule is followed. The promoting of a limited number of people throughout the operation each year will improve the outlook of the employees toward the

---

[30]Ibid., p. 25.
[31]Ibid., p. 25.

future. Annual employee evaluations greatly aid the manager in determining who will be promoted.

Encouraging job transfers within the organization will eliminate the trapped feeling in the mind of some employees and stimulate them to vie for open positions within the department.

Retaining quality people through good management techniques will always be a challenge. The manager should make it one of his highest priorities.

SELECTED READINGS

ADL SYSTEMS. "Computer Operation: A Little Attention Can Yield a 30% Productivity Increase." *Computers and Automation,* February 1973, pp. 22–24.

BIGGS, CHARLES L., EVAN G. BIRKS, AND WILLIAM ATKINS. *Managing the System Development Process.* Englewood Cliffs, N.J.: Prentice-Hall, 1980.

BROOKS, F. P., JR. *The Mythical Man-Month: Essays on Software Engineering.* Reading, Mass.: Addison-Wesley, 1975.

DEMARCO, TOM. *Structured Analysis and Systems Specification.* Englewood Cliffs, N.J.: Prentice-Hall, 1978.

DIJKSTRA, E. W. "Programming Considered as a Human Activity." In *Classics in Software Engineering,* ed. by E. N. Yourdon. New York: Yourdon Press, 1978, pp. 213–217.

DITRI, A. E., J. C. SHAW, AND W. ATKINS. *Managing the EDP Function.* New York: McGraw-Hill, 1971.

GILDERSLEEVE, T. R. *Data Processing Project Management.* Princeton, N.J.: Van Nostrand Reinold, 1974.

HASSET, JAMES E. "Hot and Cold Data Centers." *Datamation,* March 1981, pp. 176–180.

JENSEN, R. W., AND C. C. TONIES. *Software Engineering.* Englewood Cliffs, N.J.: Prentice-Hall, 1979.

METZGER, P. W. *Managing a Programming Project.* Englewood Cliffs, N.J.: Prentice-Hall, 1973.

NOLAN, RICHARD L. "Managing the Crises in Data Processing." *Harvard Business Review,* March–April 1979, pp. 115–126.

RUBIN, M. L., ED. "Data Processing Administration." In *Handbook of Data Processing Management,* Vol. 6, pp. 387–432. Princeton, N.J.: Van Nostrand Reinhold, 1971.

THOMAS, FRANK B. "Hiring and Retaining Quality Computer Personnel." *Journal of Systems Management,* October 1979, pp. 24–26.

SCHNEIDERMAN, BEN. *Software Psychology: Human Factors in Computer and Information Systems.* Cambridge, Mass.: Winthrop, 1980.

SODEN, J. V., AND G. M. GRANDELL, JR. "Practical Guidelines for EDP Long-Range Planning." In *AFIPS Conference Proceedings: 1975 National Computer Conference,* Vol. 44, pp. 675–679. Montvale, N.J., 1975.

WADSWORTH, M. D. *EDP Project Management Controls.* Englewood Cliffs, N.J.: Prentice-Hall, 1972.

WEINGBERG, G. W. *The Psychology of Computer Programming.* Princeton, N.J.: Van Nostrand Reinhold, 1971.

WILSON, GLEEN T. "Workforce Strategies: Hire, Win, Hire, Lose." *Data Management,* December 1981, pp. 27–29, 32.

6

Computer Systems Performance Evaluation

INTRODUCTION

Large amounts of money are invested by companies to acquire computer equipment and even larger sums are needed to operate, program, and maintain these systems. These investments have made computer users increasingly aware of the need to improve the efficiency of their data processing operations. Computers are used for many tasks. The range of tasks and size of the computer systems increase constantly. But computer users have difficulties in evaluating the efficiency of their data processing operations. Inability to make an accurate assessment has kept management fearful of the entire data processing area and has resulted, generally, in a hands-off attitude. This situation places a particularly heavy burden on that portion of management directly responsible for the data processing operation. They have to make recommendations on new and/or added equipment, but they lack objective techniques for evaluating the data processing operation and projecting needs.

Such a situation would be unacceptable in the management of human or mechanical resources. People are evaluated; machines are evaluated; where appropriate, their interactive performances are evaluated. But the data processing area, in many cases, remains a mystery, unresponsive to the profit and efficiency standards integral to any business. Strangely enough, data processing managers may find themselves in the unique position of gaining more prestige because they request increases in computer sizes (and costs, therefore) than because they effect sizable reductions in costs through more efficient management of current equipment.

Computer systems have become indispensable to the advancement of management science and technology. We observe growth in three main areas: computer utilization, computer technology, and computer science. More and more businesses, government, and academic organizations are using highly sophisticated technology within a field that made great progress from an art toward a science. This rapid growth has produced the requirements for a new field, the measurement of computer systems. In an atmosphere of escalating hardware and software costs and increasing budget scrutiny, measurement provides a bridge between design promises and operational performance.

Churchman[1] has stated that measurement is a decision-making activity and therefore must be evaluated by decision-making criteria. He named four aspects of measurement that are of a decision-making nature: language, specification, standardization, and accuracy and control. These are found in any performance measurement project.

A general performance evaluation approach must focus upon the isolation and characterization of significant performance parameters that characterize the rate and amount of the work performed and the availability of the various resources to perform the work. From this point of view, computer system performance evaluation can be defined as the process of analyzing and synthesizing the behavior of computer system performance parameters. Analysis includes the dividing of the computer system into components so each one can be analyzed separately. Synthesis includes the evaluation of the total system (hardware and software). To do that, techniques that provide both static and dynamic measures of resources performance are available. Improvements, which may be achieved by using computer performance evaluation tools and techniques, may be of interest for the equipment and software vendors, the data processing installation, and the users. Each one of these participants is motivated by different goals.

Users are interested in improving performance so that parameters such as response time and execution time will be improved. The computer installation management would like to maximize the system resources utilization to increase the throughput and decrease the cost of operation. Manufacturers are interested in computer performance evaluation for the purpose of meeting present and future demands.

The Purposes of Evaluation

There are three general purposes of performance evaluation: selection evaluation, performance projection, and performance monitoring.

Selection evaluation, in which the evaluator plans to include performance measurement as one of the criterion in the decision to acquire a particular system from a vendor, is the most frequent case. The procedure includes both hardware and software evaluation.

Performance projection is oriented toward designing a new system, either a

---

[1]C. W. Churchman, "Why Measure," in P. Schoderbeck, ed., *Management Systems* (New York: John Wiley, 1971).

hardware component or a software package. The goal here is to estimate the performance of a system that does not yet exist. For example, the central processing unit for a new computer or the executive system for a dedicated time-sharing system may be evaluated prior to final development to estimate the feasibility and performance of the design. A secondary application is the projection of the performance of a given system on a new work load.

Monitoring provides data on the actual performance of an existing system. These data can be used to forecast the impact of changes in the system, such as a reconfiguration of the hardware or an improvement in the frequently executed software modules. Such evaluation may also be concerned with obtaining a profile of the use of a system to make strategic decisions, for example, the characteristics of a job priority system. Because the programming system is an integral part of modern computers, the evaluation process must consider software as well as hardware in assessing performance. The capabilities of the operating system are central to the performance of the computer; particularly crucial are any multiprogramming and multiprocessing features. Application programs are a part of the computer system, and their performance is a component of the total systems performance.

MEASURES OF DATA PROCESSING PERFORMANCE

Levels of Evaluation

There are five levels of evaluation within the organization that are related to the data processing function; the following points relate to cost controls that are associated with each level.

Organization Level. This is the level that concerns top management. At this level are cost-control programs that address the question of effectiveness, as opposed to efficiency. McLean[2] distinguishes these terms by stating that effectiveness is concerned with "doing the right thing," while efficiency is concerned with "doing the thing right."

Computer Center Level. This level, dealing with efficiency, is concerned with accounting for data processing jobs. At this level, costs are perhaps better identified. They include not only gross computer costs, but also such labor costs as data entry, validation, and error correction.

Computer System Level. This level is concerned with in-the-computer accounting packages. With multiprogramming and multiprocessing, keeping track of what resources are actually used by a job becomes a complex matter. Some of the accounting packages discussed in this chapter address methods for evaluation at this level.

---

[2]E. McLean, "Assessing Returns from the Data Processing Investment," in F. Groenberg, ed., *Effective vs. Efficient Computing* (Englewood Cliffs, N.J.: Prentice-Hall, 1973).

Computer Subsystem Level. This level brings us to the performance moni-tors. Performance monitoring is thus only a portion of the overall subject of measuring computer systems. These monitors aim at a level of detailed measure-ment that is not currently possible with job accounting packages. Most of the work in the hardware and software monitoring is concentrated on measurement at this subsystem level.

Job Level. This level is of concern to the individual user. Areas such as programming optimization techniques, compiler efficiency, and automated pro-gramming fall in this level.

What to Measure—Some Measures of Performance

There are not yet any standards developed for measures of performance. This is because a theory of computer performance does not exist and the quantitative values from different computer systems are difficult to compare. However, certain loosely defined measures are generally accepted.

Response time

This is a measure of how long a user's job must await a service from hardware units such as the CPU or channels. Under optimum conditions, the response time is almost zero because there are no other jobs competing for service. As load increases in terms of the number of users, the rate at which the users are interacting, and the volume of hardware resources required, the re-sponse time worsens. A traditional measure of response time is the delay between submitting the job and receiving the job output. Computing a measure of re-sponse time is difficult in a multiprogramming design where two or more jobs can be using hardware resources simultaneously.

Throughput rate

This is a measure of the amount of useful work performed by the system. One way of measuring it is to find the ratio of the amount of elapsed time required to complete a job in a normal time-sharing environment as compared with the elapsed time in a batch environment. The closer this ratio is to one, the better the throughput. Another measure might be the number of specific tasks performed per time interval. However, the significance of this measure is ob-served only when the measurements are taken on different load levels of the time-sharing systems, thus including the variance in the measure.

Overhead percentage

This is the measure of the amount of CPU and channel time the operating system requires versus the amount of resources required of the user programs. This measure is clouded by the different functions performed by the operating system for the user (e.g., file maintenance). Some operating systems may perform useful computations for the user program. Time for this function should not be computed as overhead.

Component overlap measure

This measure determines whether or not the use of a hardware component is being overlapped to a significant extent with other components. If it is found that one is not, then there is good reason to suspect that the nonoverlapped component is a bottleneck to the system.

Software time measure

The amount of time that is spent in the different areas of a large program should be explored so that those areas with high utilization can be examined for potential improvement.

Software transition measure

The sequence of transitions within a program or within a program's data space is important for optimizing overlay designs. By transitions we mean the frequency in which the software program goes from arithmetic to I/O call, which may result in waiting time for data being read in and out.

Tuning

Tuning is the process of measuring the system, understanding effects, and making changes in hardware and software that may cause large increases in system performance.

User satisfaction

It is important to capture the user's feelings about the system so that his or her subjective frustrations may be tabulated and additional trends determined. Automatically correlating this information to the jobs he or she is operating and to the general system load and reliability significantly increases the usefulness of the measure.

Reliability measures

These measures statistically determine the reliability of the system and its subsystems. This is accomplished by maintaining a log (manually or automatically) of the errors and failures. These data are statistically analyzed to determine correlations and significance. The results are used to decide when sufficient effort has been invested in testing and whether a modified component is as reliable as its earlier versions.

System utilization measures

These measures include the amount of time the system is occupied with useful work, the setup time required to initiate operation of the system, the time required to set up a job, and the job rejections caused by poor procedures.

Raw time

Raw time is the actual speed of performance of any part of a computer; clock speeds, add rates, and memory speeds are typical examples.

TOOLS AND TECHNIQUES

Performance Evaluation Techniques

Performance evaluation techniques may be divided into five categories: audiovisual, time accounting, models, programs, and monitors. Brief descriptions of these techniques are presented in the paragraphs that follow.

Audiovisual

It is an effective technique that could be very useful in some situations. For example, a bell rings when a part of the system or the whole "crashes." This audio effect is important because the operator may not always be in a position to look at the console lights. Some idea of the behavior of a computer can be obtained by observing the status lights—in particular the WAIT indicator. Some examples are the CPU is idle if the WAIT indicator is on. Some part of the system is active if the SYSTEM indicator is on. A WAIT indicator on with a blinking SYSTEM indicator usually indicates an inefficiently used CPU, an I/O-bound system. A dim WAIT light usually means a CPU-bound system. This mode of measurement is a very limited one but nevertheless was and is used to gain some knowledge of the status of the system.

Time accounting

Logs.   Most installations have printed forms on which the user enters job name, submission time, and other job parameters. These forms also record the time that the job exits the computer center. This information can provide a gross total turnaround time in the center as opposed to turnaround time on the computer system itself.

Cycle and Add Time.   Early evaluations of computer equipment were often based on a comparison of CPU and add times. Speed was the dominating criterion, and the shorter the memory access time, cycle time, and add time, the higher the computer was rated. This technique was used primarily when programming was done in machine language and thus can be criticized for a number of reasons. In general, it ignores the organization of the machine, special hardware features, and software.

Instruction Mixes.   Instruction mixes have been used to provide a broader range for evaluation than do cycle or add times. The frequency of execution for typical instructions is used to specify a weighted average of execution times. Again, the machine with the lowest total time is judged superior. The mixes do consider more instructions than a simple add; however, they are subject to the same criticisms as cycle and add time for their inadequate consideration of special hardware features and the omission of any consideration of software.

Analytic models

An analytic model is a mathematical representation of a computing system. A number of such models have been developed, particularly those based on queueing theory. Models vary according to the type of mathematical analysis used. They are frequently employed to provide performance data on one particular component of a system, such as a disk unit.

It is difficult to evaluate these models as a class because of their diversity; a new model is usually created for each system or case. An analytic model is useful as an additional point of reference in hardware and software analysis. Some models can be altered easily to reflect new parameters, making this the first evaluation technique so far discussed that can be of a value in monitoring existing systems. In general, models are very important in the design of new systems.

Analytic models do not generally include a comprehensive set of operating system functions, nor do they consider the quality of software performance. The development and, particularly, the revision of models are tedious and time consuming. In many cases, the entire system may be too complex for modeling, given the interaction among hardware, software, applications programs, and the data base. The simplifying assumptions necessary to develop models in these instances tend to reduce their validity.

Programs

Kernel Programs.   A kernel program is a program that has been partially or completely coded and timed. The timings are based on the manufacturer's stated execution times for instructions that compromise the kernel program for a given machine. Both simple algorithms and elaborate data processing applications have been coded and timed as kernel programs. A kernel program may use the entire instruction set of a machine permitting consideration of characteristics that may be unique to the particular computer, such as differences in addressing logic, special index registers, number of addresses, and so on, that are overlooked by the previous techniques. However, most kernel programs do not include adequate I/O, and the timings are based on hardware specifications. With this method, there is no attempt to evaluate software.

Benchmarks.   A benchmark run consists of several programs run together as a representation of the existing or expected work load. A comprehensive series of benchmark runs can demonstrate differences in machine organization and evaluate the performance of I/O equipment and secondary storage as long as a variety of instructions is used by the test program. The benchmark may be constructed by selecting typical programs from the existing work load. Using the known characteristics of these programs, a benchmark is constructed that has a "distribution function" similar to the distribution function characterizing the real work load. A technique for constructing a benchmark is given in Chapter Two.

Synthetic Programs.   Like a benchmark, a synthetic program is one that is coded and executed, but it differs in that it does not necessarily exist beforehand. Like a kernel program, the synthetic program does not represent a real program, but, unlike a kernel program, it is coded and does include I/O considerations, files, and the environment provided by the operating system. Thus, in a sense, it combines the attributes of a kernel program and a benchmark.

The activities represented in a synthetic program must cover a wide range; some segments of the program will have to depend heavily on computational facilities, while others will have to make high I/O demands. The programs can be written in both assembly and higher-level languages to demonstrate the speed of the compiler output code. As with benchmarks, throughput can be evaluated by running a series of synthetic jobs sequentially and then using full multiprogramming capabilities, the comparison between the two times indicating the increased throughput for multiprogramming.

The major advantage of a synthetic program is the flexibility it provides, since jobs can be designed to include almost any desired measurement parameters. However, some of the problems of benchmarks also apply to synthetic programs. These difficulties include the representation of the current or projected job mix, run priority, run selection, weighting of different synthetic programs, and adequate attention to the effects of the programming system. It is also difficult to develop synthetic programs for terminal-based systems that respond on line. This technique requires a mobilization of personnel to code and debug the appropriate synthetic programs. Without any overall coordinating authority, there is the danger of a lack of standardization.

Simulation

Simulation, if used correctly, may be a good technique for evaluating the performance of computer systems. Not only is the present system modeled, but a simulation model provides a test bed in which different parameters can be varied experimentally. Simulation models can be used for selection, design, tuning and expansion studies of computer systems. Two types of simulation have been used in studying computer performance.

Simulators have generally been offered in proprietary software packages such as SCERT and SAM.[3] The simulators use some type of table look-up and equations to estimate the behavior of a simulated job mix. The results from using these packages have been reported to be very good in the batch environment, but their validity in multiprogramming or real-time systems has been questioned.

A simulation can also be developed using one of the popular simulation languages, such as SIMSCRIPT, GPSS, DYNAMO, SIMULA, and GASP, to write a model specific to the system being evaluated. The advantages of using simulation language rather than other programming languages, include the following: the simulation language helps the analyst to formulate the model, it simplifies the task since flow charting and programming are easier, it is easier to debug the programs, it permits easy manipulation of the model, it aids in explaining the model and the results to others, and it allows faster preparation of the simulation model.

The major drawback of simulation is its relatively high cost. Many of the simulations used for evaluation have been designed specifically around existing or proposed systems, and major changes to include other systems would entail a complete rewriting. Deciding how many items to include in the simulation is a difficult design question. If the level of detail in the simulation is too fine, the simulator may be too expensive to use; too much machine time or capacity may be required. If the level of detail is too gross, the results may be misleading because important details might be aggregated to such an extent that their impact is lost. It is difficult to consider adequately the effects of software, multiprogramming, time-sharing, and terminal-oriented operations. It is also possible that adequate time may not be available for the development of a simulation model. Determining the validation of the simulation model is very difficult task.

Simulation provides excellent results for selection evaluation of a new computer and software system, configuration enhancement studies, work load scheduling, and system tuning. However, the effort and cost of preparing simulators for these specific systems is usually prohibitive. Simulation offers the greatest advantages for projecting performance on proposed systems.

Usage of evaluation techniques

The performance evaluation techniques can be used in computer selection, projection design, and performance evaluation. For selection evaluation the user should analyze the job mix and develop appropriate weights for the particular situation. In the computer selection process, it is best to use programs where simulation may be used as a secondary tool. Simulation may be used as the prime technique for projected design. Monitors are viewed as the primary technique for evaluation of operations.

---

[3]"Simulation: Its Place in Performance Analysis," *EDP Performance Review,* Applied Computer Research (November 1973).

Performance Evaluation Tools

Free tools—accounting packages

A tremendous amount of information that can lead to improved computer performance is contained in accounting data. This ability to collect accounting data is provided by the hardware vendors as part of the operating system, usually at no additional cost. Most vendors will also supply special software for analyzing these data free of charge or for a nominal fee.

Commercially available tools

A very large number of tools is available for computer performance measurement and evaluation. These products may be divided into three categories: accounting package reduction programs, hardware and software monitors, and simulation models. These products are discussed in more details later in this chapter.

Accounting packages

Accounting packages are the most often used technique for describing the performance of computer systems. Accounting systems can be used for estimating the resource utilization of specific tasks, and they are provided by most vendors with their basic software.

The important thing to bear in mind is that the prime objective of the accounting packages is to charge users for their usage of the various resources of the computer system; accounting packages were not intended as tools for computer system performance evalulation. Since these packages are developed for accounting purposes, not all information required for performance evaluation is collected. Perhaps the most serious shortcoming of accounting systems is that they do not account for the behavior of the operating system itself.

However, accounting packages contain a great deal of useful, crude information that can be used in the initial phase of computer system performance measurement and evaluation. Using accounting data systems, three types of performance data may be collected: performance indicators, performance diagnostics, and performance enforcement. Performance indicators include percentage of time system is idle, number of jobs processed, turnaround time of jobs, CPU wait time, cost of jobs, paging rate, and trend analysis. Performance diagnostics are divided into four types: system, files, operations, and programs diagnostics. System diagnostics include CPU activity, percentage of time I/O devices are busy, total memory allocated, number of tapes allocated, number of disks allocated, and potential disk contention. Files diagnostics include file blocking, disk file fragmentation, cylinder boundry alignment, frequently mounted files, file placement, inactive files and low-activity tape files. Operations diagnostics include downtime, disk mount frequency, tape mount frequency, operator file mount time, device error statistics, operator errors, and scheduling errors. Programs diagnostics may include elapse time, run frequency, core wasted, CPU time versus I/O time, tape allocated but not used, paging rate, and abnormal termination. Performance enforcement is divided into two categories: external and internal. External performance includes reporting to user management and charging for the services. Internal performance enforcement includes reports on core wasted, tapes mounted but not used, poor block sizes, files not on cylinder boundries, disk space wasted, and use of low-activity tapes.

Monitors

Monitoring is a method of collecting data on the performance of an existing system. It is generally used to locate the bottlenecks limiting performance when either reconfiguring the existing hardware or improving the execution of software. Monitoring is also useful in gathering a profile on the use of a system, for example, the percentage of computer-oriented jobs. These data can help in determing priorities and which system should be supported by a computer installation.

Hardware monitors

These techniques of monitoring are based on the fact that most performance characteristics of computer systems can be measured directly from signal voltage transmissions in the digital circuitry of the computer hardware. All hardware monitors, therefore, consist of high-impedance probes that are connected to counters, generally through some selectable arrangement of AND, OR, NAND, and NOR circuitry, with the output generally stored on magnetic tape or disk. The high-impendance probes draw negligible power from the computer circuits to which they are attached, as an oscilloscope probe is. By sensing electrical signals in the computer, the monitor is able to count events during a period of time and/or to count time between successive events. These circuitries allow the detection of specific simultaneous events, such as CPU BUSY and CHANNEL BUSY. The conceptual overview of the hardware monitor is illustrated in Figure 6.1.

The hardware monitors, therefore, employ (1) probes, or sensors, for sensing changes of state in digital signals, (2) a device for accumulating these changes over long periods of time (counters or distributive memory), and (3) some means of recording accumulated data for later reduction and analysis (tape, printer, CRT, or disk).

Hardware monitor advantages are

- Passive data acquisition
- Computer independence
- Operating system independence
- High-precision detailed measurements
- Simultaneous multiple measurements

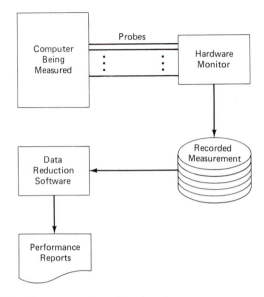

Figure 6.1 Hardware Monitor—Conceptual Overview

Hardware monitor disadvantages are

• Cost
• Difficulty of use
• Lack of logical data relation
• Monitor attachment that can crash system
• Hardware monitor that can malfunction

Software monitor

Software monitors perform the data gathering functions by means of a program that is resident in main memory during the measurement period. The conceptual overview of the software monitor is illustrated in Figure 6.2. This program can either be "passive" or "active." It is passive if it waits for some other operation, such as an input/output operation, to cause an interrupt, at which time it samples the status. It is active if it uses a timer and causes the interrupt. When the interrupt occurs, the software samples the status of designated components, for example, Is the CPU busy? Is channel 1 busy? Is the printer busy? What are the queues in each device? The raw data are accumulated briefly in main memory and are then recorded on a magnetic tape or disk.

Software monitors are usually divided into four categories:

A computer configuration monitor is usually time-driven and it is loaded into the operating system. This monitor measures component utilization and overlaps. Typical measurements may be CPU busy/wait, CPU busy in OS/users, channel busy, device busy, CPU/channel overlap, and CPU wait on channel or device.

A problem program monitor is either time- or event-driven and is usually

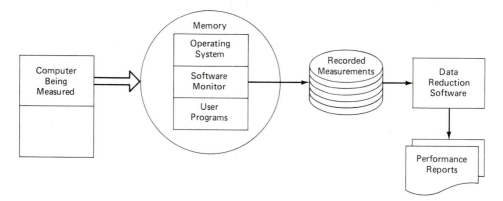

Figure 6.2   Software Monitor—Conceptual Overview

loaded as part of the problem program. This monitor measures computer activity associated with a specific problem program. Typical measurements of this monitor may be instruction execution frequency distributed by memory location, program wait time distributed by data set or memory location, SVC usage, OP code execution frequency distribution, and program execution trace.

An operating system monitor is either time- or event-driven and is loaded into the operating system. It measures operating system features. Typical measurements may be initiator/terminator activity, memory allocation utilization, operating system module activity, and queue lengths and activity.

A data set monitor is either time- or event-driven and is usually loaded into the operating system. This monitor measures direct access activity. Typical measurements of this monitor are direct access device arm movement, direct access file activity, and impact of direct access file organization.

Software monitor advantages are

- Ease of use
- Ease of installation
- Relatively low expense
- Output in "logical" or programmer terms
- Ability to report on many different areas

Software monitor disadvantages are

- Degrades system performance
- Requires system resources
- Runs only on specific machine (machine dependent)
- Measures only information available to computer instructions
- Sample data may be invalid

Comparison

The degree of difficulty and complexity of these tools varies, and therefore the ease of learning also varies. It is customary to rank these techniques in terms of the least to most training required as follows: accounting systems, software monitors, hardware monitors, simulation languages, and simulation packages. Other characteristics that need to be considered when comparison of these tools is made include cost, dependency, overhead being added to the system being measured, flexibility in measuring, ease of use, ability to monitor peripheral equipment, what can be measured and analyzed, and the expected life of the technique. Table 6.1 presents a comparison of the three types of monitors discussed, according to these characteristics.

TABLE 6.1   MONITORS—COMPARISON CHART

	Accounting System	Software Monitor	Hardware Monitor
Cost	Free	High	Low/medium
Dependency	Total	Total	Probe tips
Overhead	Low	Variable	None
Flexibility	Limited	Limited to design	Much
Ease of use	Excellent	Good	Poor
Peripheral monitoring	No	No	Yes
Training required	Limited	Limited	Extensive
Application	Work load definition	Trends—are there any problems?	Answering specific questions
Expected life	Same as the operating system	Same as the operating system	Good

Procuring tools

Some of the available CPE (computer performance evaluation) tools are very sophisticated and difficult to learn and use. Therefore, it is not wise to start the CPE activity by acquiring tools. As part of the learning and implementation of the CPE activity, available accounting data should be used first. Then, once the CPE is ready, acquire a software monitor or accounting data reduction package, develop a simulation capability and/or analytical models. Then, when the CPE activity is matured and there is a justification, acquire a hardware monitor. The introduction of new products and new features into the market is very rapid; therefore, it might be very useful to survey the field prior to acquiring new technique or tool.

Choosing a monitor

Noe[4] lists minimum technical specifications for hardware monitors to aid not only the user but also the designer of the monitors. In the same article he provides the user with an extensive list of questions that should be asked when issuing an RFP for a hardware monitor. The following are the major critieria for choosing a monitor:

Cost.   Purchasing of a hardware monitor requires a relatively large investment.

Speed/Timing.   These are dictated by the system to be monitored. It is clear that when monitoring a fast computer, data collected by a slow monitor are meaningless. Two dimensions are used here: pulse rate (measured in megahertz) and pulse width (measured in nanosecond).

Monitor Clock.   This clock provides master pulses for automatic operation and for counters operating in the time mode. The clock rate should be on order of 10 MHz (which gives a resolution of 0.1 μsec).

Number of Counters.   A counter is a device that counts the number of intervening clock pulses between events being measured. The number is also dependent on the machine being measured, with a range of 4 to 64 counters.

Probes.   Since these are directly conected to the computer, they must be compatible and designed for minimum interference with the computer being measured. They must also support long cables so that signals may be picked up from various points physically distant from each other and from the central monitor console. There is also the option of comparator probes that compare the signals to a given value.

IMPLEMENTING THE MEASUREMENT PROGRAM

Starting the Computer Performance Evaluation

Computer performance evaluation is usually initiated when the organization plans to expand its data processing resources and would like to analyze its present system as well as the proposed system. Another common reason might be the existence of problems with the present system, as when a new application is to be added to an already highly utilized computer, projected work load growth has been underestimated, or operations wants to install a new computer or add components to the existing one, in which case solutions to these problems are sought. The third reason is the need for continuous measurements to keep improving the services provided and reduce the cost of providing these services.

Attention should be exercised in organizing the CPE team. This team may consist of one or more persons, depending on the size of the data processing activity and its needs. The members of the CPE group need to be highly skilled in

[4]J. D. Noe, "Acquiring and Using a Hardware Monitor," *Datamation* (April 1974).

their respective fields, hardware and software. Since this group actually acts as in-house consultants, its members should be congenial and have the ability to present their findings and recommendations orally and in writing. The CPE team members should be open minded and eager to examine suggested changes.

This team should be located as high as possible within the organization structure, so that they can conduct their work with no interference, such as internal politics and authority. This placement ensures that recommendations that are accepted will also be implemented. It is common to consider this group as part of the management of the data processing activity, in which case the CPE manager reports at the least to the data processing director. Ideally, the CPE manager should report to the organization's controller.

The charter of the CPE group should be clearly defined and should be formal and signed by the highest possible corporate officer. This charter should state that no new programs and substantial changes will be implemented without first having it reviewed by the CPE team. It should also state that, before ordering, replacing, or adding any new equipment, the CPE team must measure and evaluate the activities and conditions of the system that will be affected by the new equipment. This type of charter will allow the CPE group to examine both existing and proposed systems or changes.

Continuing the Evaluation Activity

The continuing of the measurement and the evaluation activity should at least include acquiring of new tools to keep up with the developments; determining the frequencies of measurements with respect to capital investment, work load, and availability of personnel; planning of work load changes based on new systems and new users; maintaining a close watch on the distribution of the computer activity by device and by program to relate equipment costs to level of use and to determine trade-offs possible between cost and performance; developing and maintaining the CPE data base, so that historical data can be used to predict trends in work load, usage, and so on; integrating of operations with the measurement activities, mainly by educating the operations personnel on how can they use these tools to improve operation; and establishing good working relations with the hardware and software vendors, since in many cases their help is needed as is their permission to attach hardware monitors.

The framework of the performance evaluation consists of the following steps:

1. Characterize the purposes of the installation.
2. Define the management objectives.
3. Identify the environment in which the installation exists.
4. Select the necessary CPE tools.
5. Collect required performance data.
6. Analyze the collected data and results.
7. Take recommended actions.

Data processing installations are usually one of three types: production shop, users-oriented shop, or a mixture of these two. Production shop invests in computer capacity to maximize the work processed. This type of shop uses maximum system potential, and therefore, individual programs may suffer. A user-oriented facility is one whose objective is to provide fast response and turnaround time. The investment in this case is in people time, and therefore, maximum system availablity is desired. System utilization is relatively low in this type of shop. In a mixed shop, the objective is to provide good service to the users as well as to maximize the work processed.

Before initiating the CPE study, the objectives should be defined clearly. The objective for such study may be to increase throughtput, reduce costs, improve turnaround, reduce response time, identify reserve capacity, evaluate new hardware or software, and evalute need for new or additional capacity.

When identifying the environment, a number of factors should be considered: the hardware, which includes computer components and anticipated additional hardware; the software, which includes the operating system features, system utility software, anticipated additional software, and distribution of program time; past and current CPE studies, which includes data used to evaluate performance, techniques used to improve user programs, exception reporting, evaluation of system changes, and the use of accounting data; the work load, which includes the number of jobs processed, backlog of work, and historical trends in work load; the users, which includes the types of users, specific applications, use of disks and tapes, and the method of charging for computer services; the operation, which includes idle time periods, number of shifts, distribution of operation time, and the type of shop (closed or open shop); the scheduling, includes type of schedule (established or demand), job classes, and job priorities; and the organization, which includes the position of the installation within the organization and the installation's organization.

A number of tools should be considered before deciding on which of them will be used in the CPE study. These tools, most of which were discussed previously, include visual inspection, accounting data, software monitors, hardware monitors, benchmarks, and simulation.

The performance data to be collected during the CPE study may be divided into four types: operational data, resource allocation data, resource utilization data, and predicted performance data. Operational data usually include system idle, CPU wait or idle, job scheduling, console activity, tape mounts, disk mounts, and number of job reruns. Resource allocation data include information about the memory, tape drives, disk space, multiprogramming level, and unit records equipment. Resource utilization data include CPU activity, problem program activity, program code efficiency, file access efficiency, memory utilization, channel busy, tape busy, and unit record busy. Predicted performance data, which may be collected using benchmarks or simulation, may include work load processing time, resource requirements, multiple-job interaction, multiple-component interaction, file structure/access implications, and capacity level and constraints.

Table 6.2 presents the objectives usually found in a CPE study and possible actions to be taken.

The possible actions require making changes, additions, or deletions. Changes usually include file location, device location or speed, job scheduling, program code, operating system, and record blocking. Additions or deletions usually involve channels, control units, devices, memory, operations, and operation shifts.

Managing the CPE Group

An effective CPE group usually operates on a project basis. These projects tend to be adhoc in nature; each study has a single purpose. Therefore, it is important to consider the following five aspects in managing the CPE projects.

Plan. A plan needs to be developed before starting a new project. This plan should identify all the resources required for the project, such as people, facilities, and equipment. A schedule for the project is to be prepared including milestones and deliverables.

Organizaton. All necessary resources need to be available and structured so that the project can be managed.

Direction. The project may be directed by using the schedule, including the milestones, developed in the planning phase.

TABLE 6.2 TYPICAL OBJECTIVES OF CPE STUDY AND POSSIBLE ACTIONS

Objectives	Possible Action
Reduce response time	Eliminate bottlenecks Increase availability Increase capability Increase capacity Redesign the system
Increase throughput	Increase component utilization and overlap Improve bottlenecks to utilization ratio Improve level of multiprogramming Improve efficiency of large jobs
Reduce turnaround	Eliminate bottlenecks Increase capacity Increase capability Examine priority levels Redesign the system
Reduce costs	Check for underutilized components Downgrade components/features Eliminate components/features Consolidate functions

Control. Controlling is measuring performance against the plan. Corrective measures need to be taken when deviation from the plan occurs.

Coordination. Coordination of the project ensures that all involved are aware of, and are receptive to, the project's effort, goals, and recommendations.

PERFORMANCE ANALYSIS

A number of techniques have been developed for evaluating the performance of computer systems, hardware, and/or software. Three techiques for analyzing the performance data collected will be discussed: Kiviat charts, cost/utilization analysis of hardware, and cost/utilization analysis of the total information system.

Kiviat Charts

One of the best known techniques for analysis of performance data is the Kiviat chart.[5] These charts display the various aspects of computer hardware performance, allowing the user to determine visually whether the system under consideration is being used properly. The Kiviat charts are prepared by first listing system parameters and the actual (measured) and the ideal percentage utilization of the system with respect to each parameter. To demonstrate this technique, eight system parameters are listed in Table 6.3. Note that the number of parameters for which the ideal is 0 percent should equal the number for which it is 100 percent. These parameters values are then plotted on the radii of a circle, the center representing 0 percent and the circumference 100 percent. Each radius represents one parameter. Parameters with 0 percent and 100 percent ideal values alternate around the circle. The example in Table 6.4 yields the Kiviat chart in Figure 6.3(a).

In a well-utilized system, the shaded area is star shaped, with points close to

TABLE 6.3 SYSTEM PARAMETER UTILIZATION—AN EXAMPLE

Parameters	Percentage Utilization	
	Ideal	Actual
1. Memory used for control programs	0%	10%
2. Memory used for production programs	100	90
3. Bulk storage units inactive	0	20
4. Channel utilization	100	50
5. CPU wait time	0	30
6. CPU active	100	70
7. CPU active on control programs	0	20
8. CPU active on production programs	100	80

[5]M. F. Morris, "Kiviat Graphs—Conventions and Figures of Merit," *Performance Evaluation Review* (ACM SIGMETRICS Newsletter), Vol. 3, no. 3 (October 1974), pp. 2–8.

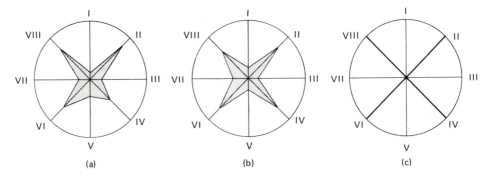

Figure 6.3 Examples of Kiviat Charts.   *Source:* Reprinted with permission from I. Borovits and P. Ein-Dor, "Cost/Utilization: A Measure of System Performance," *Communications of the ACM,* Vol. 20, no. 3 (March 1977). Copyright 1977, Association for Computing Machinery, Inc.

the circumference of the circle as exhibited in Figure 6.3(b). In the ideal case, the shaded area is reduced to alternate radii of the circle as shown in Figure 6.3(c).

One of the shortcomings of this method of analysis is that the parameters are not scaled according to their economic significance. Thus it is possible to find a system that seems to be utilized satisfactorily at the expense of grossly underutilizing some other dimension that may be extremely significant in terms of its costs.

Cost/Utilization Analysis

The cost/utilization measurement was first introduced by Borovits and Ein-Dor.[6] This method is an expansion of the technological aspect of system performance evaluation to cover some of the economic aspects in the form of cost/utilization evaluation. This technique assumes the existence of performance data collection devices to provide the basic data. The cost of the hardware components is used to weigh the significance of each component.

This concept of cost/utilization applies utilization figures indirectly to the costs of physical units rather than to the units themselves. Cost is a common dimension that permits the integration of utilization data for all components of a system. Then a single measure of cost/utilization for the entire system may be computed.

The cost/utilization factor measures the extent to which the outlay on the total system is actually utilized. It is computed as

$$B = 2\left[\sum_i (F - U_i)^2 P_i\right]^{1/2}$$

where P_i is the cost of the ith component in the system as a percentage of total cost and U_i is the percentage utilization of the ith component.

Thus F can vary from zero, in a system not utilized at all, to one in a

[6]I. Borovits and P. Ein-Dor, "Cost/Utilization: A Measure of System Performance," *Communications of the ACM,* Vol. 20, no. 3 (March 1977). Copyright 1977, Association for Computing Machinery, Inc.

perfectly utilized system. The cost/utilization method includes both computation of the cost/utilization factor and visual representation of this measure.

This method make it possible to also compute a measure of system imbalance. This measure is computed as

$$F = \sum_i P_i U_i$$

where B is the measure of imbalance and F, U_i, P_i are as previously defined. The expression inside the brackets measures the variance of the degree of utilization of individual components, U_i around their weighted mean, F. Multiplying these squared deviations by the relative cost of the components gives the variance of utilization of units of costs rather than of physical components. The scaling factor, 2, normalizes B so that it varies between zero, for perfectly balanced system, and one, for maximally unbalanced system.

Cost/utilization analysis may be shown in a rectangular graph representing the maximum possible cost/utilization in the system. The horizontal axes of the graph represent the percentage of total system cost distributed by each type of hardware component. The vertical axes represent percentage utilization of hardware components. A histogram is then constructed within this graph, the bars of which represent utilization of system cost and the area above the bars representing slack in the system. Once this histogram has been constructed, the cost/utilization factor is calculated, relating cost utilized to total system cost.

To illustrate this method of cost/utilization analysis, a typical computer system is used, and the distribution of the total cost among the various components is presented in Table 6.4.

Figure 6.4 presents four types of systems. In (a) the system is well balanced and well utilized. In (b) the system is well balanced but underutilized. In (c) the system is relatively well utilized but somewhat unbalanced. In (d) the system is both unbalanced and poorly utilized.

This method may also be used as a control device. Tracing the trends in

TABLE 6.4 PERCENTAGE OF HARDWARE SYSTEM COST CONTRIBUTION BY COMPONENTS—AN EXAMPLE

Component	Percentage of cost
1. CPU	41%
2. Memory	23
3. Disks	13
4. Tapes	12
5. Card Reader	2
6. Printer	9
	100%

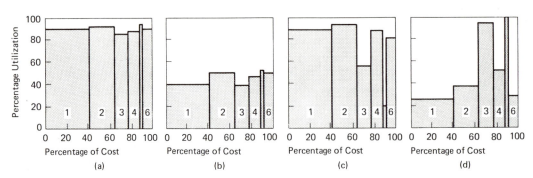

Figure 6.4 Illustrative Cost/Utilization Histograms.   *Source:* Reprinted with permission from I. Borovits and P. Ein-Dor, "Cost/Utilization: A Measure of System Performance," *Communications of the ACM,* Vol. 20, no. 3 (March 1977). Copyright 1977, Association for Computing Machinery, Inc.

cost/utilization and balance factors can indicate where potential bottlenecks are developing and at what rate the system is approaching saturation. Consider the example in Figure 6.5 relating to six periods for a hypothetical system composed of three components.

It is clear that the system will be fully loaded within two or three periods because of a bottleneck developing in component 2. An increase in the capacity of this component could delay saturation for some time. The utilization of component 3 is increasing at a lower rate than *F,* indicating that it is a potential source of system underutilization.

Software Performance Analysis

Borovits and Chmura[7] developed a method for software performance analysis that is an extension of the cost/utilization model described previously. It also provides the two measures of performance that measure utilization and imbalance. In addition to the basic assumptions of the previous method, this technique assumes the knowledge of planned (budgeted) software component utilization.

The system is said to perform optimally, if all software components are utilized according to plan. Unlike hardware component utilization, software component utilization has no absolute 100 percent other than the hardware capacity. Therefore, the planned utilization is used as the base for comparison. As it was done in the previous method, weights are assigned to the software components under consideration. The percentage of the total plan represented by the plan for a software component is that component's weight.

The plan/utilization concept applies utilization figures indirectly to the plan for the software components rather than the components themselves. The plan/

---

[7]I. Borovits and A. Chmura, "Cost/Utilization: A Measure of Computer Information System Performance," in Robert Goldberg and Harold Lorin, eds., *The Economics of Information Processing* (New York; John Wiley, 1982), pp. 35–37.

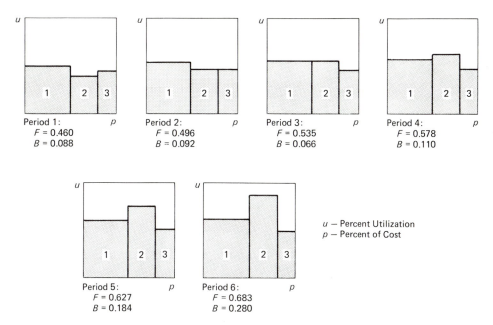

Figure 6.5 Trace Cost/Utilization Criteria Source: Reprinted with permission from I. Borovits and P. Ein-Dor, "Cost/Utilization: A Measure of System Performance," *Communications of the ACM*, vol. 20, no. 3 (March 1977). Copyright 1977, Association for Computing Achinery, Inc.

utilization factor measures the extent to which the outlay on the total software system is actually utilized. It is computed as

$$S = \sum_{j=1}^{m} (Q_j V_j) \left(1 \bigg/ \sum_{j=1}^{m} Q_j^2 \right)$$

where S is the software plan/utilization factor, Q_j is the planned allocation of the jth software component as a percentage of total software plan, and V_j is the percentage utilization of the jth software component.

S varies between zero in a totally unused system and more than one in a system with total software use exceeding plan, consuming total hardware capacity. When S is equal to one, net plan/utilization equals total plan.

The software system imbalance measure indicates the extent to which software system component utilization is balanced. It is computed as

$$C = 2 \left[\sum_{j=1}^{m} (V_j - Q_j)^2 Q_j \right]^{1/2}$$

where C is the software imbalance measure and V_j and Q_j are as defined previously.

The expression in brackets measures the variance of the degree of utilization of individual components, V_j as compared with budget. Multiplication of the

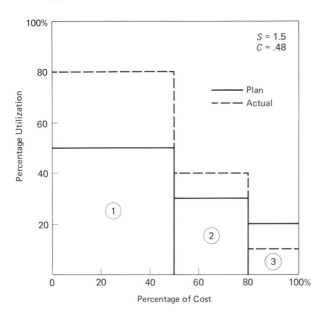

Figure 6.6 Software Plan/Utilization Chart

squared deviations by the relative plan for the components yields the variance of utilization in units of plan (budget) rather than of software components. The scaling factor (2) normalizes C so that it varies between zero in a system with perfect net balance and one in a perfectly imbalanced system. In a perfectly balanced system, $V_j = Q_j$ for all j. This means that software components are utilizing hardware according to plan.

The software plan/utilization may be shown in a graph, with a square representing total hardware capacity. The horizontal axis indicates the percentage of software system cost contributed by each software component. The height of each histogram bar showing plan should equal the width of the component's base. Figure 6.6 shows a typical chart based on the illustrative values given in Table 6.5.

This technique, as was the previous one, may be used to trace trends. Consider the example in Figure 6.7, showing charts of a hypothetical system for four periods. The system is constantly consuming resources at variance with plan.

TABLE 6.5 PERCENTAGE OF SOFTWARE SYSTEM PLAN CONTRIBUTION BY COMPONENT—AN EXAMPLE

Component	Percentage of Plan
1. Inventory management	50%
2. Timekeeping	30
3. Payroll	20
	100%

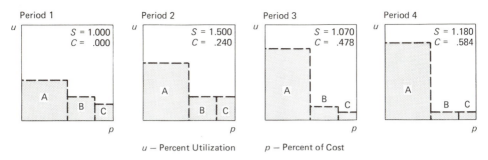

Figure 6.7   Illustration of Trace of Plan/Utilization Criteria

This might indicate any number of problems: plan was not accurate, the software supplier's rates have changed, and management attention has been inadequate.

Combined Performance Analysis

Borovits and Chmura[8] have suggested a method by which both the hardware and the software models may be combined so that a measure for the total system, hardware and software, may be obtained. To do so, it is necessary to weight each major component (hardware and software) by the fraction of the computing budget it represents.

The measure of total system utilization is computed as follows:

$$T = (F \cdot W_h) + (S \cdot W_s)$$

where T is the measure of total system utilization, F and S are as defined previously, W_h is the fraction of total computing hardware cost and software plan consumed by hardware, and W_s is the fraction of total computing hardware cost and software plan consumed by software.

This is illustrated in Figure 6.8. By convention, the horizontal axis and the vertical axis equal one. The rectangle for hardware occupied the lowest portion of the square, while the rectangle for software occupies the next higher portion. When utilization exceeds plan, the top of the rectangle for the software may extend beyond the bounds of the square. The value of T varies between zero in a totally unused system and more than one in a system in which software utilization exceeds the plan. When utilization exactly equals plan, T equals one.

The measure of total system imbalance may be computed as follows:

$$X = (B \cdot W_h) + (C \cdot W_s)$$

where X is the measure of total system imbalance, and B, C, $W_{h, and} W_s$ are as defined earlier.

This is illustrated in Figure 6.9. By convention, the horizontal axis and the vertical axis equal one. Imbalance may never extend beyond the bounds of the square. The value of X varies between zero in a system with perfect balance and one in a totally unbalanced system.

[8]Borovits and Chmura, "Cost/Utilization," pp. 37–38.

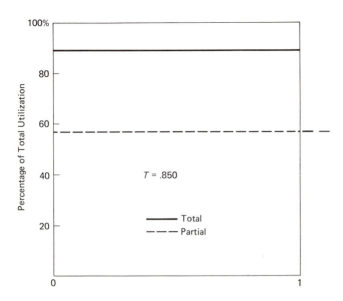

Figure 6.8 Typical Total System Utilization Chart

IMPLICATIONS

Information derived from the three methods described may indicate a number of possible management actions:

1. If cost/utilization and imbalance are within acceptable bounds, corrective actions other than continued monitoring may be unnecessary.
2. If cost/utilization for hardware exceeds acceptable bounds, redesign or reconfiguration of the system may be required.

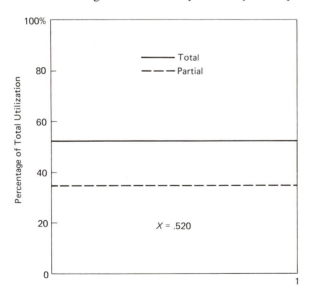

Figure 6.9 Typical Total System Imbalance Chart

3. If imbalance for the hardware exceeds acceptable bounds, upgrading of some of the components may be necessary.

4. If cost/utilization of the software exceeds acceptable bounds, budget changes may be required.

5. If imbalance for the software exceeds acceptable bounds, changes may be required in the software, such as improving software running time. There may be, also, a need for change in the charging rates to take advantage of price elasticity of demand.

SELECTED READINGS

BELL, T. E. "Computer Performance Analysis: Measurement Objectives and Tools," R-584-NASA/PR. Santa Monica, Calif.: The Rand Corporation, February 1971.

BOROVITS, ISRAEL, AND SEEV NEUMANN. *Computer Systems Performance Evaluation.* Lexington, Mass.: Lexington Books, 1979.

DRUMMOND, M. E., JR. *Evaluation and Measurement Techniques for Digital Computer System.* Englewood Cliffs, N.J.: Prentice-Hall, 1973.

FERRARI, DOMENICO. *Computer Systems Performance Evaluation.* Englewood Cliffs, N.J.: Prentice-Hall, 1978.

KOBAYASHI, HISASHI. *Modeling and Analysis: An Introduction to System Performance Evaluation Methodology.* Reading, Mass.: Addison-Wesley, 1978.

KOLENCE, K. W., AND P. J. KIVIAT. "Software Unit Profiles and Kiviat Figures." *Performance Evaluation Review,* September 1973.

LUCAS, H. C., JR., "Performance Evaluation and Monitoring." *Computing Surveys,* Vol. 3, no. 3 (September 1971).

NORTON, D. P., AND K. G. RAU. *A Guide to EDP Performance Management.* Wellesley, Mass.: Q.E.D. Information Sciences, 1978.

"Survey of User Performance Experience." *EDP Performance Review,* Applied Computer Research, March 1974.

7

Planning and Controlling the Data Processing Activity

INTRODUCTION

Too often the phrase "managing information systems" is used synonymously with project management. This misconception has led to shortsightedness in system projects and misunderstanding of the role of the computer in business organizations. To differentiate project management from information systems management, it is necessary to distinguish between implementation and planning. Project management is that set of activities involved with the development and installation of computer systems (hardware and software). In contrast, the management of information systems is concerned with planning and controlling the data processing activity so that it meets the organization's data processing needs. It is the subject of planning and control that is the focal point of this chapter.

Business Systems

To understand how information systems fit into business organizations, it is necessary to understand how an organization operates and then determine the functions that allow those operations to be controlled. To view the entire business, a methodology or approach must be employed that relates the actions of the various parts of the organization to each other and to the external environment. The systems approach satisfies the need for such a methodology. It is possible to define a business organization as a system, that is, as an assemblage or set of related elements.[1] An alternate definition of a system is "a body composed of a number of subsystems that are interrelated, each system or subsystem interacting

[1]John P. Van Gigch, *Applied General Systems Theory* (New York: Harper & Row, 1978).

with other systems and with the external environment." Systems and, in turn, businesses can in fact be classified according to how they interact with the environment.

Closed systems are entities unto themselves that have no regard for the environment. *Open systems* are entities that accept inputs from the environment and, after processing, produce outputs that are returned to the environment.

Operational processes in a business act as open systems. Data processing as an example, receives inputs from the environment, processes them within the data processing organization, and produces outputs that are returned to the environment.

Static systems are entities that accept inputs and return outputs to the environment. *Dynamic systems* are entities that accept inputs and return outputs to the environment with a feedback loop from the environment to the system.

The control function in a business allows the organization to remain dynamic. It is able to monitor performance via a control loop and adjust performance accordingly as it varies from desired results.

Nonadaptive systems are entities that do not change as the environment changes. *Adaptive systems* are entities that study the environment, predict the future, and then try to make changes to meet future requirements.

The adaptive function in a business includes forecasting, planning, and resource development. It receives inputs from the control system, the operation system, and the environment; utilizes these inputs to plan for the future; and then changes the business's subsystems through its outputs.

Planning and Control Function

The planning and control function should vary in scope and intensity with the level of management within the data processing organization. For example, top management has much more planning responsibility than lower management, where, on the other hand, lower management has broader control responsibility than upper management. Figure 7.1 illustrates the planning and control responsibilities by level of management.

It is important to have all levels of management participating in the planning process.

PLANNING

To develop long-range plans for data processing, there needs to be a specific long-range plan with stated goals and objectives for the organization as a whole as well as for the individual users.

In developing the data processing plan, the organization's data processing requirements over a variety of time periods must be considered. Just as the overall business plan must consider the short-term as well as the long-term business requirements, so must the organization's data processing plan. The data

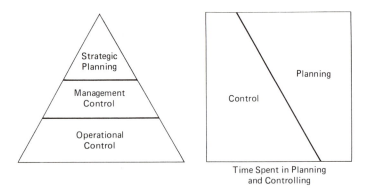

Figure 7.1 Time Spent in Planning and Controlling by Level of Management

processing plan can be subdivided according to the time horizon considered. The issues addressed in each subplan will vary according to the time frame considered. McLean and Soden[2] distinguish between the various types of plans as follows.

Long-range information systems planning

Long-range planning deals with meeting the future data processing needs of the host organization. It is largely conceptual and can have a horizon of five, six, seven, or more years. It does not deal with specific projects or even groups of projects but, rather, with emergent types of user needs and services that might be useful in addressing these needs. It must also plan for the data processing organization of the future and for the skills and capabilities that will be needed in developing and managing the system of the future.

Medium-range planning

This is what many organizations call their long-range plan. It is the planning that is necessary to meet the host organization's present data processing needs, projected two to five years into the future. It is, on one hand, a portfolio of projects, ranked by importance, coupled with projections for their implementation. It also involves technical planning for systems and data-base network architecture, for hardware and software acquisitions and conversions, and for the staffing of multiyear projects and development activities.

Short-range planning

It is generally equivalent to the data processing annual plan. It involves detailed budget preparation, personnel scheduling, and the creation of timetables for individual projects. It also often includes quantitative statements regarding performance targets for the data processing department. It is relatively operational.

[2]Ephraim R. McLean and John V. Soden, *Strategic Planning for MIS* (New York: John Wiley, 1974), pp. 3–30.

Data Processing Planning Process

Data processing planning attempts to answer the following questions:

1. What are the objectives for the data processing effort in the organization?
2. By what strategy will the data processing function seek to achieve these objectives?
3. How is the data processing function going to organize the data processing effort to carry these objectives?
4. How is the data processing function going to decide how much to spend on data processing?
5. How is the data processing function going to decide how to allocate scarce resources to various projects and services?

To answer these questions, a process must be implemented by which the organization can evaluate and define the framework within which its data processing activity will operate. Six activities should be included in the planning process methodology.

Formally assess the environment

An assessment of the environment results in identification of opportunities and risks associated with the organization's present and future position. This assessment should include a consideration of the following:

1. The objectives, strategies, policies, and plans of the organization
2. The competitive position of the overall organization
3. The user groups within the organization—their own management systems needs, the current share of data processing resources they use, the fit of data processing services with their own plans
4. The position within the system life cycle of the systems organization
5. The present and emerging technologies in information processing
6. The ability of the data processing function to effect change in the organization

Set data processing objectives and develop strategies

Objectives define what is to be accomplished by the data processing organization, whereas strategies determine how those objectives will be met. The data processing function's objectives should be closely connected with the strategic objectives of the organization. The choice of appropriate objectives is critical, since all subsequent planning is oriented toward successfully meeting these goals. The activities of defining objectives and determining strategies are closely interconnected. They should deal with the following issues:

1. The fit of the data processing's objectives with the overall organization's objectives

2. The data processing's services attributes (i.e., the classes and types of systems and services to be offered)

3. The growth, continuity, and level of contribution of the data processing function within the organization

4. The role of users in systems development efforts

5. The types of technology to be employed

6. The type of management and staff to be developed

7. Steps taken to ensure security of the organization's assets

Define policies

Once objectives and strategies have been defined, guidelines on how best to carry out these strategies can be prescribed. Policy decisions include but are not limited to the following:

1. Organizational structure of the data processing function

2. Procedures for resource allocation

3. Funding criteria

4. Data management structure

5. Vendor selection guidelines

6. Use of outside services

7. Selling services to outside organizations

Develop data processing plans

As previously mentioned the data processing plan can be subdivided according to the time horizon of the plan. The long-range plan identifies general courses of action, types of resources to be employed, and subpolicies necessary to achieve strategic objectives. The long-range plan, which by its nature is highly conceptual, includes the following: (1) data processing architecture to meet future organizational needs; (2) description of emerging data processing concepts, and (3) identification of broad types of potential resources needed.

The medium-range plan is directed at the marginal planning level. It identifies goals, action priorities, resource levels, standards, and specific procedures to achieve strategic objectives. It outlines the following:

1. A data processing architecture to meet the present organizational information needs

2. A ranking of computer applications within the project portfolio

3. A consolidated projection of project implementation

4. Projections of software and equipment acquisitions

The short-range plan is directed at operational planning. It specifies performance targets and task schedules and identifies specific requirements necessary to achieve strategic objectives. It includes the following:

1. An annual plan
2. A schedule of individual computer application developments
3. Expense budgets
4. Personnel budgets
5. Timetables

The outcome of this process should be the strategic data processing plan, which outlines the objectives, strategies, policies, and implementation procedures. It should identify projects to be undertaken, hardware and software projections, personnel projections, and financial requirements. A typical outline of a plan should include at the least the following.[3]

I. Introduction
   A. Summary of major goals, a statement of their consistency with the organization goals, and current state of planning vis-à-vis these goals
   B. Summary of aggregate cost and savings projections
   C. Summary of total personnel requirements
   D. Major challenges and problems
   E. Criteria for assigning development projects and production priorities

II. Projects Identification
   A. Maintenance projects, all projects proposed, and development projects
   B. Estimated completion time
   C. Personnel requirements, by time period and job category
   D. Computer capacity needed for system testing and implementation
   E. Economic justification by project development costs, implementation costs, running costs, out-of-pocket savings, intangible savings
   F. Project control tools
   G. Tie-ins with other systems and master plans

III. Hardware Projections
   A. Current applications—work loads and compilation and testing requirements
   B. New applications—work loads and reruns
   C. Survey of new hardware, with emphasis on design flexibility that will allow the organization to take full advantage of new developments in hardware and software
   D. Acquisition strategy, with timing contingencies

[3]Ibid., p. 17.

E. Facilities requirements and growth in hardware, tapes and disks storage, offices, and supplies

IV. Personnel Projections
  A. Personnel needed by month for each category
     General: management, administrative, training, and planning personnel
     Development: application analysts, system designers, methods and procedures personnel, operating system programmers, and other programmers
     Operational: operators, data-entry personnel, and input/output control clerks
  B. Salary levels, training needs, and estimated turnover

V. Financial Projections by Time Period
  A. Hardware expenses, maintenance, depreciation, floor space, air conditioning, and electricity
  B. Personnel training and fringe benefits
  C. Miscellaneous building expenses, outsider services, telecommunications, and the like

Summary

Data processing planning is not a static activity. It is a process of continuous assessment and reassessment to ensure that the direction of the project development and daily operation fit the objectives, strategies, and plans of the organization. As required, the plan is modified to fit the changing needs of the organizaton. It is only by being open, dynamic, and adaptive that the planning process can be a useful and relevant tool for the organization.

CONTROLLING THE DATA PROCESSING ACTIVITY

Control is defined as the process of assuring that objectives, plans, policies, and standards are being attained. Therefore, it is necessary first to develop those objectives, plans, policies, and standards and to communicate them to those managers who have the responsibility for their accomplishment.

The control function include the following activities.[4]

1. Measurement of performance as compared with planned objectives, plans, and standards
2. Reporting of the results obtained in the measurement process
3. Analysis of the deviations from the predetermined objectives, plans, and standards to determine the underlying causes

[4]Glenn A. Welsch, *Budgeting—Profit Planning and Control* (Englewood Cliffs, N.J.: Prentice-Hall, 1971), pp. 23–24.

4. Evaluating alternative courses of action required to correct the indicated deviations

5. Selection and implementation of the "best" alternative

6. Follow-up to determine the effectiveness of the corrective action and recording of the information so improvements can be made in future planning and control cycles.

Effective control must be performed before it is too late to take corrective action about deviation from the plan. To be able to detect variations, performance reporting is necessary. These reports compare actual results with the predetermined objectives and standards.

The measurement and analysis process involves reporting of the (1) actual results, (2) budget or planned data, and (3) the difference between the two. This type of reporting is known as the exception principle. Using the budget as a tool for controlling the data processing activity is discussed in details in the following section.

THE DATA PROCESSING BUDGET

Budgeting and Control of Data Processing

As mentioned previously, control is defined as both management planning and control of the data processing activities, such as development of new applications and the regular operations. This type of control is usually exercised by setting goals, approving plans, and measuring performance against these plans or budgets. Budget is the financial plan for certain time periods, and it represents the authorization to utilize organization resources to operate existing information systems, develop new applications, and add new capacities, such as hardware, software, and personnel, to be used for the regular operation and the development activities. Budgets are usually defined in terms of money amounts and the allocation of these amounts to certain time periods by organizational units. Although this task is normally done on a short-range basis, it is one of the most difficult tasks to be performed by management. There is always competition for scarce resources among potential users, mainly for developing of new systems. Therefore, setting goals and priorities for the requirements must be negotiated between users and the data processing function.

There are two types of budgets; the variable budget and the fixed budget. A fixed budget assumes no variance in the level of activity. A variable budget establishes a series of standard costs for various activities levels. When using the fixed budget approach, it is impossible to report any variation from the projected level of activity and the fact that the cost of supplying the data processing services is different from the one that was used in preparing the budget. For these reasons the use of fixed budget for data processing is not recommended. Fixed budget is recommended only for situations where there is no meaning for measuring the level of activity, which is not the case of data processing. A variable budget anticipates various activity levels and required computing of the variances between standard and actual costs at the data processing activity.

Variable Budget

The variable budget is concerned only with expenses. It provides data expenses that make it possible to allocate allowances to the various functions of the data processing activity according to the level of work performed. The variable budget is referred to in the literature also as the flexible budget, sliding scale budget, expense and control budget, and formula budget. The variable budget provides a procedure (formula) for the relationship of each expense classification to the volume of work done by each function. The formula includes two elements: the constant factor (fixed cost) and a variable rate (variable expense). In the case of fixed costs, the variable factor is equal to zero; in the case of variable cost, the fixed factor is equal to zero.

Fixed costs are those that remain constant in the short run regardless of the level of work performed, for example management salaries. Variable costs are those that vary directly (proportionally) with changes in the amount of work performed, for example, the cost of printed forms that is directly related to the volume of forms used. Semivariable costs are those that are neither fixed nor variable, for example, usage of communication lines that usually include fixed charge per period of time, plus charge for actual use.

The potential of the variable budget approach to costs control, in a dynamic environment such as data processing, should be obvious. It is significant in situations where it is difficult to budget volume or rate of work accurately. When using the variable expense budget, a dynamic cost control should be used.

Using the Budget as a Control

Implementation of the budget approach entails the need for continuous and dynamic control. The control is administered through the use of performance reports. These reports are grouped according to responsibilities and display a comparison of actual performance to planned performance, and thus provide performance variations analysis from the budgeted levels. These reports usually are produced and distributed on a monthly basis or when special requests are made. Performance must be measured and reported to each level of management. Actual performance statistics are not enough; results must be compared with a realistic standard (budget) to be evaluated competently. These reports may be divided into three distinctly different classifications: statistical reports, special reports, and performance reports.[5]

Statistical reports are accounting reports that exhibit the vital historical data concerning all aspects of the data processing activity. Special reports are reports that are prepared for ad hoc needs, each one being related to a specific problem. Performance reports are usually prepared on a monthly basis. These reports are designed to facilitate managerial control.

[5]Ibid., p. 497

Performance reports should be designed according to the data processing structure and should implement the exception principle in management. They need to be simple, easy to understand, and selective (displaying only the relevant information). These reports may be presented in three forms: they can be written reports (including narrative and tabulated statistics), they can be presented in graphical form (charts and diagrams), and they can be presented orally. A typical format for a performance report is shown in Figure 7.2. This is only an example. The level of detail should be determined by the organization's standards and requirements.

Typical Data Processing Budget

A typical budget for a data processing department will include costs items about personnel, hardware, software, communications, supplies, occupancy, training, and other expenses. The budget should define as many cost elements as possible.[6]

Salaries and Other Personnel Expenses. This element usually includes salaries; overtime costs; benefits; hiring, firing, and moving expenses; education; and training.

Hardware Expenses. Data processing equipment expenses include rental, leasing, purchase, depreciation, overtime charges, if any, maintainance costs, and insurance.

Office Equipment Expenses. This element includes all office equipment expenses, such as typewriters, copying machines, telephone equipment, and so on.

Software Expenses. Expenses of software include purchasing costs of software, rental costs, and maintenance costs.

Supplies Expenses. This item includes the budget for purchasing disks, tapes, printed forms, and the like.

Communication Expenses. Here we find charges for communication lines and communication equipment, such as modems.

Housing Expenses. Included here are office space rent, electricity, air conditioning, depreciation, cleaning, insurance, and so on.

Other Expenses. All other expenses not covered in previous items appear here, for example, travel, postage, books, conventions, and general insurance.

The Budgeting Process

The data processing budget involves a number of steps[7]: projection of the work load, including development projects, constructing of the formal budget, and preparing of the pro forma statements. There are two types of budgets at the

---

[6]James W. Cortada, *EDP Costs and Charges—Finance, Budgets, and Costs Control in Data Processing* (Englewood Cliffs, N.J.: Prentice-Hall, 1980), pp. 231–234.

[7]John W. Buckly and Kevin M. Lighter, *Accounting: An Information Systems Approach* (Encino, Calif.: Dickenson, 1973), pp. 998–999.

Figure 7.2 A Typical Performance Report

	Budget		Actual		Variance	
	This Month	Year-to Date	This Month	Year-to Date	This Month	Year-to Date
Personnel						
Salaries						
Overtime						
Training						
.						
.						
.						
Hardware						
Rental						
Maintenance						
.						
.						
.						
Office Expenses						
Equipment						
Telephone						
.						
.						
.						
Software						
Rental						
Purchase						
Maintenance						
.						
.						
.						
Supplies						
Forms						
Disk packs						
.						
.						
.						
Communications						
Rental						
Modems						
.						
.						
.						
Housing						
Rental						
Electricity						
.						
.						
.						
Other:						
Travel						
Postage						
.						
.						
.						
Totals						

operating level: operating and financial. Operating budgets are formal statements of the expected activities such as work load quotas, supply usage budget, direct labor budget, overhead budget, data processing equipment budget, and so on. Financial budgets are budgets of cash receipts and disbursement and, therefore, are concerned with the financing of the data processing activity. The pro forma statements exemplify the end results of the budgeting process and as such represent the financial objectives of the organization. The pro forma statements contain budget values rather than actual values.

OPERATIONS PLANNING AND CONTROL

Introduction

Data processing operation and control is similar in many respects to that found in manufacturing shops. The general process consists of input data, data preparation, job setup, processing, and outputting the final product, such as reports, updated files, and so on. It is possible to use management techniques applied in the manufacturing environment to improve data processing operations. Operations planning and control uses the users' requirements as the basis for the planning, which in turn yields the operation plan. This plan, of course, needs to be controlled. The following discussion presents the planning and controlling processes required for data processing operations.[8]

Planning the Work

The operation plan consists of three parts: the long-range plan, the daily plan, and the current plan.

The operation long-range plan

The operation long-range plan is a tool for planning the work to be done by the operation function and for projecting future work load. This plan is essentially a list of all jobs to be processed. This plan should take into account the dependencies between specific occurrences of jobs.

The operation daily plan

This plan contains the work to be performed by the operation function on a particular day and/or shift. It is based on the long-range plan, type of work, application description, and the calendar. The daily plan is also based on the various resources capacities.

[8]International Business Machines, *Operations Planning and Control—General Information,* Document No. GH19-6120-0 (White Plains, N.Y.: IBM, 1980), pp. 8–16.

The current plan

The current plan shows the status of work completed and work still to be done. The basis for this plan is the daily operation plan, which is continuously updated. It should provide the ability to modify the daily plan, as a result of having to rurun jobs, change priorities, and so on.

Figure 7.3 outlines the the functions of the operations planning and control and by whom these activities should be performed. The time periods used here—month, day, and current—are only examples. Each organization should choose its appropriate time intervals taking into account the type of work, the work load, and the availability of resources.

Controlling the Operations

Once the three plans are completed, they become the basic tool for controlling the data processing operation. The important task is the monitoring of the work flow. Each work station, a small group that specializes in a particular phase of the production process, is presented with a list of tasks to be performed. It is the responsibility of the work station to report all activities taking place, including completed work, arrival of nonscheduled jobs, and so on. Based on this reporting, the current plan needs to be modified. Work not completed on time is also

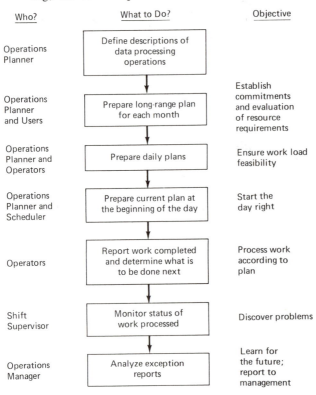

Figure 7.3 Functions of the Operations Planning and Control

reported, so corrective action can be taken by management. At the end of each cycle, a summary report showing all exceptions is produced, so that operations management can analyze the causes for these problems and thus prevent their recurrence. Reports showing completed work and actual resources utilization may be generated to help determine future capacity requirements.

This procedure, if used correctly, provides a mechanism for controlling operations and makes it possible to act immediately. Tools are commercially available for planning and controlling data processing operations. The data processing operation is similar to the manufacturing activity and it is possible to use planning and control tools that are available for different industries.

ACCOUNTING CONTROL OF DATA PROCESSING[9]

Emerging requirements for providing better control of all corporate activities have focused attention on improving cost control of data processing operations. Data processing departments have grown in their scope of applications; consequently, these operations comprise an increasing share of corporate expenses. Thus equitably distributing the costs of data processing among user departments has become a necessity. This requirement has motivated a study of methods for integrating the measurement of data processing resource utilization into the corporate accounting system. The restructured system to accommodate all phases of accounting control, including data processing, is the subject of this discussion.

The special problem of data processing accounting is that of analyzing and charging for jobs processed. For sequential job processing, charges have been previously based on a fixed rate and elapsed-time basis. Multiprogramming has further complicated the elapsed-time method of measuring system utilization in billing the user. In the past, a widely used method of charging users for data processing services was to pro rate the total data processing expense among the users. This method, by which all users absorbed the full costs of data processing, is commonly known as "full-absorption costing."

In a multiprogramming environment, however, elapsed time for any given job is affected by the interference of other jobs being processed concurrently. Therefore, the elapsed time for each job typically exceeds the time it would have required in a nonmultiprogramming environment. Elapsed time is, in general, a poor basis for data processing job accounting because jobs usually use less than all available resources. The objective toward which the data processing accounting method discussed in this presentation is aimed is to charge each user in a multiprogramming environment the amount he or she would have paid in a nonmultiprogramming environment and to eliminate fluctuations in job costs caused by variations in system utilization.

The accounting method presented here, termed the "resource utilization

[9]R. C. Rettus and R. A. Smith, "Accounting Control of Data Processing," *IBM Systems Journal*, no. 1 (1972), pp. 74–92. Reprinted by permission from *The IBM Systems Journal* © 1972 by International Business Machines Corporation.

system," measures the system resources and personnel used for each job and the times for each of these factors in determining and controlling their costs to departments and to the corporation. The data processing resource utilization system is integrated with the whole corporate accounting system, which also includes the general ledger and budget. This integration is presented in Figure 7.4. The basic technique for relating these three accounting procedures involves a cost center corporate configuration, standards rates for system components, and resource utilization measurement. Inputs, processing, and output requirements of the component accounting system are discussed.

Corporate Accounting System

All companies have a general ledger system—either manual or automated—that furnishes an income statement and balance sheet. The costs of the data processing equipment was relatively small when it was being used primarily to perform these accounting functions and when the manager in charge of data processing usually reported within the accounting structure. All associated costs were therefore charged to the accounting department and were included on the income statement as part of general and administrative expenses. Accompanying the development of broader computer capabilities, other departments, such as sales and production, began automating functions they previously performed manually.

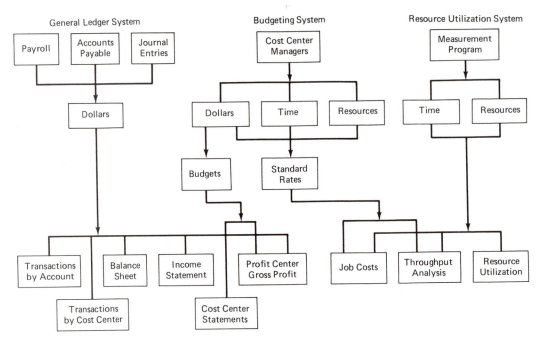

Figure 7.4 The Integrated Accounting System.   *Source:* R. C. Rettus and R. A. Smith, "Accounting Control of Data Processing," *IBM Systems Journal,* Vol. 1, 1972, pp. 74–92. Reprinted by permission from *IBM Systems Journal.* © 1972 by International Business Machines Corporation.

Data processing has now evolved into service departments that provide services for the entire company. It follows, therefore, that the using departments should be charged for this transfer of work. One of the objectives of this presentation is to discuss a cost-center-oriented accounting system whereby the objective of charging departments for data processing can be accomplished equitably.

"Cost centers," which are defined more rigorously later in this presentation, are points where dollars, time, and resources of the corporate budgeting system are expended and recovered. One of the primary functions of a corporate budgeting system is to provide standards against which actual performance can be measured. The budgeting system described here provides such standards for each cost center. The budgeting system can also be used to develop standard rates for measuring resource utilization and determining the cost to perform the data processing service. The budgeted time that each resource is available to perform chargeable work is known. Also the budgeted dollar value of the resource is known. Therefore, the budgeted unit cost of each resource—defined here as the "standard rate"—can be determined. The purpose of the standard rate is to eliminate price and usage fluctuations from the costs of jobs and to provide an accurate cost of each job on which user billing can be based.

Companies whose data processing costs are a large part of their total expenses wish to know and account for the utilization of their computing center. This is particularly important to a company whose data processing costs are charged on the basis of the amount of service provided to several different users. In such a situation, an accurate measure of the cost of work processed should be determined because this provides the basis for billing users.

Techniques for measuring analysts' and programmers' productivity are not subjects of this presentation, since they have analogies throughout the business world. Further, accounting for resources of a computer system by jobs is relatively simple in a nonmultiprogramming environment (running only one job at a time on a central processor). Computing centers that operate a multiprogramming environment find that a resource utilization system is essential. Such a system is directed toward determining the cost of each job that is run in that environment so that the charge for each job is not affected by other jobs being processed concurrently. Equally important is the measurement of the overall throughput of the system. The company that is not doing multiprogramming may also be able to use much of the information presented here and later be able to make a smooth transition into the multiprogramming environment.

These three subsystems are presented as an integrated accounting system. The component subsystems—general ledger, budgeting, and resource utilization—can be used independently. That is, a company can install the resource utilization system without developing standard rates if it is concerned only with measuring resource utilization and does not want to assign costs to individual jobs or measure overall systems throughput. Similarly, standard rates can be developed for use by the resource utilization system without adopting the budgeting system. Further, the general ledger system can be installed without the budgeting system, provided that management does not need to measure variances from the budget.

The methods presented here should be thought of as a guide to the development of the integrated accounting system, which may require modifications to fit a particular company that is seeking to achieve better control of its data processing activity.

Cost Center Identification

A cost center is a group of resources designated for accounting control of the particular operation being performed. Cost centers differ from departments in that a department is a grouping of resources for reporting and managerial control purposes. Cost centers can exist independently of departments or within departments and can even coincide with the existing departmental organization. The first requirement for merging the computer resource utilization system into the integrated accounting system is to identify the data processing cost centers.

We now give a method for identifying data processing cost centers in a typical company. Assume that we have a data processing department that is presently divided into the following three areas: operations, systems, and programming. Each area has a manager who reports to the data processing manager. The company presently has a three-digit departmental identification number and desires to renumber these departments as cost centers. The 600 series numbers is allocated for use by the data processing center. For example, in analyzing the accounting requirements for data processing, we determine that the following cost centers are required:

1. Operations
   Model X
   Model Y
2. Systems
3. Programming
   Maintenance
   Development

Functions and groups

In addition, assume that there are several supporting activities within operations that must be segregated because they cannot be identified with the model X and model Y cost centers. Assume further that these activities are to be separate cost centers. Also, there is a requirement for the secretarial pool and the technical library as separate cost centers. The overall data processing department is defined as a cost function, which is divided into cost groups. "Cost groups" consist of one or more cost centers, and they comprise all cost centers performing a similar activity. In the data processing example, the cost groups are operations, systems, programming, and support.

The results of this analysis of the data processing example are presented in Table 7.1. Cost centers are only functional areas that can accumulate charges and, therefore, are the only entities identified by three digits. The data processing

TABLE 7.1 DATA PROCESSING COST CENTERS

Cost Center Number	Cost Center Description	Level
6XX	Data processing	Function
60X	Data processing support	Cost group
601	Management	Cost center
602	Secretarial pool	Cost center
603	Technical library	Cost center
62X	Operations	Cost group
621	Systems programming	Cost center
622	Tape/disk library	Cost center
623	Control desk	Cost center
624	Model X	Cost center
625	Model Y	Cost center
65X	Systems	Group/center
67X	Programming	Cost group
671	Maintenance	Cost center
672	Development	Cost center

function and the four cost groups do not accumulate charges but receive combined financial statements of their component cost centers; for example, the programming cost group (67X) receives a combined statement for cost centers 671 and 672. The systems cost group (65X) is also designated as a cost center because it is the only entity within the group. The numbers assigned allow for expansion as more cost centers or cost groups are added.

Corporate chart of accounts

Accumulated cost center expenses are numerically classified into a corporate chart of accounts, which is a general ledger coding structure that includes both the balance sheet and the income statement accounts. The structure and classification of accounts today are well standardized in formats supported by the Securities and Exchange Commission and the American Institute of Certified Public Accountants. Because it is so basic, the subject is extensively treated in most accounting texts and handbooks. The data processing cost center is integrated to the general corporate chart of accounts via the 600 series, as discussed.

Standard Rate

After segregating data processing resources into cost centers, one can determine what the costs are and provide a standard rate for each resource. "Standard rates" are factors based on expected resource utilization and expected resource cost. The use of standard rates for data processing resources provides consistent cost and utilization data on which to base the pricing decision. Any cost or utilization fluctuations are reported as variances from the budgeted cost or utilization so that the specific area of variance can be acted upon.

The standard rates for the data processing resources are developed at the same time the budget is developed. However, they can be developed independently of, or in the absence of, a corporate budget. The standard rate development consists of the following three procedures: resource identification, derivation of the available time for each resource, and budgeting the cost of each resource. The determination of standard rates is discussed here by using a specific data processing configuration as an example.

Resource identification

In this explanation, a computer system is discussed, although the same general method applies to other resources such as programming and system analysis. We define the following four general categories of computer system resources: main storage, CPU cycles, channels, and input/output devices with their associated control units.

- Main storage is the amount of addressable storage available measured in thousands (K) of bytes.
- CPU cycles are a measure of the operational time available, for the central processor.
- Channels consist of three categories: byte multiplexor, selector, and block multiplexor.
- Input/output devices are grouped by like units called component groups

The following central processor and devices are assumed in our example:

- One CPU unit with 512 Kbyte main storage
- One Model A direct access storage device with eight drives, yielding 4,000 available tracks, for a total of 32,000 tracks
- Four Model B tape drives
- Four Model C tape drives
- One Model D card read/punch
- Two Model E printers
- Twenty Model F display consoles

A special characteristic of main storage and direct access storage devices (DASD) is that they are not allocated to jobs by individual devices in the same way as other component groups are allocated because they can be used by two or more jobs concurrently. Therefore, the measurement unit for main storage is "Kbytes," and direct access storage devices are measured by tracks. For all other devices the measurement unit is the number of devices. Also, not all main storage and DASD are available to perform productive work because of system requirements. Therefore, the measurement unit for main storage is the total bytes minus the number of bytes used by the nucleus supervisor. For DASD, the measurement unit is the net available tracks. In Table 7.2, the 10 component groups in our example with their measurement units are identified.

Budgeted time

Next, determine the time that each component group is available to do productive work. The standard rate is the same for the entire year unless some event occurs during the year that necessitates a change. Thus, one can define total time, TT, for each component group as

$$TT = \text{total available hours per year per component} \times \text{measurement unit}$$

Nonproductive conditions are then identified. A component is considered as nonproductive during the following time:

- Preventive maintenance, PM, time regularly scheduled.
- Down time, DT, time lost due to failure of hardware or system software.
- Idle time, IT, time during which a component is not used by a job.
- Rerun time, RR, time during which a component is performing nonbillable work.
- Multiprogramming degradation, MP, time during which a component is waiting and is ready to work but is not being utilized because another job is impacting it. (The CPU and channels cannot be nonproductive as a result of multiprogramming degradation because they are never allocated to a specific job. There is no MP in nonmultiprogramming environment.)

Companies are not limited to the categories in this example; initial program load, IPL, could be a category for another company.

Budgeting PM, DT, IT, and RR is relatively easy. MP is derived empirically using the resource utilization system discussed later in this presentation in connec-

TABLE 7.2 I/O COMPONENT GROUP MEASUREMENT FACTORS

Group Number	Description	Measurement Unit
0	Main storage	Kbytes (net)
1	CPU	Number
2	Byte multiplexor channel	Number
3	Selector channels	Number
4	Direct access storage device	Tracks (net)
5	Tape drive Model C	Number
6	Tape drive, Model D	Number
7	Card read/punch	Number
8	Printers	Number
9	Visuals displays	Number

tion with developing cost information. Productive time, *PT,* can now be derived for each component according to the following formula:

$$PT = TT - (PM + DT + IT + RR + MP)$$

Budget cost

The budget cost of each component group consists of direct cost of the component group, allocated indirect costs in the cost center, and allocated overhead costs in the operations cost group and the data processing function.

Direct costs are costs that can be specifically identified with the component group. They include such specific costs as equipment rent or lease expenses of devices and their control units, maintenance contracts, and depreciation of purchased equipment. Other costs might include printer forms, rent or depreciation of tapes and disk packs, and telecommunications charges.

Indirect costs are costs charged to a productive cost center that cannot be identified specifically with a component group. A productive cost center is one that charges users for its services. The allocation of indirect costs to component groups is based on the major manufacturer's monthly rental of all equipment in the component group or some other equitable method. An allocation based on direct costs of the component groups is equitable only if the equipment is rented. Examples of indirect costs are rental (depreciation, lease, etc.) of devices that are not available to perform useful work. The console typewriter, main storage allocated to the nucleus (supervisor), and unavailable DASD tracks also generate indirect costs.

Overhead costs consist of all costs residing in the nonproductive centers in the operations cost group. Referring to Table 7.1, overhead costs might be the following:

- •621 Systems programming
- •622 Tape/disk library
- •623 Control desk

Additionally, overhead costs consist of all costs residing in the nonproductive cost groups such as data processing support (60X). Although operations do not receive all these costs, they must be allocated among the three productive cost groups—operations, systems, and programming—based on an appropriate method such as budgeted costs or budgeted revenue.

The basis for combining and allocating overhead costs to productive centers is the major manufacturer's total rental value of all components residing in each of these centers. Because overhead costs are allocated to component groups in the same manner as indirect costs, they can be combined and allocated together.

Standard rate

The standard rate, *SR,* for the component group is determined by dividing the annual budget cost, *BC,* for each component group by the annual productive time, *PT,* for the component group as follows:

$$SR = BC/PT$$

The standard rate for each component is determined by dividing the standard rate for each component group by the measurement unit for the component group. In this sense, a track on a DASD and 1 Kbyte of main storage are devices because these are the smallest units that can be allocated to a job.

Resource Utilization Measurement

The measurement of multiprogramming degradation for components of a computer system is considered to be nonproductive because it detracts from the time that the component is available to perform work on the job. The underlying assumption on which the theory of multiprogramming is based is that in this environment the degradation suffered on certain components is offset by increased utilization of other components, primarily the central processing unit. Therefore, the objectives of multiprogramming are to increase overall system utilization and throughput and thereby decrease the cost of each job. Achieving these two objectives requires the accurate measurement of resources used by the jobs.

Wait-ready status

The possible conditions regarding a job at any moment are the following:

- CPU alone is executing.
- CPU and I/O devices are executing concurrently (overlapped).
- I/O devices alone are working on the job.
- The job is in the wait-ready status when it is ready to continue executing, but it is waiting to obtain the CPU, which is working on another job.

The wait-ready period is the time during which the main storage and I/O devices allocated to the job cannot be used. The execution time of the job is, therefore, degraded by the multiprogramming environment in which it operates.

If one measures the total time a job is in the wait-ready status, *WR*, one determines the multiprogramming degradation, *MP*, experienced by the main storage and I/O devices allocated to the job because

$$WR = MP$$

And, because the total elapsed time of the job is known, one can measure resource utilization by subtracting the wait-ready time from the elapsed time, thereby obtaining productive time:

$$PT = ET - MP$$

Techniques, however, are not commercially available to measure the amount of time each job is in the wait-ready status. Thus it is the user's responsibility to program and maintain the operating system modifications necessary to measure this status.

Theoretical resource utilization

Since users cannot readily make this modification, we present an alternative method for obtaining the approximate *MP* by calculating the theoretical stand-alone time of a job. This method attempts to find the theoretical amount of time that systems resources are used by each job, based on the speeds of the devices used and the amount of processed data. If the theoretical resource utilization (*TRU* time) and the elapsed time of a job are known, multiprogramming degradation applicable to main storage and I/O devices allocated to the job can be derived as follows:

$$MP = ET - TRU \text{ time}$$

The information necessary to determine *TRU* time is usually provided by the accounting package supplied by the mainframe manufacturer.

We now discuss the theory underlying the measurement of resource utilization and also give further specialized consideration in the appendix. Given that today's data processing environment provides modern language structures, double buffering, and sufficient channels on the system to take advantage of these facilities, we can assume that for most jobs the CPU and I/O times can be overlapped and that any I/O time can be overlapped with any other I/O time. On this basis, we can define *TRU* time for main storage and I/O devices used for any job as the greater of the theoretical time required to process the longest data set or CPU time.

To determine the theoretical time required to process the longest data set, we must compute the theoretical time required to process each data set. The theoretical measurement of utilization of the various components is the following:

- Main storage and device utilization equals job *TRU* time.
- CPU utilization is the actual time, *AT,* the CPU is executing the job. *AT* is supplied by the accounting package.
- Channel utilization is based on the number of execute channel program, *EXCP,* commands processed by the channel, the physical record length, *PRL,* of the records transferred across the channel, and the transfer rate, *TR,* of the device channel is servicing. The computation is:

$$\text{theoretical channel utilization} = EXCPs \times PRL \times TR$$

The *EXCPs*, *PRL,* and the address of the device and channel are supplied by the accounting package. The *TR* is supplied externally.

Standard job cost

By using either method of determining the component utilization formula just described, and applying the standard rates described in the previous section, we can determine the standard cost of each job. Figure 7.5 shows the utilization of all components required by a hypothetical job.

The following standard rates for components are assumed for this example:

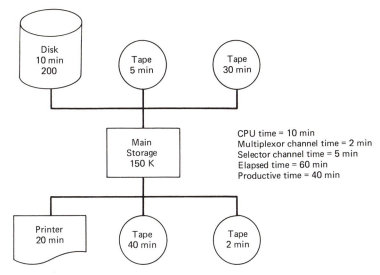

Figure 7.5 Hypothetical Job Times.   *Source:* R. C. Rettus and R. A. Smith, "Accounting Control of Data Processing," *IBM Systems Journal,* Vol. 1, 1972, pp. 74–92. Reprint by permission from *IBM Systems Journal.* © 1972 by International Business Machines Corporation.

Tape	$0.30/device minute
Disk	0.01/track minute
Printer	0.20/printer minute
Main storage	0.01/1 Kbyte minute
CPU	2.90/CPU minute
Multiplexor channel	0.40/transmission minute
Selector channel	0.50/transmission minute

The standard cost of the example job is computed as shown in Table 7.3.

TABLE 7.3 STANDARD JOB COSTS

Component Group	Utilization (minutes)	Number of Components	Standard Rate for Group	Total Cost
Tape	40*	4	$0.30	$48.00
Disk	40*	200†	0.01	80.00
Printer	40*	1	0.20	8.00
Main storage	40*	150††	0.01	60.00
CPU	10	1	2.90	29.00
MPX channel	2	1	0.40	0.80
SEL channel	5	1	0.50	2.50
			Job Total	$228.30

*Productive time.

†Tracks.

††Kbytes.

TABLE 7.4   RECORD OF SYSTEM COMPONENT UTILIZATION

Component Group	PT	MP	PM	DT	RR	IT
Tape	160	80				(240)
Disk	8000	4000				(12000)
Printer	40	20				(60)
Main storage	6000	3000				(10)
CPU	10					(10)
MPX channel	2					(2)
SEL channel	5					(5)

(header of table: Time measurement Categories (minutes))

Component utilization

To record component utilization for this hypothetical job, it is convenient to record the times for system components in various measurement categories in a table such as Table 7.4. The credits to idle time are entered because each component was debited with a device/day at the start of processing. Although Table 7.4 indicates minutes, smaller time measures may be used.

Component utilization information is accumulated for each job processed by the system. At the conclusion of the measurement cycle, resource utilization and system throughput are then reported.

Integrated Accounting System

The previous section discussed the measurement of resource utilization based on the concept of productive time. The input requirements, processing, and expected outputs of the systems are now presented for the three systems that constitute the integrated accounting system depicted in Figure 7.4: general ledger, budgeting, and resource utilization.

General ledger system

Input.   Three primary areas furnish financial inputs to the general ledger system: (1) payroll; (2) accounts payable, which records all payments that will be made to suppliers of services; and (3) journal entries, which record all other transactions. These transactions are coded in accordance with the corporate chart of accounts. In the case of payroll, if the application has been automated, individuals are normally coded to costs centers and distributed directly by the payroll program. If these three applications are already automated but the company wishes to change to five-digit chart of accounts, the existing programs should be altered to accept a five-digit code. During processing, all inputs are verified so that only valid accounts are accepted. Entries for these applications are done at least once a month.

Output.   The following reports are recommended to be produced by the general ledger system.

Transaction by account. Each transaction, with a description and source is listed for each account so that the accounting department can verify the validity of all transactions and account balances.

Transactions by account within cost centers. Each cost center manager receives a report that enables him or her to examine the details supporting each account balance.

Balance sheet and income statement. These reports are listed by detailed account and in the summary for each month and the year to date.

Cost center statement. Each cost center manager receives a cost center statement in detail and in summary, showing the current month and the year-to-date balances by account. A report in summary form is depicted in Figure 7.6. Managers of cost groups and functions receive the total of costs centers for each group or function under their control. If a budgeting system is used, actual figures are compared with budgeted figures. Any variances are reported.

Profit center gross profit. Each production cost center and sales unit receives a report showing actual sales of their service, cost of those sales, and gross profit. This report is also prepared for functions and groups. If the budgeting system is used, budget and variances also are shown.

Budgeting System

Input. Cost center managers supply the budgeting information. Detailed expenses by account by month are necessary. Revenue budgets are prepared by the sales department with the assistance of the productive cost center managers. Other income and expenses are supplied by accounting. Time and resource inputs used for developing standard rates are the responsibility of each productive cost center manager.

Outputs. The budgeting system provides monthly budgets with an annual recap reported by cost center group, cost function, and total company. Revenue and gross profit budgets are also provided. If standard rates are developed, all component groups within the system are analyzed to show total cost and expected utilization by category: *PT, MP, RR, DT, PM,* and *IT.*

Resource utilization system

Input. The first input required is actual utilization data, which are supplied by any one of the programming measurement systems discussed. Utilization data consist at the least of the following:

- Job identification
- Beginning and end time of each job
- Device used, by
    Type
    Physical record length
    Number of READs or WRITEs (EXCPs)
    Address

Figure 7.6   Format for Summarizing Cost Expenditures

	This Month		Year to Date	
Corporate Information Processing Center Cost Analysis	Hours	Cost	Hours	Cost
01—659 Corporate General Accounting				
00459 Appropriation Report				
System 360 M-30				
Unit Record				
Card punching				
30111 Moving and Living Expenses				
System 360 M-50				
System 360 M-30				
Unit record				
Card punching				
40047 Special References				
System 360 M-155				
System 360 M-30				
Programming				
Systems				
Card punching				
40073 Accounts Payable				
System 370 M-155				
System 370 A&T				
System 360 M-30				
Programming				
Systems				
Unit record				
Card punching				
Other card punching				
40077 Authorized Signatures				
System 360 M-50				
Unit record				
Card punching				

- Access method (DASD)
- CPU cycles used
- Main storage allocated

Also, other data are needed such as those contained in the equipment file, or the program resident table identifies each component group by physical device address and component group number. The program resident table further contains standard unit rates and expected utilization by category (*PT, MP, PM, DT, RR,* and *IT*). Input regarding downtime (*DT*) and preventive maintenance (*PM*) is furnished daily. A method of identifying reruns, presumably built into the job identification number, is also required.

At least two processing programs are required. The primary functions of the daily processing program are to

1. Read utilization data for each job
2. Compute job TRU time
3. Compute component utilization to utilization table
4. Write job cost
5. Add component utilization to utilization table
6. Format and write utilization reports
7. Write utilization data

The monthly processing program reads, sorts, and combines job costs and utilization data and writes the monthly reports.

Output. The basic reports produced by the system are (1) resource utilization, (2) throughput analysis, and (3) job costs. Other reports can be also generated such as summary utilization and operating system analysis reports. These reports should provide utilization information by department and by function as well as information about scheduled time, actual time, preventive maintenance, unscheduled maintenance, and so on.

The resource utilization report, produced daily and monthly, provides for each component group the actual and budgeted hours as a percentage of total available hours. Percentage variation is given for *PT, MP, RR, DT, PM,* and *IT*.

The throughput analysis report provides the following information by component group and total for the system:

- Number of devices
- Standard rate
- Budgeted dollars (*PT* extended based on budgeted utilization)
- Actual dollars (*PT* extended based on actual utilization)
- Variance
- Actual hours of *PT, MP, RR, DT, PM,* and *IT*

The job cost report gives the standard cost by job within function by user of

- CPU
- Main storage
- Channels
- DASD
- Tape
- Printer
- Card read/punch
- Teleprocessing devices
- Other devices
- Total

Concluding Remarks

Measurement of the use of data processing resources is necessary for allocating the cost of these resources to users. This is becoming more important because the cost of data processssing is making up an increasingly larger percentage of each user's budget. Traditional measurements of the cost of data processing resources, such as the full-absorption method, are unsuitable because users are not charged according to their actual resource utilization and because data processing departments are not held accountable for fluctuations of efficiencies and inefficiencies of their operations.

Systems and programming resources are measured by any of the common personnel measurement systems used throughout industry. The measurement of computer sytems resources, however, is more difficult, particularly if the computer is used in a multiprogramming mode. A system that measures resource utilization is required to furnish actual usage data to a program that calculates the cost of components used by a job. In addition, data processing cost centers are identified, and budgeted utililization and cost data are supplied so that a standard rate for components can be calculated. Jobs are costed at a standard rate to isolate cost and usage fluctuations from job cost data.

Two methods determine component utilization. Measuring wait-ready time experienced by a job is the more accurate method, but the user may not be able to make the operating system modification necessary to measure it. An alternate approach is to compute theoretical resource utilization using algorithms based on the speed of devices and the amount of data being processed.

The resource utilization system described here provides not only job data, but also system throughput and component utilization. It is presented with general ledger and budgeting systems to assist the company that desires to install an integrated accounting system or simply to aid one in understanding how the utilization system interfaces with a general corporate accounting system. The systems presented in this discussion pertain to the historical aspects of computer system utilization. An additional use of the cost data developed is a predictive one. New and revised applications can now be evaluated because standard costs of the proposed applications can be developed.

In developing theoretical resource utilization, other factors such as on-line jobs, spooling, and consecutively processed data sets regarding job type and resource identification may be considered.

On-line jobs

By definition, on-line jobs require the availability of all resources while the job is resident in the computer. The on-line job bears the cost of all allocated resources (I/O devices and main storage) for the elapsed time the job is resident.

Spooling

Spooling, or writing of report files after the job creating the files has terminated, presents another special situation. If the costs of the spooling program are identified and are allocated to the programs creating the records on a per record basis, this results in a full-absorption cost system that is subject to price fluctuations. Therefore, the development of a standard rate for spooling operations is recommended since spooling is considered a resource of the total system.

Consecutively processed data sets

In the measurement of TRU time, the assumption that all I/O is overlapped with all other I/O is not true when two or more data sets are processed consecutively because one or more data sets is completely processed before one or more subsequent data sets is processed. It follows that consecutively processed data sets are identified and I/O transfer time is calculated as if those data sets were one. Thus they are added together and are treated as one data set before being compared with other data sets.

SELECTED READINGS

BAHR, D. "Capacity Planning for EDP Systems." In *Proceedings SEAS Anniversary Meeting 1973,* Leuven, Belgium, September 11–14, 1973, pp. 303–312.

BUCKLY, JOHN W., AND KEVIN M. LIGHTER. *Accounting: An Information Systems Approach.* Encino, Calif.: Dickenson, 1973.

HAND, A. B., AND W. L. RIVERS. "Constructing a Data Processing Cost Accounting System." *Magazine of Bank Administration,* April 1974, pp. 34–44.

KRAUSS, L. *Adminstrative and Controlling the Company Data Processing Function.* Englewood Cliffs, N.J.: Prentice-Hall, 1969.

MAIR, W. C., D. R. WOOD, AND K. W. DAVIS. *Computer Control and Audit.* Altamonte Springs, Fla.: The Institute of Internal Auditors, 1978.

NOLAN, R. L. *Management Accounting and Control of Data Processing.* New York: National Association of of Accountants, June 1977.

SMIDT, S. "The Use of Hard and Soft Money Budgets and Prices to Limit Demand for Centralized Computer Facility." *Proceedings AFIPS Fall Joint Computer Conference,* Monvale, N.J.: American Federation of Information Societies, 1968, pp. 499–509.

STATLAND, N., ET AL. "Guidelines for Cost Accounting Practices for Data Processing." *Data Base,* Vol. 8, no. 3 (Winter 1977), supplement.

8

Data and Physical Security

Internal control is vital to almost any company. Management relies on the presence of internal controls to ensure that its records are accurate, its business is not interrupted, its assets are protected, its competitive advantages are maintained, and so on. Controls found outside of an EDP environment will not suffice in the data processing area.

The data processing function is responsible for the handling, processing, and storing of data from the time it is received until the delivery of results to users. Additionally, data processing is responsible for the design of systems to carry out their activities. As a result, controls are implemented to prevent, identify, and correct human errors, hardware/software failure, catastrophes, and computer abuse.

Computers can be the object or tool of an act of abuse as well as constitute the environment in which such an act occurs. If the computer is an object of abuse, services may be used without authorization, contents of computer files may be stolen, or the computer may be subject to vandalism. Computers may also be used as a tool to design or implement an abusive act against a company. Within the computerized environment, acts such as fraud, embezzlement, invasion of privacy, and intentional alteration of records might also occur.

Assets to be protected include data (files, programs, and documentation), equipment, supplies (which cannot be acquired easily, such as printed forms), utilities, personnel (such as safety), buildings and facilities, means of access (perimeter security).

Computer abuse may represent the greatest area of exposure to the data processing department. Internal controls should be developed to safeguard adequately against such abuse. Data processing management must be aware of this threat to the installation, impose cost-effective countermeasures, and strive to make the cost of penetration greater than the expected value of information obtained.

The objective of this chapter is to identify and discuss security threats and controls that are available to ensure security. A general review of the most frequent types of computer fraud and their impact on the organization is also presented. As technology changes, so will the security techniques. New hardware and software will be marketed for these purposes. However, the philosophy behind the security system should remain relatively constant. There are three areas of information security that must be addressed[1]:

- *Data confidentiality*. Data confidentiality ensures that data are not given to unauthorized users either accidentally or intentionally. This area has both legal and proprietary ramifications.
- *Data integrity*. Data integrity concerns both accidental and intentional data alteration or destruction.
- *Availability of service*. Availability of service deals with denial of service to authorized users.

EVALUATING SECURITY NEEDS

It is agreed that there will be a greater need for increased internal controls as our reliance upon EDP systems grows. Prerequisites of good security are good management, formal documented procedures, and common sense. As a first step in determining the type of security required, management should evaluate the computer operations environment. A cost-benefit analysis of potential controls should then be completed.

Considering the Environment

Management should first attempt to identify all threats that exist within the computer's environment. The areas of general threat were alluded to in the preceding discussion, where it was pointed out that the computer can be the object of an act of abuse as well as constitute the environment in which such an act occurs.

In determining the extent to which exposure might exist in these areas, consideration should be given to the complexity of services. Complex capabilities were introduced with the advent of third-generation computers. As a result, concurrent processing, extensive sharing of resources, and remote terminals were

---

[1]Cadambi Srivansan and Paul Dascher, "Computer System Security," *Infosystem* (May 1981), p. 116.

available. These complex systems have many benefits, but they present a substantial security problem, since numerous opportunities for accidental or deliberate acquisition of information exist.[2] The threats to security include the following:

- Errors, omissions, and accidents
- Failures of the infrastructure (equipment, utilities, such as power and communications, heating systems, etc.)
- Natural disasters and actions of the elements (flood and water leakage, fire, earthquake, windstorm)
- Hostile insider action: (a dishonest employee who may gain a personal advantage by modification or disclosure of records or theft of data or assets and then endeavor to eliminate any trace of the action; a disgruntled employee who, because of dissatisfaction, may cause damage by modification, disclosure, or destruction of data or other assets.)
- Impersonal outsider action (such as riot and war)
- Hostile outsider penetration

Cost-benefit analysis

Security costs for protection against all hazards are high. There is no sense in spending $20,000 to guard against the possible loss of $10,000. An analysis of costs versus value should therefore be conducted before determining the specific internal controls that are to be implemented.

Differences in the type of information processed and the potential threats require diverse security measures. Consideration should be given to the fact that information has a distinct value that varies with the perception of different interest groups. As an example, the organization that has and uses information would place a different value on it than would the individuals who generate the information. On the other hand, an intruder might place a very different value on such information.[3] As part of the cost-benefit analysis, a risk analysis should also be performed. In this analysis, all possible threats to the system should be identified with the areas that may be affected by these threats. The expected loss value is then taken into consideration in the cost-benefit analysis.

As a result of computer abuse, service may be interrupted or information stolen, altered, or destroyed. In evaluating the cost of these threats, a probability should be associated with each. A security risk assessment study should be performed to quantify the risk and establish a potential or expected impact.

However, due to the subjective nature of the factors noted, such an assessment may be quite difficult and actually have the primary benefit of directing

[2]K. S. Shankar, "The Total Computer Security Problem: Overview," *Computer* (June 1977), p. 51–52.

[3]Stuart E. Madnick, "Management Policies and Procedures Needed for Effective Computer Security," *Sloan Management Review* (Fall 1978), p. 65.

management's attention to the highest exposure areas. With this background in mind, the organization can begin to focus on the nature of the internal controls desired.

Organization and Administration

During the security evaluation process, the following questions should be answered:

- Has anyone been appointed to be responsible for the security of data and other assets of the data processing installation?
- When has the company's security system undergone its last independent audit of compliance and adequacy?
- Does insurance exist for the data processing resources if security measures fail or do not adequately cover insurable risks?
- If the company's data processing installation were severely damaged by fire or other calamity, are there recognized, tested plans to continue providing the data needed to keep the company operating?

Appointing a person to be responsible

The organization should appoint a high-level security officer who will be in charge of the security administration. Since it is impractical to assume that a large installation will have only one security manager, there may be a need to appoint a number of security managers, mainly in remote locations. Persons to whom security control is delegated should have complete control over resources for which they are responsible so that alterations to such control cannot be made by any other security officer unless he or she is so authorized, regardless of his position in the organizational structure.

Security control group

As in accounting organizations, separation of duties is important in data processing organizations.[4] This is especially true with respect to the security control group. Wilkins[5] recommends that each key area of data processing be assigned a security representative. Together, these security representatives should constitute the security control group. As mentioned, to give this group authority, these individuals must report to top-line organizational management. If they re-

[4]Srivansan and Dascher, "Computer System Security," p. 116; Cadambi Srivansan and Paul Dascher, "Computer System Security," *Financial Executive* (June 1980), p. 28; and U.S. Department of Defense, *Industrial Security Manual for Safeguarding Classified Information* (Washington, D.C.: Defense Supply Agency, 1970), p. 3.

[5]Barry J. Wilkins, *The Internal Auditor's Information Security Handbook* (Altamonte Springs, Fla.: The Institute of Internal Auditors, 1979).

port only to the data processing management, they lose much of their regulating strength.

Design of the security policy

An organization must review all its information as the first step of security policy design and evaluation.[6] Not all information is worth protecting. Also proprietary data are not all of equal value. The more valuable the data are, the tighter the security controls should be. One must take care not to rate too much data at a high classification, as this will result in an overly costly security system; at the same time it will lead to inefficiency and will undermine the credibility of the program.

The process of identifying valuable information must involve top management. An inventory of data from all activities of the organization must be compiled. What is vital about each piece much be determined.

Once the valuable information has been determined, it can be classified. Wilkins[7] suggests the classification system used by the Department of Defense. This system classifies information into the following four categories[8]:

- *Unclassified*. At first glance this may seem unnecessary. However, making data unclassified shows that a conscious decision was made to label it as such.
- *Confidential*. These are data that should not be distributed outside the company but have large distribution within the company. If they were released, no serious damage would be done.
- *Priority*. This category includes most information with value. Distribution is usually limited to authorized personnel.
- *Top priority*. Few pieces of information fall into the top-priority category— generally only those that would directly result in extremely serious damage to the company. Sometimes the collection (or viewing) of a set of data results in a top-priority rating because together they tell the "whole story."

DATA SECURITY

Data security is defined as a plan and the application of measures designed to protect information (data, files, programs) from unauthorized or accidental modification, destruction, and disclosure as well as to protect the continuing ability to process data. Data security includes, also, the ability to contain damage and recover from failure. As for other assets, the owner of the data, programs, and computing facilities is responsible for their security.

[6]Ibid.
[7]Ibid.
[8]U.S. Department of Defense, *Industrial Security Manual,* p. 3.

Internal Controls

Internal controls can be classified into three basic areas: those that prevent a cause of exposure from occurring, those that detect something that has already happened, and those that correct the effects upon detection. Preventive controls are established to guide the company's operations. Detective controls alert the organization to problems. Corrective controls are designed to aid in investigating and correcting the origination of exposure.[9]

Traditional classes of preventive controls

In the area of computer abuse, preventive controls are designed to limit access to the computer, data files, programs, and system knowledge.

Organizational Controls.   Much of the security risk may be minimized by using correct organizational controls. Steps that may be taken include separation of the data processing function from the users, separation of duties within the data processing function, and separation of duties among the users themselves; individual security responsibility should be assigned, and security staff may be used where appropriate.

Personnel Procedures.   Individuals with the greatest amount of control within the data processing operation also have the greatest potential to commit computer abuse. Generally, these key people are also the most likely to be above suspicion. Before hiring a responsible person, an investigation should be performed. A background check is inexpensive and may provide useful information. Current employee habits should also be reviewed. The personnel procedures include hiring procedures, vacation control, and job rotation. A very important procedure that has to be developed and maintained is the termination procedure. The termination procedures should provide a checklist for what to do when an employee departs the organization, such as canceling his or her account number, reclaiming his or her identification card, and so on.

Operational Controls.   Generally management's basic goal should be to minimize the vulnerability of the computer operation. By defining the actions a person is authorized to take, the organization limits its vulnerability. As a first step, consideration should be given to[10]

- Determining the individuals that wish to access or alter information
- Establishing the information that will be accessed or altered
- Defining the operations to be performed on the information

Each individual should be assigned a specific set of responsibilities to carry out a particular function. In the case of a security violation, this will aid in pinpointing the individual. Care should be taken to establish responsibilities for

---

[9]William C. Mair, Donald R. Wood, and Keagle W. Davis, *Computer Control and Audit* (Altamonte Springs, Fla.: The Institute of Internal Auditors, 1978), p. 36–37.

[10]Madinick, "Management Policies and Procedures," p. 62.

the work to be accomplished and the resources that are to be used. Provisions for adequate supervision are also essential for effective control.

Predetermined procedures should be established for all transactions. Infrequent transactions, irregular handling, and nonstandard treatment are frequently embezzlement. Compare output with input, use control totals, control error corrections, supervise recovery and restart, and control job input/output media.

Development Controls. Development controls, an absolute necessity, should at the least include continuously reviewing the programming, having more than one person make changes to the library, controlling access to the program library, logging all changes to program library, and comparing additions to the library with authorizations. It is useful to compare library and programs with earlier version.

Functional duties

In defining responsibilities, management should be acutely aware of the need for properly segregating duties. As a minimum, management should ensure that no one individual is exclusively responsible for the complete processing of any transaction. Such a policy may be difficult to implement in a small company where processing is centralized.

Incompatible duties and conflicts of interest should be avoided. An independence should be maintained between data processing and other departments that initiate or approve transactions. However, a dangerous situation arises if knowledge of computer operations is limited to the data processing department. Management outside the EDP function should have a basic knowledge of computer systems.[11]

Systems analysts, programmers, computer operators, and librarians should be independent from each other and also from input and output functions. Machine operators should not have access to programs. Programmers should be denied access to computers except for test purposes, at which time their action should be monitored. A library of computer files and programs should be developed and released only upon proper authorization and for normal processing. Personnel should also be required to rotate and to take mandatory vacations.

Data security design

During the system design, data processing decides the best approaches to converting the decisions that have been identified by the user into electronic media. When final detail design is completed, the system is approved by each area involved. To discourage attempts of computer abuse during the design phase, technical reviews and approvals should be made; management and users should review and approve; internal audit should participate; and the system should be tested upon completion of the design.[12]

---

[11]W. Donald Georgen, "Rating Internal Controls," *Financial Executive* (April 1975), p. 46.

[12]Mair, Wood, and Davis, *Computer Control and Audit*, p. 298.

Supervisors of system analysts and programmers should review the results of each phase before submitting them to management and users for approval. All system documentation should also be reviewed.

All phases, except for programming should be reviewed by management and/or the users. Management is responsible for the development of sound computer systems and the prevention of fraud and embezzlement.

Internal auditors should review each stage of development. Management may delegate responsibility for review to internal auditors. An internal auditor can best exercise his or her responsibility by reviewing programs while they are being designed and developed. A second choice is to establish adequate controls in completed programs. A third, but worse, choice is to audit a system that has been made operational.

Internal audit's most commonly performed design phase activities are composed of reviewing audit trails and control requirements. However, some audit departments concentrate on reviewing the control standards during the development process, such as establishing that the degree of documentation is in compliance with company practice. A large portion of internal audit's time might be spent during the design phase.

Normally, users should direct an overall test of the system after the final design to detect and correct errors before implementation. All discrepancies should be properly investigated and resolved.

ACCESS CONTROLS AND COMMUNICATIONS SECURITY

Physical security has by far received the greatest attention from management since costs are easily calculated and potential losses can be quantified. Preoccupation with physical security, however, ignores the expanding horizon of decentralized data processing. The following is a discussion of access control techniques for remote terminals, including communication security. To gain access to a computer system, a perpetrator must fulfill the following three requirements.[13]

1. Have access to a remote terminal connected to the system
2. Be able to obtain authorization to access the system
3. Utilize the proper communication sequence to obtain the desired system response.

Access control security measures seek to block the unauthorized user by (1) identifying the user, (2) identifying the terminal, and (3) identifying the level of authorization for that user.

[13]Charles F. Hemphill, Jr., and John M. Hemphill, *Security Procedures for Computer Systems* (Homewood, Ill.: Dow Jones-Irwin, 1973), p. 130.

User Identification

Identification of valid users is accomplished with a combination of software and/or hardware. Common methods include passwords, physical characteristics of individuals, and mechanical devices.[14]

Passwords

A password is used in an information exchange between the computer system and the remote terminals to identify users that log on. Once identified, proper access restrictions can be applied. There are several password forms:

1. Single password—a semipermanent code that can be used repeatedly.
2. Changeable or random password—an improvement over the single password. The computer generates random numbers that may be stored on cards or any magnetic media. At each log on, the user transmits the next random number, which is compared with the computer's list. After one use, the password is discarded.
3. Mathematical transformations—the user calculates the value (a pseudorandom number) of a known equation with variables supplied by the computer. For example, $X=5$ $Y=6$ WHAT IS YOUR ANSWER? If the equation is $2X + 3Y + 6$, then the password is 34.
4. Functional password—the password structure may be divided into levels. For example, the first level may specify the processing function, the second level may unlock a number of files or records within a file, and a third may define the user's security clearance.
5. Extended handshake—sometimes referred to as question and answer. The computer requests personal data such as mother's maiden name, place of birth, and so on.

Passwords are relatively inexpensive forms of access security. Effective use of passwords requires assignment of individual user codes, changing these codes frequently and randomly, inhibiting the printed display of these codes during log on, and making the password short enough to be memorized. Writing a password down is the most common cause for its accidental disclosure.

Several points of discipline should be exercised by the system. First, if a password identification sequence is initiated but not completed by the user within a given amount of time, the terminal should be automatically disconnected. Second, the entire password and account identification transaction should be completed before the information supplied by the user is verified. If the user supplies incorrect information, the system can respond with an INVALID INFORMATION message. Systems that respond with messages such as INVALID PASSWORD or INVALID ACCOUNT NUMBER provide the prospective intruder with information about the log sequence.

---

[14]Ibid., pp. 130–138.

Remote terminal users should be given a limited number of tries (for example, two tries) to complete the log sequence correctly. After that number of unsuccessful tries, the terminal should be automatically disconnected and the attempts recorded to give insight into potential security problems.

Physical characteristics

Physical characteristics may also be used to identify terminal users. Several devices are currently available to identify fingerprints, voice prints, lip prints, retinal patterns, brainwave forms, and hand geometry.

These techniques are expensive and inconvenient to users and are subject to practical limitations. For example, a legitimate user with a sore throat and blood-shot eyes would have a tough time trying to gain access through these devices.

The most promising technique is hand geometry. Each person has a slightly different hand width, finger length, and skin translucency. By scanning the hand with a laser, these characteristics can be matched with stored images for positive identification.

Mechanical methods

Mechanical methods such as keys, punched badges, and magnetically or optically encoded cards have been used successfully in banks for many years. When users' identification is required frequently, these methods are fast, economical, and practical.

A problem with this technique, however, is the possibility of users losing keys or cards, which can then be used or reproduced by unauthorized individuals. It is difficult, but not impossible, to reproduce a magnetically encoded card. For this reason, cards and keys are usually used in conjunction with other identifiers, such as passwords, to provide added security.

Terminal Identification

Once the user has been identified, it is important for the specific terminal being used to be authorized to make access. This step is increasingly important with the growth in personal computers and communication networks. Without terminal identification, anyone, anywhere, can access the system by masquerading as a valid user.

Autointerrogation is one method used to identify a terminal automatically. Some terminals are now equipped to respond to computer-generated queries with a unique tamperproof identification code. This may also be done with a user-entered code, verified by programming the computer to "hang up" automatically on that terminal, and then reconnecting the line, ensuring that an intruder at an invalid location is not connected. A problem with this approach is inflexibility when a terminal stops working or the user desires to move to another location.

The terminal itself can also have interlocks that allow only certain types of files and/or information to be output at that location. This is similar to software locks where only users providing a password are allowed into certain files.

A simple and inexpensive way to verify terminal identification is to telephone the user at the terminal location during log on.

Authorization Level Identification

Once the user and terminal have been identified, authorization level and processing restrictions can be applied.

Security or authorization tables are widely used in multiprocessing, database systems. Their purpose is to prevent authorized users from seeking to subvert system controls for unauthorized system use. The password, account number, and terminal identification are used as keys to the table. The table can restrict users to certain programs and files and provide protection from reading, writing, copying, and deleting.

File acccess authorization is further enhanced with the use of lockwords. Lockwords are generally issued by the creator and owner of a file to authorized individuals much like passwords. By adding suffixes to the lockwords, limitations on reading and writing can be imposed by the owner.[15]

Other Considerations

A problem not addressed by these techniques is the use of an authorized but unattended terminal, particularly within a business organization. Individual curiosity leads to browsing, but it can be eliminated by automatic timed log off. After several minutes of I/O inactivity, the operating system automatically logs off an unattended terminal.

Several obvious, yet often ignored, procedural steps should be followed. First, users should not be allowed to supply or change their own passwords. The duty of security should be to maintain separate system operations. Second, discharged employees' passwords, lockwords, and/or mechanical identifiers should be immediately destroyed.

Finally, an audit log of all unsuccessful log-on attempts and authorized security overrides must be kept to detect any evidence of improper access.

DATA SECURITY: WHAT, WHY, AND HOW?

Threats to Data Security

Data information can be considered as assets or representations of assets to any business, just as personal property is to the individual. It is an instinct that assets of value should be protected against any harmful threats. To understand how to protect our data, we should first understand the threats to data security.There are two kind of threats to data security; accidental and intentional disclosures.

---

[15]Dennis Van Tassel, *Computer Security Management* (Englewood Cliffs, N.J.: Prentice-Hall, 1972), pp. 150–151.

Accidental disclosures

This refers to the unintentional disclosure, as opposed to an intentional one, and can be divided into three categories.[16]

Hardware Failures.   No machine can work continuously without breaking down. Murphy's law states that "if anything can go wrong, given enough time, it will." In computer systems, power failures can occur, components can go bad, or the system simply cannot perform the way we expect it to. As a result, the machine can drop bits, add digits incorrectly, mistakenly overwrite data, or present us with other unexpected errors. Thus data may be lost, exposed, or altered. Security measures are needed to assure that data quality is above a required standard, to recover data when lost or altered, and to make sure that data will not be exposed to unauthorized persons because of such failures.

Software Failures.   Just as the hardware can fail, by the same token software can fail too. In the case of software failures, they are usually caused by bugs existing in the programs unnoticed until something goes wrong. A bug may cause the data to be easily retrieved by unauthorized persons, jam the system, or lose or alter data in an unexpected manner. On complex systems, programs usually contain traces of rarely occurring errors. As the programs become more complex, the chance of having such errors increases dramatically.

Human Errors.   No human is perfect. Everyone can and will make mistakes. In any kind of data handling, people will make mistakes while performing documentation or communicating or transacting data. This will cause data alteration, exposure of data to unauthorized persons, or simply loss of data. Usually there are more operators in an on-line system than in a batch system, thus increasing the chance of error making in transacting data in an on-line system. Yet errors can be detected more quickly in an on-line environment since the system acquires its data closer to its source.

Deliberate infiltration

This refers to the intentional disclosure, destruction, or alteration of data to benefit certain persons or organizations at the expense of others.[17] Sometimes this is also refered to as computer crime. In this discussion, we emphasize this issue. The objectives of deliberate infiltration are fourfold:

Gaining Access to Information in Files.   Sometimes, the information may be of value; sometimes it may not. A user may access the information just "for the heck of it" or because he or she is driven by curiosity as to the contents in the files.

Discovering the Information Interests of Users.   This is a major objective of deliberate infiltration. The information may be valuable to the user, who, by stealing such information, will benefit.

---

[16]Mair, Wood, and Davis, *Computer Control and Audit,* pp. 347–352.
[17]Ibid., pp. 412–420.

Altering or Destroying Files.   In this case, the information contained in the files is usually unfavorable to the users. By destroying the files or altering them, it will benefit the user.

Obtaining Free Use of System Resources.   By accessing the system, an unauthorized user can use the system free. In this case, no files are stolen or altered. The user simply uses the resources of the system at the expense of the company.

There are many ways of accessing information deliberately. In general, such infiltration can be classified as active or passive.

Passive Infiltration.   This type includes such techniques as electromagnetic pickup, both from the CPU and input/output devices, wiretapping, and concealed transmitters. In all these cases, information is stolen but not altered. Sometimes, the "trash can search" is also practical. A user may search the trash can, hoping to get the printout of information that may slip into the trash can unnoticed.

Active Infiltration.   Active infiltration can be further divided into five types:

1. *Browsing.* Browsing involves the use of legitimate access to the system to obtain unauthorized information. This usually happens within an organization in which one user may legitimately access the system and obtain information on files belonging to other users.

2. *Masquerading.* Masquerading refers to the practice of obtaining proper identification through improper means and then accessing the system as a legitimate user. An unauthorized person may steal the identification or password of a legitimate user and thus, without being noticed, can have access to the system and obtain information.

3. *Trap doors.* An unauthorized user may successfully test the various combinations of system control variables. After repeatedly testing, using the trial-and-error method, the user may find the proper identifications and passwords neded to gain access to the system and become a legitimate user.

4. *Entry via active communication lines.* In some networks, it is possible to attach a special terminal to the active communication channel to gain access to the system. In most cases, this is done by professional people who have a good knowledge of the system.

5. *Physical means.* This involves the physical access to the system through a position with the data center. A person may be an employee of the company, yet unauthorized to enter the data center. By misuse of his or her position, this person may be able to enter the data center and gain information on files.

Countermeasures in Data Security

Purpose of countermeasures

The purpose of countermeasures is to protect the data files against all threats noted in the preceding discussion. Countermeasures should be designed to protect the data both against accidental disclosures and deliberate infiltrations.

Factors to be considered

When designing countermeasures against threats to data, there are four important factors to be considered.

Information Content.   This refers to the sensitivity of the data. Certain data will require no special data security, others may require "normal" need-to-know restrictions, while some highly sensitive information may require extensive precautions. Thus, different countermeasures will be needed on different occasions.

Environment.   This refers to the types of users and the methods they use to gain access to the system. Users may be classified into different types depending on their level of authorization. So the system may be utilized in different manners, such as on-line or off-line mode.

Communication.   This refers to the use of data communication facilities. With different types of facilities, different countermeasures will be required. This is especially true when the communication networks are transmitting and receiving data in a remote manner, over which active infiltration can be performed without being noticed.

System Facilities.   This refers to the services provided by the computer system, including such areas as remote programming support, total information system, and interactive problem solving. In certain facilities, infiltration is easy; in others, it may be difficult.

The Implementation of Countermeasures

In the implementation of countermeasures, all the factors discussed previously should be considered to protect against threats of both accidental disclosure and deliberate infiltration. It is practically impossible to design a security system that is perfectly protected, but it is possible to achieve a high level of security. The main objective of countermeasures is not to protect the data totally from infiltration but, rather, to make the costs of infiltration exceed the benefits of obtaining the information. On the other hand, it may not be worthwhile to have a highly secure system, when the cost of obtaining it exceeds the benefits of utilizing it. Moreover, the countermeasure has to be updated to cope with the continuous changes in programs, data, and hardware.

There are six commonly used countermeasures:

1. *Access control.* Identification is required from the users to access the resources or obtain data. Methods that are in use include passwords, keys, badges.
2. *Processing limitations.* Restrictions should be installed to protect jobs from poking into each other's programs and data while they are being processed.
3. *Auditing and threat monitoring.* To have the ability to discover attempts to access or problems with the security system, it is necessary to audit and monitor the system continuously.

4. *Privacy transformation.* This involves establishing a set of techniques by which the information is coded so that its contents are concealed. This countermeasure practice is used mainly in distributed systems where information, data, and programs are moved by using communication lines.

5. Integrity management. This refers to the total integrity of the equipment, programs, physical security, people, and the operating process. All important documents, data, and files have to be protected in a secure place, such as a vault. All activities in the computerized system should be logged, so they may be analyzed later.

6. *Level of authorization.* A specific user may access only his or her own data and programs.

PHYSICAL SECURITY

Physical security involves the protection of computer equipment, programs, and files from destruction, tampering, fire, flood, windstorm, earthquakes, snow, lightning, building collapse, explosion, theft, vandalism, sabotage, war, and utility outages, including breakdowns in air conditioning and communication. Locks, guards, badges, and controlled access are employed in the physical security program. At a minimum, management should consider the foregoing occurrences and make an informed decision about protection. A risk analysis should be performed where critical areas are identified and the probabilities and costs associated with the potential occurrences are considered.

Protective Measures

The following strategy applies to various physical risks, such as fire, trespassing by outsiders, flood and water leakage, and so on, and is designed to minimize exposure, enable prompt detection, stop penetration and limit damage, recover, plan a vital records program, and develop computer room procedures..

A first level of security is provided by limiting access to the data processing facility. This can usually be accomplished by manual recognition or an ID card check. Consideration should also be given to inspecting personnel entering and leaving the facility for cameras, recording devices, transmitters, receivers, and documents.[18]

More elaborate systems can be devised for establishing a person's identity before allowing access to the data processing facility. A person might be required to know a password, or a combination of facts about his or her personal background. Entrance could require a machine-readable badge or keys to the facility. Finally, an individual's fingerprints, hand geometry, voice, or signature could be used as a basis for access.[19]

[18]Hal B. Becker, "Securing Distributed Systems: Gaining by 'Losing Control,'" *Data Management,* Vol. 16 (March 1978), p. 25.

[19]Shankar, "The Total Computer Security Problem," p. 55.

Generally, a low level of exposure for the facility should be desired. The computer facility's location does not have to be listed in company telephone directories or building lobbies. External signs should be discouraged. Additionally, the number of access entrances should be limited.[20]

Planning a Vital Records Program

It is the organization's responsibility to protect its assets, which include all debts, programs, and files. The vital records program has two objectives: protection and reconstruction. The second objective is to make sure that the organization will have the ability to continue the data processing operations. The first step is to decide what is vital and then determine the means by which the vital records will be protected. This can be done by storing vital data files and programs in vaults as well as storing duplicates of records in another location.

Computer Room Procedures

The computer room procedures should include at least the following basic elements: access to the computer center, personnel requirements, location of the control area, submitting and processing jobs, dispatching, operations, magnetic media library, and emergency procedures.

Choice of the EDP site

If the luxury of choosing an independent site for the EDP process is available, the following factors should be considered. To begin, if an appropriate environment is chosen, much expense and risk can be minimized. An independent building or a room constructed with the EDP function in mind would be best. It should be located away from high traffic so it can maintain a low visibility. Trouble spots and obvious environmental hazards should be avoided (e.g., geological fault lines, airports, fire and flood areas). Outer walls should be avoided as should common walls that are accessible to the public. Peripheral facilities should therefore be controlled; there should be no generators, boiler rooms, safes, water mains, or restrooms immediately adjacent to the computer center. It is suggested that surrounding the center on all sides by data processing controlled activities. A ground floor location should be avoided. Underground utilities are best as roof access is limited. Shrubbery should be limited so intruders cannot be concealed. If night shifts are necessary, a "nice" neighborhood would be welcomed by employees. Surrounding industrial activity should be considered with respect to its effect on the facility.

The immediate enclosure of the center should be constructed of fire-resistant materials. The walls should be true walls so that there is no ceiling crawl space that would allow entry. The common walls should have high fire rating. The floor above the center should be watertight. Doors should remain closed, and vaults should be self-closing. Ventilation ducts should have dampers and heavy

---

[20]Mair, Wood, and Davis, *Computer Control and Audit*, p. 344.

steel grills. Windows, if they exist, should be bricked up or wire mesh should be used. All apertures should be considered, including mail slots. Trash chutes and dumbwaiters should have fusable metal links and restrictive oneway valves. The facility should have its own independent air-conditioning system; this will minimize the spread of fire from external sources. Temperature and humidity should be kept within the allowable range. Air-conditioning also filters out potentially debilitating air contaminants. It is recommended that the temperature and humidity be monitored and charted. Utilities should also be secured, especially power and communications.

Handling and storage of magnetic media

Simple rules, if followed, will help to maintain the storage media's viability. Disks packs should always be encased if not on disk drives. Disks should be stored and mounted appropriately while drives should be kept closed. Smoking should be prohibited near open disk drives or packs.

Tapes should be handled by the hubs, thereby avoiding crimped edges. They must be handled carefully, as damaged tapes will cause signal dropouts. All dropped tapes should be examined. Body salts and oils contaminate tapes. As with disks, drive doors should be kept closed, and heads should be cleaned regularly.

The library itself should be checked and cleaned periodically. Access is to be restricted, and when unattended, the library should be locked. Temperature and humidity levels should be similar to those in the computer center. A thorough inventory must be kept and certified periodically. Old storage media should be purged before it is disposed of. Since sensitive information needs to be secured, all waste should be shredded.

Four basic categories of storage are available: safes, vaults, record storage, and closed areas.[21] All should be fitted with alarms. Safes should be certified for fire, explosion and fire, and impact. Vaults must be built-in or nonremovable and completely fire sensitive. No work is to be done inside. The vault doors are the most critical feature and should be rated equivalently with the walls. Record storage rooms are larger and less secure than vaults. Sprinklers are usually a mandatory feature. Closed areas are simply those that are kept locked, such as the computer room. All important records should be kept outside the computer room. Files that reconstruct records along with duplicates should be stored off the premises.

Unauthorized physical access

As noted before, our desire is to minimize the probability and damage that could occur, along with planning for an effective recovery. Therefore, every door should have a lock; open areas should be fenced in, and dark areas should be lit.

---

[21]James Martin, *Security, Accuracy, and Privacy in Computer Systems* (Englewood Cliffs, N.J.: Prentice-Hall, 1973), p. 281.

Lights have been found to be very effective, inexpensive deterrents. Other measures besides lights and locks include door and window barriers, guards, and intrusion detection devices. Guards must be well trained and monitored. A single entrance to a closed shop with a receptionist/guard on duty is the rule. Visitors must be logged in, issued a badge, and be given an escort. This all follows from the goal of low visibility. Outputs should be kept within the center, with the appropriate authorization procedures fulfilled prior to release.

Locks are a fairly inexpensive protection. If keys are used, they need to be guaranteed nonduplicative. They should also be issued strictly on the basis of need and be appropriately safeguarded. Combination locks, magnetic badges, and voice or handprints authorizations are more rigorous and more expensive. There should be three perimeter barriers: the first is a wall or fence; the second is interior walls, windows, and doors; the third is locked cabinets and vaults that should have alarms for deterrent and warning purposes. Other factors to be considered include manholes, doorframes, common walls, the roof and ventilation ducts.

A variety of intrusion detectors is available.[22] If possible, battery operation is preferable.[23] An electric circuit could be broken by opening a door. Current-carrying tape or wire is recommended over microswitches, since the latter are more easily defeated by a thief. Alternatively, a circuit could be created by a microswitch in the floor or switching on of the lights or computer. A light or a laser beam could be broken. Modulated light is suggested so that a flashlight cannot be used to defeat it. Mirrors as well as the monochromatic light of a laser could be used to extend the area of coverage. Ultraviolet or infrared light cannot be detected visually. Sound or vibration monitors and alarms have the disadvantage of incurring false alarms. Ultrasonic and radar waves can detect movement whereas variation in an electronic field will detect a presence. Magnetic detectors have the potential to erase data and are usually bypassed. Theft detectors, as found in retail stores, could be affixed to tape or disk labels. Closed-circuit T.V. could be monitored and controlled from a remote location. Time-lapse cameras can snap one frame every preset interval of time.

After a detection device is triggered, an alarm of some sort should go off. The alarm could be located locally and/or remotely at a guard or police station. In addition, doors could be locked to implement a trap. One must consider, however, the possibility of accidental entrapment of an innocent party when no one is present to release them.

Often all the detection devices are linked to a central station system console. This console could even alert the guard as to the location of the intrusion. It is, thus, an efficient implementation of personnel. Detectors can be connected over private or public (telephone) cable. Reliability of the system is paramount and should be checked regularly.

---

[22]Ibid., pp. 259–299.

[23]American Federation of Information Processing Societies, *System Review Manual on Security* (Montvale, N.J.: AFIPS, 1974), p. 26.

The potential for damage from within should not be overlooked. The backup storage location should be kept secret. Fired employees should either be restricted or immediately escorted to the door. Finally, the local police and fire departments should have ready access and familarity with the EDP center so that they can respond efficiently to an alarm.

Fire

Fire is the most feared disaster that can beset an EDP installation. It is often the secondary result of other natural catastrophes such as earthquakes and hurricanes. A fire usually starts via electrical shorts in hidden locations, aided by a good supply of oxygen, assured by the air-conditioning system. To help minimize the potential damage by fire, it is appropriate to decrease the hardware density within the center. If there are two computers, separate them rather than install them side by side. The same goes for input/output devices, disk drives, and so on. As previously mentioned, critical records and documentation should be stored in vaults. Proper housekeeping is also an excellent preventive tool. Flammables, such as paper, with low flashpoints should be stored outside the computer room. Paper should be removed frequently and the space below the raised floors should be cleaned out regularly. Screens positioned above the cables would also help. If possible, a no smoking rule should be put into effect. All furniture should be of noncombustible construction.

There are two major types of fire detectors: heat and smoke. Heat detectors can be set off by rate-of-rise or level of temperature. Water sprinklers have temperature-level heat detectors called fusable links. Since electric fires are localized, this detection system is generally triggered too late. Smoke detectors are therefore the more prevalent type used. To position them, air flow patterns should be studied, but basically detectors should be placed on ceilings, in ducts, in vaults, and under raised flooring. One minor disadvantage of smoke detectors is that they are more prone to false alarms, which, when used along with automatic extinguishers, could create problems. Besides setting off automatic extinguishers and alarms, there should be a built-in delay to permit stopping the extinguishers if appropriate. The detector should alert the computer operator and designate which detector went off. The delay should allow for the power and air conditioning to be turned off before the extinguishers are released.

There are three types of automatic extinguishers: sprinkler, carbon dioxide, and Halon. Sprinklers are the most common and are sometimes required by insurance companies. Their drawbacks include the inherent water damage and their ineffectiveness with electrical fires. It is an inexpensive method and it does cool the fire, so that flashbacks are prevented, but water will not effectively penetrate the equipment and the steam that is often created will ruin magnetic media. Carbon dioxide extinguishers are usually activated by a thermostat and will suffocate the fire and also the people. Appropriate training of personnel is obviously important. Safeguards include the close proximity of exits, delayed release of the gas, oxygen availability, and initiation of a buddy system. This is considered the best method when the facilities are unattended. Halon, which is a form of freon, is safe for humans if kept under low concentrations for short periods of time. But once the fire becomes intense, the gas starts decomposing into a toxic substance. For this reason, fast flooding of the area is suggested so that the fire does not have a chance to build. A major disadvantage of Halon is its expense. One should note that both Halon and carbon dioxide are colorless and odorless.

Hand extinguishers should be clearly marked and on an open path. They should have nozzles or hoses so that they may be used under the raised floor. They should also be tested regularly. Pull-type master switches should be clearly marked and unobstructed at all main doors. Personnel should be trained in an orderly powerdown procedure so that storage loss is kept to a minimum. An emergency system should also be available. Water- and fireproof equipment covers, along with at least one floor panel filter, should be easily accessible. Fire doors should only be opened from the inside and should trigger an alarm. Personal safety is extremely important, so a first aid kit along with the appropriate training in emergency procedures should be mandatory. Finally, expert advice can usually be obtained free from your insurance company.

Floods

This phenomenon can be minimized best during site selection. Areas near lakes, rivers, coasts, and mountain bases should be avoided. Roofs and pipes should be maintained and water pressure monitored. If the center is above ground, it should be water tight; if below ground, there should be adequate sump pumps and drains. There should be drainage under the raised floor. The cable should be water resistant.

Earthquake

Again, appropriate site selection is the best protection. The building's structure itself must be considered. Sway bracing and flexible joints within should maintain the equipment's upright nature. Fuel transmission and storage along with an on-site water supply are also considerations.

Windstorm

The meteorological history of the locale should be checked for tornadoes, hurricanes, and high winds with the appropriate precautions taken. Windows, trees, utility poles, and so on, should be avoided.

Wiretapping

Passive, active, and piggyback entries are used in hooking into the communication system. Analog scramblers, digital cryptography, and teleprocessing control procedures are the current methods of protection. A public line tap requires phone company cable access or expensive microwave interception. A premises tap at the connection box is much easier. Simply locking these junction boxes may be sufficient.

Maintenance procedures

During the maintenance and unplanned downtime, care should be taken that no real data and files are active. It is also important to monitor the technicians' activities and all repairs that they make.

Regulation of system access

Identification and Authentication.   The identification and authentication function identifies users and resources and then verifies the identifying data.

Authority.   It is not enough for users to identify themselves; users should also be checked for the acceptable level of authorization. The authorization function should contain data that associates users, resources, and rules of access.

Delegation.   This function is responsible for establishing and maintaining the set of rules for access and authorization.

Logging.   To measure the system's effectiveness, all attempted and successful accesses should be recorded, including all identification data, such as user and terminal IDs. This log should then be analyzed periodically, culminating in an exceptions report showing all activities, including improper attempts.

Monitoring (Surveillance).   A good data security system should be capable of monitoring the system and maintaining records of all accesses to various resources of the data processing operation, such as terminals, files, and so on. As a result of this exception, reports will be generated. These reports provide an audit capability and make it possible to trace an intrusion after it has taken place.

CONTROLLING AND AUDITING THE SECURITY SYSTEM

Controls and audits include the separation of duties (incompatible duties), personal accountability, controls on development, controls on computer center operations, system controls on applications, verification of status, and assessment of adequacy and use of controls by review and audit. The security system should provide tools to enable security management to detect attempted violations.

Contingency Plans

In the event that remedial action is necessary, management needs to develop contingency plans with backup and recovery capabilities. Fidelity insurance may be used to recover losses.[24] A contingency plan should be sufficiently detailed to limit the amount of decision making in the event of an abusive act. Each phase of

[24]Mair, Wood, and Davis, *Computer Control and Audit,* p. 415.

the contingency plan should be periodically tested. The basic elements of the plan should include emergency plans, backup plans, and recovery plans.

Emergency plans

Emergency plans are developed to handle problems that occur during and right after the disaster. They should include alarms for saving people and property and safeguarding survival of the organizational unit. Considerations in preparing this plan are establishing contact, assigning secondary locations (assembly locations), and determining the need for medication, transportation, water, and food. The elements of this plan should be published and displayed so that all employees are familiar with the procedure. This plan should be comprehensive and exist in all departments and at each level of management. The emergency plan should have the ability to handle natural threats, such as fire, wind, rain, rising water, and earthquake, as well as human threats, such as riots and bomb threats.

Backup plans

The purpose of this plan is to handle the continuation of the data processing function after the disaster. It is usually effective for one to three days. This plan requires a mutual contract for backup purposes with a similar installation. Since there are going to be some constraints on the work load, predefined work priorities should be established. The requirements for performance include work sites, personnel, programs, files, data (protected in secure storage), forms, communications, and transport. Personnel assignments are an important part of the backup plan as is making sure that these assignments do not interfere with the recovery plan. This plan should be tested periodically.

Recovery plans

The purpose of this plan is to establish the capability of recovery of the data processing mission. It is usually effective for one to three months. The plan should cover the location, personnel, equipment, and forms. In preparing this plan, the organization should identify an alternate site for the data processing activity, and identify the source of replacement equipment and the replacement of communication facilities. The recovery plan should also provide for availability of data, supplies, and the recovery plan itself.

In designing and developing contingency plans, the following elements should be considered:

Planning Team. Members of the data processing department, personnel department, and users should be included. Users should normally establish priorities for jobs to be run.

Data. Applications and jobs should be classified. Priorities as to which jobs are to be run first should be established.

Personnel. Clear instructions should be given to keep the company functioning. An emergency organization chart should outline responsibilities. A roster of telephone numbers for the planning team, company officers, equipment vendors, and so on, should be maintained.

Hardware. Equipment needed to support high-priority applications should be listed.

Supplies. Special forms and supplies should be stored off premises.

Data Distribution. An alternative to distributed data processing should be established if telecommunication equipment is not available.

Facilities. Equipment and procedures needed to establish a new data center should be outlined.

Backup and Recovery Plans

To ensure that the contingency plan can be carried out, backup and recovery capabilities need to be established. At least three generations of records should be maintained with at least one generation kept off site. Normally, the grandfather file and input details for the last two generations are stored off premises as backup.

In some critical on-line systems, built-in equipment and file duplication should be used. There are cases when duplicate and even triplicate systems are necessary to ensure against a major loss of revenue or confidence (e.g., airline reservation systems).

Contracts for the use of backup facilities at other locations should be obtained. If remote storage is used, a supplemental computer should be installed at the same location.

The company should also ensure that software stored at the backup facility corresponds with stored data files. When it becomes necessary to use older data files, the associated software and equipment should also be available.[25]

Insurance

Insurance is obtained to provide for loss of money due to the destruction or theft of assets. Generally, coverage should be obtained in situations where risks cannot be substantially eliminated or absorbed. Risks that are normally covered in a data processing facility include

- Computer equipment damage
- Storage media damage
- Recovery costs for data stored on the media
- Business loss due to interruption
- Damage to outsiders

[25]Ibid., p. 351.

Potential dollar losses of each exposure should be established and an insurance agent informed. In some instances, the extent of the risk cannot be established and thus the exposure is not insurable. All forms of data processing insurance are negotiated, with a charge for each instrument established. Insurance companies should be informed of any equipment changes. Most policies cover only those items and perils specifically stated in the contract. However, "blanket policies" are available. In this instance, all perils are covered unless specifically excluded.

Initiation of the Security Program

The following are the major steps needed to be taken to establish the security program:

1. Get management approval for a data security program.
2. Establish and train the data security organization.
3. Provide an orientation for all personnel affected.
4. Carry out priority actions, such as the following:
   a. Identify vital records/programs and keep updated backup in secure storage.
   b. Identify and protect sensitive records/programs (records that could be used to victimize).
   c. Establish a system of classified (confidential) records/programs and provide protection by level of confidentiality.
   d. Provide insurance coverage, bonding, and emergency instructions.
   e. Arrange for alternative data processing capability.
   f. Inspect facilities and establish required rudimentary physical and procedural controls.
   g. Limit access to the data processing installation and other sensitive areas.
   h. Separate conflicting duties.
   i. Insist on good housekeeping practices.
   j. Train personnel (in evacuation procedures, firefighting, first aid, etc.).
   k. Assure that no long-term decisions are made that will weaken security in the future.
5. Plan the design and implementation of the security systems.
6. Keep management informed and involved.

General Security Rules

1. If no one is responsible, it does not get done.
2. Security personnel should have a security outlook, and be able to observe, recognize unusual events, be sensitive to risks, and perform well under stress.

3. Security is a series of trade-offs. The intangible costs of inadequate security are reduced efficiency, inconvenience, and lowered productivity.

4. Security depends mainly on people; if employees do not cooperate, the security system will not work. Employees will defend a good place to work. A person who was not hired never needs to be fired.

5. Reliance on automatic processes, without any human control, is risky.

6. Security usually has gaps and weaknesses when operating under emergency conditions. Consider safeguarding of confidential records during equipment failure and security procedures during bomb threat evacuation.

7. Criminal acts involving computer data and facilities are mainly committed by insiders.

8. Most so-called "computer crimes" do not involve technology but use methods that have been known for centuries; sometimes the ignorance of the computer is used as a weapon by the criminal.

9. The direct results of a disaster are frequently not as debilitating as the secondary effects.

SELECTED READINGS

AMERICAN FEDERATION OF INFORMATION PROCESSING SOCIETIES. *System Review Manual on Security*. Montvale, N.J.: AFIPS, 1975.

BEQUAI, AUGUST. *Computer Crime*. Lexington, Mass.: D. C. Heath, 1978.

ENGER, NORMAN L., AND PAUL W. HOWERTON. *Computer Security: A Management Approach*. New York: AMACOM, 1980.

HEMPHILL, CHARLES F., JR. *Security Safeguards for the Computer*. New York: AMACOM, 1979.

HOFFMAN, LANCE J. *Modern Methods for Computer Security and Privacy*. Englewood Cliffs, N.J.: Prentice-Hall, 1977.

HONEYWELL, INC. *AFIPS System Review Manual on Security*. Montvale, N.J.: American Federation of Information Processing Societies, 1974.

MAIR, WILLIAM C., DONALD R. WOOD, AND KEAGLE W. DAVIS. *Computer Control and Audit*. Altamonte Springs, Fla.: The Institute of Internal Auditors, 1978.

MARTIN, JAMES. *Security, Accuracy, and Privacy in Computer Systems*. Englewood Cliffs, N.J.: Prentice-Hall, 1973.

VAN TASSEL, DENNIS. *Computer Security Management*. Englewood Cliffs, N.J.: Prentice-Hall, 1972.

WALKER, B. J., AND IAN F. BLAKE. *Computer Security and Protection Structures*. New York: Academic Press, 1977.

9

Costing of Computer Services

INTERNAL PRICING OF COMPUTER SERVICES

Introduction

The purpose of this chapter is to analyze various methods for determining internal pricing for computer services.[1] The methods considered are those that are in popular use or are recommended in the literature. This discussion deals with the pricing of computer services for internal users operating a computer. The issue of price determination for external users is not considered.

From the viewpoint of an organization, internal prices are a necessary tool for allocating scarce computer resources among internal users so that total benefits of these services for the organization as a whole will be maximized. It will be shown that it is difficult to apply classical microeconomic theory to internal pricing for computer services, since the computer industry is characterized by increasing returns to scale and by a factor of production whose value of marginal product is difficult to determine.

The first section discusses the implication of increasing returns to scale and their effects on the cost function of the industry and the demand function of users of computer services. The second section presents the "classical" theory for internal pricing and the conditions that a system of internal prices has to obtain to form a basis for optimal resource allocation in the short and in the long run. The third section analyzes three alternative pricing methods and the degree to which

[1]This discussion is taken with permission from I. Borovits and S. Neumann, "Internal Pricing of Computer Services," *The Computer Journal,* Vol. 21, no. 3 (1978), pp. 109–204.

they fulfill those conditions: (1) average cost pricing, (2) flexible pricing, and (3) incremental cost pricing.

Market Characteristics of Computer Services for the Individual Firm

The market of computer services at the individual firm's level can be analyzed, as can any market of goods and services, by a model based on supply and demand functions. The analysis actually relates to market of a factor of production, where, in the absence of intervention, an equilibrium price would be determined according to supply and demand curves. If prices of computer services are in practice determined by the firm's management, then this determination can be seen as an intervention in the operation of the market. In such a situation, the pricing policy of management can be evaluated in relation to the goal of achieving optimal allocation of the scarce factor of production. The purpose of this discussion then is to describe the specific conditions that characterize the market for computer services; these conditions will form the basis for a theory of price determination for computer services.

Supply characteristics

The supply function of computer services reflects the cost function of producing the service in a computer center environment. Most empirical findings indicate that there are increasing returns to scale in producing computer services that stem from the behavior of three main independent variables of the production function of computer services: hardware, software, and personnel.

Returns to Scale in Hardware. Studies verify[2] that the mainframe manufacturers set up prices that behave according to Grosch's law.[3] The law states that equipment performance is a quadratic function of its cost and thus reflects increasing returns to scale. For some computers (particularly small ones), returns to scale are expressed by a cubic function, so that doubling the cost of equipment will increase its performance by a factor of eight.

Returns to Scale in Software. Returns to scale in software result from the fact that software supplied for small computers, whose memory size is limited, is usually a subsystem of the software available for large computers. Therefore, users of large computers can benefit relatively more from the use of software systems containing compilers, advanced operating systems, and the like.

Returns to Scale in Personnel. Increasing returns to scale pertain also to the personnel employed in computer centers. Solomon,[4] for instance, found that average wages go down as computer size goes up, where the size is represented by

[2]B. Schwab, "The Economics of Sharing Computers," *Harvard Business Review,* Vol. 46, no. 5 (1968), pp. 61–70.

[3]The law is used here as a starting point for our discussion. This does not imply that the law is applicable to all computer centers at all times and for all measures of performance.

[4]N. E. Solomon, "Economics of Scale and Computer Personnel," *Datamation,* Vol. 16, no. 3 (1970), pp. 107–110.

monthly rental payments. Due to increasing returns to scale in utilizing hardware, as noted, average wages decrease as performance capacity of the computer increases. In spite of the decreasing average wage outlays versus increased performance, Solomon also found that wages per employee are higher in larger computer centers. As a result, better and more skilled personnel can be employed in such centers. Since a large center employs more personnel than do smaller ones, the former can also better utilize particular specialization of employees.

Characteristics of the cost function

If the variables affecting the production of computer services are subject to increasing returns to scale, the cost function derived from the production function will show that for any given production level, the rate of growth of cost is lower than the rate of growth of output. Such a schematic cost curve is exhibited in Figure 9.1. The total cost curve, *TC,* in Figure 9.1 is typical of the case of increasing returns to scale. Negatively sloping average cost, *AC,* and marginal cost, *MC,* curves are derived from it. These cost curves are characterized by marginal costs that generate lower than average costs for any given output level.

Demand characteristics

Demand of a Single User. The demand for computer services in an organization is a demand for the services of production factor. The demand function for a production factor is derived from the value of marginal product function, which is obtained by multiplying marginal physical product by marginal revenue. The identification of the demand function of a single user thus relies on the estimation of the marginal physical product and the marginal revenue that will be generated following execution of computer jobs. Since the product under consideration—information—is not usually sold as a final product but is used as an input in the production processes of organizations, the price of the product cannot be determined.

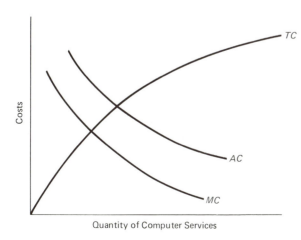

Figure 9.1 Cost Curve of Computer Services. *Source:* I. Borovits and S. Newmann, "Internal Pricing for Computer Services," *The Computer Journal,* Vol. 21, no. 3, 1978, pp. 109–204. Reprinted with permission from *The Computer Journal.*

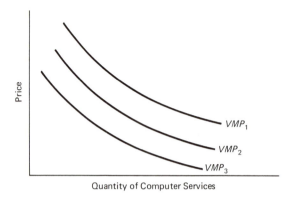

Figure 9.2 Demand Curves of Single Users. *Source:* I. Borovits and S. Newmann, "Internal Pricing for Computer Services," *The Computer Journal,* Vol. 21, no. 3, 1978, pp. 109–204. Reprinted with permission from *The Computer Journal.*

The current development of economic theory dealing with the pricing of information does not permit its application for determining the value of information at the level of organizations. The value of information is equal in principle to the expected value of profit that will be attained by the use of that information, but that expected value is incalculable in most practical situations.[5]

It is therefore evident that the demand function for computer services of a single user cannot be estimated empirically. An acceptable surrogate basis for estimation is the assumption that the value of information is subject to the phenomenon of decreasing marginal product. A negatively decreasing hypothetical demand curve can be derived based on this assumption.[6] A value of marginal product curve of this type, *VMP,* is exhibited in Figure 9.2. The curve may serve as the demand curve of a single user for computer services.

Aggregate Demand Curve. The aggregate demand curve for computer services is an aggregation of the demand curves of single users. The aggregation, however, involves further difficulties, since parameters assumed to be constant for a single user are subject to changes that take place during the process of aggregation. It is an acceptable assumption, for instance, that the value of information for a user is dependent and inversely related to the reaction time of the system.[7] The demand curve of the single user is defined for a given reaction time, which itself is a function of the demand for the system. Reaction time, assumed to be given, will thus vary during the aggregation of the individual demand curves.

Even if empirical data were available and demand curves of single users for a given level of service could be estimated, then for estimating the aggregate demand for computer services, one would have to portray a curve analogous to a demand curve for a factor of production that takes into consideration industrywide changes. But while industrywide effects usually cause a reaction in the price

---

[5]J. Marschak, "Remarks on the Economics of Information in Organizations," *Proceedings of the 4th Berkeley Symposium on Mathematics and Statistics,* Vol. 1 (1961); and R. A. Howard, "Information Value Theory," *IEEE on Systems Science and Cybernetics,* Vol. SSC-2, no. 1 (1966), pp. 22–26.

[6]J. J. Sobczak, "Pricing of Computer Usage," *Datamation,* Vol. 20, no. 2 (1974), pp. 61–64.

[7]Streeter, "Cost-Benefit Evaluation."

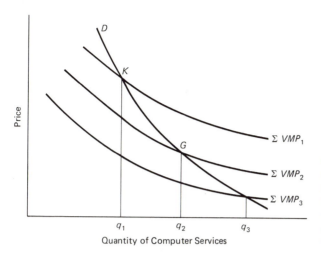

Quantity of Computer Services

Figure 9.3 Aggregate Demand Curve for Computer Services. *Source:* I. Borovits and S. Newmann, "Internal Pricing for Computer Services," *The Computer Journal,* Vol. 21, no. 3, 1978, pp. 109–204. Reprinted with permission from *The Computer Journal.*

of the finished product, in this case the effect is more complex, since the nature of the factor of production (i.e., computer services) changes during the process of aggregation.

The problem of aggregation is described in Figure 9.3. The single user is faced with different demand curves for any given reaction time of the system. The longer the reaction time, the lower the demand curve.[8] Curve MVP_1 assumes a reaction time t_1, which is shorter than t_2, the reaction time assumbed by VMP_2. The process of aggregation means therefore a horizontal summation of all individual demand curves for each reaction time i separately, $\Sigma\ VMP_i$. The aggregate demand curve, $D,$ is the collection of points lying on the $\Sigma\ VMP$ curves, where an increase in quantity of computer services induces a transfer to a lower demand curve.

When the computer center provides quantity q_1 of services, the reaction time is t_1, and K is the relevant $\Sigma\ VMP_1$ curve. Supplying quantity of services q_2 increases reaction time to t_2 and induces a shift to point G on curve $\Sigma\ VMP_2$. Curve D is the collection of points K, G, and others lying on different $\Sigma\ VMP$ curves. This is an aggregated demand curve for computer services taking industry-wide changes into consideration. Curve D is naturally sloping from left to right.

The Theory of Pricing Computer Services

Classical microeconomic theory establishes the conditions that pertain to an optimal internal pricing system for computer services. An optimal price system from the organization's point of view is the one that allocates the limited resources in a way that maximizes utility for the organization.[9] The specific conditions prevailing

[8]A user wil not pay, of course, for computer output whose reaction time is longer than a certain threshold that he or she defines as the deadline.

[9]For a complementary discussion of pricing dictated by internal policy decision, see J. Dearden and R. L. Nolan, "How to Control the Computer Resources," *Harvard Business Review,* Vol. 51, no. 6 (1973), pp. 66–78.

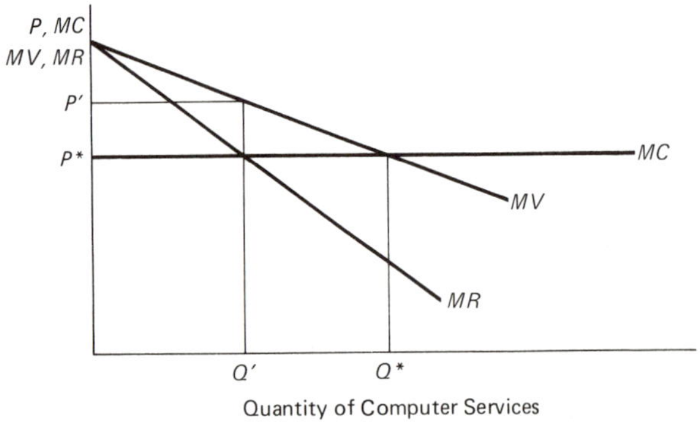

Figure 9.4 Price Determination of Computer Services. *Source:* I. Borovits and S. Newmann, "Internal Pricing for Computer Services," *The Computer Journal,* Vol. 21, no. 3, 1978, pp. 109–204. Reprinted with permission from *The Computer Journal.*

in the market for computer services, described in the preceding section, lead to difficulties in applying the tenets of the classical theory. After reviewing these difficulties, a list of requirements of an optimal price system is presented. The third section compares some pricing methods that are used in practice with the list of requirements.

The classical model of price determination

An attempt to apply the classical model of microeconomic theory to price determination of computer services is presented in Sharpe and in Sobczak.[10] The model is based on supply and demand functions where a key to internal pricing is the consideration of a computer center as a profit center. The computer center has a total cost curve, *TC,* and a marginal cost curve, *MC.* The users have a curve representing marginal value of computer services, *MV. MC* and *MV* are the relevant curves for the organization as a whole, comprising the various internal users and the computer center alike. Optimal price determination is described in Figure 9.4. From the organization's point of view, the optimal quantity of services and the internal price will be Q^* and P^*, respectively. It is evident that this is the optimal solution and that at any other quantity, total profit of the organization as a whole will be lower. Sharpe and Hirchleifer[11] express the concern that the selling department, in this case, the computer center, will try to utilize its monopolistic position and determine a price P' leading to a quantity demanded Q'. The computer center will then increase its profits, but the output P' is obviously not optimal for an organization as a whole. To overcome this temptation, both Sharpe and Hirschleifer suggest an exposure of the organization to external computer facilities and other mechanisms.

The conclusion is that the optimal price must be equal to the marginal cost of the selling department. The price will determine the optimal output of the

[10]Sharpe, *Economics of Computers;* and Sobczak, "Pricing of Computer Usage."

[11]Sharpe, *Economics of Computers;* and J. Hirschleifer, *Internal Pricing and Decentralization Decisions, in Management Controls: New Directions in Basic Research* (New York: McGraw-Hill, 1964).

computer center that must be allocated judiciously among the various users. An optimal allocation prevails if the value of the output for the organization cannot be increased by a different allocation. To achieve optimal allocation, price has to be identical for all users in the organization. Every user equates the marginal value of computer services with the price demanded from him or her. If a certain user faces a price higher than that for other users, the marginal value of services for him or her will be higher than it will be for the other users. In such a case a new allocation of computer services and the allocation of a larger quantity to the user paying the higher price will increase total output of computer services in the organization.

Limitations on the applicability of the model

Application of the model is limited because of the special supply and demand conditions characteristic of the services of a computer center.

It was established at the outset that the production of computer services is associated with increasing returns to scale. These returns are expressed by average costs, AC, that are sloping downward with increased production. The marginal cost curve, MC, will then lie below the average cost curve. For a given output, the price will be established at the intersection of the marginal value, MV, and the marginal cost curve, so that the computer center will not cover its total costs, as reflected in Figure 9.5. The price P_1 and the quantity q_1 are determined at the point where $MC = MV$, but at this price the computer center will sustain losses $(C_1 - P_1)Q_1$ and will not recover its costs.

This method of price determination is inefficient with regard to the use of fixed production factors. Computer services are one of the factors of production used by organizations. When prices of final products or services do not cover total costs of production, there are production factors that were consumed in the process of production whose total costs were not reflected in the price of the final products. Since the cost of using production factors reflects their value of marginal product, it follows that decreasing the use of computer services will increase the benefits that the organization can gain from limited resources. If users do not pay for the cost of providing their demand for computer services, then the value of such services is lower than their value in the alternative use. It is thus evident that the condition of covering the total costs of computer services by their users is necessary for economic efficiency and the price determination based on marginal costs does not fulfill this condition when the production function is characterized by increasing returns to scale.

Reliance on the classical model of price determination also involves difficulties due the characteristics of the demand for computer services. Nonhomogeneity among users, in addition to the quality of increasing returns to scale, may enhance monopsonistic behavior on the user's part. Consider, for example, an organization with two users, one of which has a higher demand for computer services relative to the other. The demand of the small user can be satisfied at a lower cost due to decreasing costs, yet the large user will be aware that his or her demand

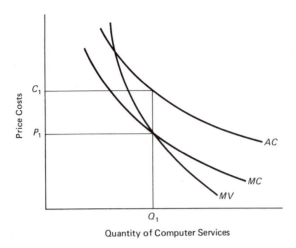

Figure 9.5 Price Determination Under Increasing Returns to Scale. *Source:* I. Borovits and S. Newmann, "Internal Pricing for Computer Services," *The Computer Journal,* Vol. 21, no. 3, 1978, pp. 109–204. Reprinted with permission from *The Computer Journal.*

affects the price paid for the services. The lack of homogeneity contradicts the conventional premise that market prices are given for a single user. The small user will equate his or her value of marginal product of computer services to the price he or she pays for them, while the larger user, who takes into account his or her influence on the price, will equate his or her value of marginal product to the marginal cost of employing computer services (marginal factor cost) which is lower than the price of the services.

Another limitation of the classical model pertains to the difficulty of estimating the demand schedules of single users. The process of internal pricing must therefore be accomplished by the authorized body in the organization that lacks adequate knowledge of the demand schedules. Moreover, it is conceivable that the single user in many cases does not know his or her value of marginal product of computer services. It is therefore possible that the users will not be sensitive to price changes and hence that the use of pricing mechanism for efficient allocation of computer resources is meaningless. A user who does not know the value of marginal product may, for any given price, consume more or less than the optimal quantity of computer services needed.

The conditions for an optimal allocation of computer service

The preceding discussion points to the following conditions as being necessary for an optimal allocation of computer services based on a system of internal prices:

1. The price of unit of service must equal its marginal cost of production; this is a condition for an optimal allocation in the short run.
2. The price of a unit of service must be equal for all users. If the price is not equal to the marginal cost of acquiring the unit (marginal factor cost), the marginal factor costs must be equal for all users. This is a condition for the optimal allocation of a given factor of production in the short run.

3. Total revenue of the computer center must cover its total costs; this is a condition for an optimal allocation of the organization's resources among the computer center and other factors of production.

4. Users should be able to determine the value of marginal product of computer services.

5. The formula for billing users for computer services rendered must be simple and understandable; this condition is required so that users can predetermine their costs and compare them with the benefits.

6. In a multiprogramming environment, the billing formula must bill jobs independently of the composition of jobs run in parallel; this condition follows the previous one.

Analysis of Conventional Methods of Pricing Computer Services

Three pricing methods that are recommended in the literature and are applied in practice were selected for analysis. Each method will be analyzed as to whether it fulfills the necessary conditions for an optimal allocation of computer services.

The average cost method[12]

The method is generally based on a cost allocation model that predetermines the cost per unit (in terms of time or performance) of every component (i.e., billing centers) of the computer configuration. Every job is billed according to the number of units of the components consumed, where the number of units is multiplied by the charge per unit. Typical billing centers are the CPU, memory, printers, card readers, keypunch machines, disks, and tapes. Total costs for the billing center are determined by calculating its direct costs and loading it with indirect costs according to a certain cost accounting formula. The costs per unit are obtained by dividing total costs by the number of units projected to be produced by the billing center.

Let

TC_i = total costs (per a given time period) of billing center i
DC_i = direct costs (per given time period) of i
IC_i = indirect costs (per a given time period) allocated to i
Q_i = projected production (per a given time period) of i
R_i = charge per unit produced by i
$q(ji)$ = number of units consumed by job j at billing center i
B_j = total charge for job j

Then

$$R_i = \frac{TC_i}{Q_i} = \frac{DC_i + IC_i}{Q_i}$$

[12]I. Borovits, "Pricing of Computer Services," *Data Processing Journal,* Vol. 16, no. 3 (1974), pp. 160–163.

and

$$B_j = \sum_i R_i \, q(i\,j)$$

The average cost method fulfills part of the conditions necessary for optimal allocation of computer services:

1. Total revenue of computer center may cover its total costs if actual production equals the projected production that was entered into the billing formula.
2. Price per unit of service will be equal for all users.
3. The billing formula is relatively simple and the users can calculate the cost of running the job (providing that the computer program and the input/output data are known to them).
4. If the billing centers are properly defined, the application of the billing formula secures identical billing to a job, independent of the time and the job mix of its execution.

On the other hand, the average cost method does not fulfill the condition that the price of a unit of service must equal the marginal cost of its production. In the short run, when the configuration is given and not fully utilized, the marginal cost may be very low. It is conceivable that jobs whose value of marginal product is higher than their marginal costs will not be submitted by users for execution. A disparity will then prevail between the organization and the users' points of view as to the economic justification for running computer jobs.

The flexible pricing method

A method of flexible internal pricing of computer services is suggested by Smidt.[13] Even when the production capacity is large relative to the demand, a priority system is necessary for resolving the scheduling problem. The average cost method, which uniformly bills all users at all times, precludes the use of a price mechanism for establishing priorities. A priority system is then by default established by an arbitrary administrative decision that does not guarantee optimal allocation. The flexible pricing method is aimed at using an internal pricing mechanism for an efficient allocation of computer services. Billing of users can then vary automatically, so that a high charge will be billed when the quantity demanded is high, relative to the production capacity, and a low charge will be billed when the quantity demanded is low, relative to the production capacity.

The simplest way to achieve this aim is to require the users to attach to every job submitted to the computer center information on the maximum price

[13]S. Smidt, "Flexible Pricing of Computer Services," *Management Science*, Vol. 14, no. 2 (1968).

per unit of service (e.g., 1 second of CPU) that they are ready to pay. This price will determine the priority level; the higher the price, the higher the priority level. The allocation of computer resources will be based on those prices.

Under such a method, the users face uncertainty as to the performance that they get, for the prices are unpredictable. To overcome the problem, Smidt proposes to complicate the method slightly by establishing two categories of users. The first category includes users who indicate the completion time demanded by them and are committed to pay the price to execute the job by the time specified. The second category includes the users who indicate the maximum price that they are ready to pay. Jobs of those users will be run when the price of service units determined by the computer center will not be higher than the users' maximum price.

Under such a scheme, computer time, for instance, will be sliced into small intervals. Jobs that require a completion time lower than the interval time will be run first. Next jobs to be run will be those that require completion time higher than the interval but that have to be stated, partially at least, to be completed within the specified completion time; a certain algorithm will have to allocate time to such jobs. If there is still time left in the interval, jobs with indicated maximum prices will be processed, starting with the highest price. The price per unit of time of the interval will be determined according to the maximum price quoted for the last job to run in that interval. To apply the method in practice, it is necessary to determine the length of the time interval, the time for which the price is fixed, the allocation algorithm, and the range for which users can indicate acceptable reaction time or prices.

The main advantage of the flexible pricing method over the average cost method pertains to its treatment of job queues at a given time in a way that increases total benefits to the organization from servicing jobs waiting in a queue. Another advantage is that the method forces users to consider the value of computer services for each job that they plan to submit, since they have to indicate the maximum price that they are ready to pay.

These advantages must be weighted against the following disadvantages:

1. The flexible pricing method does not guarantee recovery of total costs of the computer center. Prices are practically determined according to demand and are based on an assumption of a perfectly inelastic supply, so that fixed and variable costs are disregarded. The method is thus unable to secure recovery even of the variable costs of the computer center.

2. The condition of equality between prices and marginal costs is not necessarily obtained.

3. The billing formula does not enable users to preevaluate the costs versus the benefits of acquiring computer services. A user can secure price certainty, but then the user is not relieved of the uncertainty pertaining to the reaction time and hence to the value of the services; on the other hand, the user can secure certainty of reaction time but is still subject to price uncertainty.

Incremental cost method

A billing formula for computer services based on an incremental cost method is suggested by Nunamaker and Whintson,[14] following a more general application of the method in the area of pricing for public investments. (See Loehman and Whinston.)[15] The suggested method forms an integral part of the process of designing a computer center. There are four stages in implementing the process:

1. Each user specifies his or her requirements for computer services.
2. Users' requirements are converted to specific configurations.
3. Costs of the final configuration of the computer center are allocated to the users (according to a cost allocation formula presented hereafter).
4. Users evaluate the costs allocated to them against expected benefits and may consequently change their demands.

The process is of an iterative nature and results in a definition of an optimal configuration. Although the billing formula is used as a planning device, it may serve as a mechanism for internal pricing of computer services.

The incremental cost method attempts to resolve the difficulties that are inherent in a billing formula based on marginal costs in the short run. It was shown that the computer center cannot recover its total costs under such a pricing method, due to prevailing increasing returns to scale (i.e., decreasing average costs). Incremental cost pricing is therefore based on marginal costs in the long run.

The equation of determining the "marginal" user immediately arises when the computer is servicing several users. Numerous alternatives exist for arranging the users when demands are simultaneous and costs are joint. The billing formula that follows assigns an equal weight to each arrangement.

Let

N = set of user groups in the company ($N = 1, 2, \ldots, n$)
K^i = level of computing service requested by the ith user group
C^i = costs allocated for the requirement of users i
$C(N)$ = total cost of the system servicing N users

The n users can be arranged in $n!$ ways. The weight of the additional cost due to user i when his or her demand is ordered in the gth position is given by

$$\frac{(n - g)! \, (g - 1)!}{n!}$$

---

[14]J. F. Nunamaker and A. Whinston, "Design of a Corporate Computer System: From Problem Statement to Cost Allocation" (USA AD-724161 Army Research Office, Springfield, Va: National Technical Information Services, 1972).

[15]E. Loehman and A. Whinston, "A New Theory of Pricing and Decision Making for Public Investment," *The Bell Journal of Economics and Management Science*, Vol. 2, no. 2 (1966), pp. 606–625.

Further, let

G   = the subgroup of g members of N
C(G) = cost of operating a computing facility for the members of the group G

Then the billing formula wil be of the form

$$C = \sum_{G \in N} \frac{(n-g)!\,(g-1)!}{n!}\,[C(G) - C(G-i)]$$

The main advantage of the incremental cost method is that it guarantees that revenue of the computer center will cover its total costs. The method provides for optimal determination of the computer configuration in the long run. The method is well integrated in the planning process and verifies that the configuration and equipment that are optimal in the long run will indeed be acquired. The method thus is suitable for planning the establishment or expansion of a computer center.

The disadvantages of the method is that in the short run, when the size of the configuration is given, the allocation of computer resources among users may be nonoptimal.

More specifically, the incremental cost method may lead to

1. A price of a unit of computer services that does not equal short-run marginal costs
2. A price of a unit of computer services that is not equal for the users, since the price charged to a user is related to the quantity of computer services demanded by him or her.

Due to these limitations, it is possible that the allocation is nonoptimal and that a revised allocation of computer resources among various users will increase total benefits to the organization as a whole.

Conclusion

Various methods can be applied for determining prices of computer services for internal users. The organization owning the computer should use the pricing method as a mechanism for allocating scarce computer resources among its internal users in a way that will maximize total benefits to the organization.

Application of classical microeconomic theory for internal price determination of computer services is involved with difficulties emanating from the nature of the market. There are necessary conditions that must prevail for an internal pricing scheme to optimize the allocation of computer resources among the users. The internal pricing methods analyzed in this section do not meet the conditions. Their use may therefore lead to an allocation of resources that is not optimal for the organization as a whole.

THE ROLE OF PRICE

Price is defined by economists as the ratio between the amount of some good that must be given up to obtain a unit of some other good. In data processing terms, price is defined as the amount of some other resource that the user gives up in order to obtain data processing services. If the user does not give up anything in exchange for the computing services, he or she does not pay a price for this service. It is important to distinguish between cost and price: job price is the amount that a user pays for having the job processed; job cost is the amount that it costs the data processing department to process the job. Price and cost are usually defined in terms of money, which is used as the medium of exchange.

Should Users Be Charged?

In answering this question, we must first consider the objectives of the organization in which the data processing department operates. It is also important to note that the overhead incurred by the billing system itself may be relatively high. Charging for data processing services may be of two forms: charging for the utilization and services provided or charging off costs as an overhead expense. In practice, when the computer services are treated as an overhead item or free good, the incentive is to increase data processing service usage almost without limit.

Charging the user for the service usually regulates the user, and therefore, it is used as an allocation control device. Those that argue against using the charging mechanism as a control device claim that if the computer is not fully used, there is no need for control function, whereas on the other hand, if the demand for services exceeds the availability, charging serves no useful purpose since it does not guarantee availability for those users who are willing to pay. Unfortunately, application of other techniques to control the usage of the data processing services, such as rationing, usually fails.

When installing the charging system as a control device, to encourage proper use of the data processing resources, careful attention should be given to the points just mentioned. It is clear that some controls must be exercised on data processing service usage as it is an expensive and easily misused good.

COMPUTER INSTALLATION ACCOUNTING[16]

For the purpose of this discussion, a specific computer system is used. However, the concept and procedures are applicable to most computer systems. All data necessary for implementing the accounting system are available either by using an accounting package or a software monitor.

---

[16]H. M. Gladney, D. L. Johnson, and R. L. Stone, "Computer Installation Accounting," *IBM System Journal*, no. 4 (1975), pp. 314–338. Reprinted by permission from *IBM Systems Journal*. © 1975, by International Business Machines Corporation.

Much has been written on accounting for computer installations, and much remains to be written. Unsettled questions include

- What must be done to ensure that computational resources contribute to the strategic objectives of the organization?
- What are the economic effects of different pricing policies on the effectiveness, efficiency, and growth of an installation?
- What must be done to comply with government guidelines for procuring computation as part of research and development contracts?
- How can those guidelines be reconciled with internal objectives?
- Is pricing effective in the allocation of computer resources?
- To what extent are complicated accounting methods acceptable to users, and how much do they encourage desirable behavior?
- To what extent is price reproducibility necessary and feasible?

In addition, complex technical problems are involved in measuring the resources delivered in multiprogramming and multiprocessing installations. Few installations can afford to wait for such issues to be resolved, particularly since, for many of them, resolution in the sense of a definitive policy is not to be expected.

Fortunately, it is possible to define an accounting mechanism that does not implicitly assume specific policies but is helpful in focusing attention on policy questions that must be addressed. This can be done in a way that does not require individuals or groups responsible for setting policy to understand the more arcane details of measurement and charging and that gives the individual user enough information to make reasonable decisions in structuring his or her application to be economical.

Commonly, each computer installation has its own locally developed accounting program, primarily because computer manufacturers do not supply such software. Also, local development sometimes is rationalized by arguments that each installation has its own peculiar financial policies, equipment, and user requirements. We argue that there is a generalized approach by which an accounting system can be designed to satisfy the requirements of most, if not all, medium, to large-scale installations. It must be designed "top-down" to support cost center, profit center, or line funded installations and be independent of the choice between fixed and dynamically adjusted prices. The installation's policy options can be implemented either with parameter changes or with self-contained procedures that make use of specific rate formulas. For illustration, we will use a program developed jointly by two installations between 1969 and 1972 and used for about three years in various versions in a very large installation (the System/360 Model 195 at the IBM Research Division laboratory in San Jose, California).

Occasionally, the need for detailed accounting analysis has been questioned as an unnecessary administrative task. It is our belief that resource allocations will be made, if not by conscious and informed decision, then by default. Even if the final decision is to implement a simplified scheme for measurement, accounting, and allocation, analysis of the type we illustrate should be made to get an insight into how the accounting and allocation policies will affect the installation.

Once a commitment is made to collect utilization data in a computing facility, the marginal cost of running a more elaborate system to analyze the data can be small, provided that the accounting data base is suitably structured. We believe that the cost is well worth the investment, especially if a generalized package can be acquired and customized for the particular installation.

In subsequent sections of the presentation, we refer to previous contributions that address parts of the subject in more detail than we can include; we summarize objectives and problems encountered in designing an accounting program; we give an example of an algorithm for distributing costs as prices for service; we describe a method of estimating the costs of resource pools; and we describe a program that we implemented, with emphasis on minimizing the clerical effort required and ensuring optimal auditability and with comments on how it might be done better in the future.

Background

There are several complementary views of the role of pricing in a computer installation. Nielson[17] discusses it as a mechanism for decentralizing resource allocation decisions so that such decisions are made in the most appropriate parts of the organization. Extreme decentralization is common in universities, where users' objectives are heterogeneous and the major purpose of the administration is to provide an environment for independent thought and study. Accordingly, Nielson focuses on access by the individual and on establishing priorities for charging. He discussed flexible pricing in an earlier article.[18]

McFarlane et al.[19] discuss pricing as a tool with which management can translate strategic objectives into action and then examine mechanisms for control. Questions facing top corporate management are "What resource commitment should be made to computing?" "How should the resource be deployed for maximum effectiveness?" and "Are the resources being used efficiently?" The authors indicate that the accounting control system should have formal mechanisms for providing relevant information to responsible managers and that the mechanisms must include schemes for monitoring the use of computer resources and for communicating this information to decision makers and motivating them to take action. According to McFarlane et al., the accounting control system should help bring to management's attention such aspects of computer service as the high ratio of fixed to variable costs, the large economies of scale in hardware and software, the large increments in which capacity is required, the fact that

[17]N. R. Nielsen, "The Allocation of Computer Resources—Is Pricing, the Answer?" *Communications of the ACM,* Vol. 13 (1970), pp. 467–474.

[18]N. R. Nielsen, "Flexible Pricing: An Approach to the Allocation of Computer Resources," *AFIPS Conference Proceedings,* Vol. 33 (1968), pp. 521–531.

[19]F. W. McFarlane, R. L. Nolan, and D. P. Norton, *Information Systems Administration* (New York: Holt, Rinehart and Winston, 1973), Chap. 11.

demand growth can be very large, and the fact that peak and slack load cycles and flexible priorities are intrinsic.

Sharpe[20] takes an economic viewpoint in which he assumes a perfect market. He focuses on overall pricing strategies for the services provided by an installation, as compared with the distribution of prices to specific service categories. In this model, each part of a parent organization strives to maximize the total value (or benefit) it receives. Sharpe discusses the possibility that optimal strategies for part of an organization may not be optimal overall. If installation managers take this economic viewpoint, they can focus on measurements that indicate what can be done to increase the average and marginal cost-performance ratio of the system. Such formal theories provide useful background, but their practical value is limited in the daily environment since the value of computation service is difficult to determine precisely.

Singer et al.[21] consider circumstances in which prices are not the dominant mechanism for allocating computer time. They discuss whether prices should be used at all, or whether alternative, nonpricing methods can be expected to work. They identify the prerequisites of allocation based on prices: the users must have budget constraints that are not forgiven by the administration when overruns occurs; there must be a fluid market for services, with alternatives for both customers and vendors; demand must exceed capacity; and prices must be free to fluctuate without reference to costs. In this viewpoint, pricing is not to be regarded as a cost recovery method. Several interesting concepts emerge: that idle time has value in that users can buy it to ensure better response, that profits and losses are simply transfer payments between the corporate body and the installation and can be regarded as a form of line funding, and that priority mechanisms can be regarded as nothing more than another form of pricing.

Overall Objectives

Whichever viewpoint is adopted, it is necessary to have information relating the service delivered to its price and/or cost. It is pertinent to note that accounting systems explain costs, not value to the user. Perhaps a qualitative feature distinguishing a good accounting mechanism is that it allows management to focus on value, with confidence that cost is under control.

Before getting into the details involved in designing an accounting program, it is worth summarizing the objectives in broad terms. The analysis and reporting of computer installation utilization data should be an integral part of the cost accounting system of the organization and should meet the same audit requirements as other parts of the accounting function. Clearly reported costs of the various services enable functional managers to make cost-benefit decisions selectively and to "tune" economically their part of the business. In some circum-

[20]Sharpe, *Economics of Computers*, Chap. 11.

[21]N. M. Singer, H. Kanter, and A. Moore, "Prices and the Allocation of Computer Time," *AFIPS Conference Proceedings*, Vol. 33 (1968), pp. 493–498.

stances, there is a contractual or legal requirement to demonstrate that cost assignments are made within certain guidelines.

Because the computer billing system can conveniently provide system performance information, it can become a component in planning, both within the computer facility and for groups of users. The billing system should demonstrate utilization and cost trends clearly enough to permit projections to be made by customers. It can be used by installation management to plan and justify hardware acquisitions (such as additional direct access units) or discontinuances, and major changes in software.

Data made available by the accounting mechanism inevitably become an element in management's evaluation of the computer installation. The utilization data enter into dialogues both between upper management and the installation manager and between the installation manager and his or her subordinates, who are often charged with solving problems revealed by the data or with maintaining utilization statistics within specified bounds. The machine operations manager, for instance, commonly is charged with keeping unscheduled maintenance time (downtime) under control. McFarlane et al. elaborate by referring to the systems programming function, which often is difficult to manage by formal control mechanisms because it is a highly skilled activity in which obscure errors of approach or execution can have adverse effects far from the areas for which an individual programmer is held responsible. These authors suggest that management should give close attention to understanding the results intended and the extent to which they are attained and that systems programmers should be held accountable for the overall efficiency, reliability, and responsiveness of the system. Measures of efficiency, reliability, and responsiveness can be made available in the accounting system.

From the users' point of view, the accounting system is an important interface with the computer facility. Users should be able to employ it to plan their future costs, to design programs for economy, to ascertain whether they are getting their fair share (or committed share) of the resources, and to reassure themselves that the computer facility is being run efficiently. The accounting system that does not convey useful information in easily decipherable form to the cost-conscious user will quickly become an organizational issue.

Many installations, at one time or another, will contemplate partial cost recovery by selling service outside the parent organization. Establishing a basis for pricing outside service is hardly possible without an internal basis.

Selection of a pricing scheme determines the type of uncertainty to be borne by the user, who must choose between alternatives (e.g., fast turnaround versus premium prices, time sharing versus batch) that usually involve an expenditure of the user's time in varying degrees. Effective allocation calls for a structured price schedule: there must be a price for each system component that is to be regulated or cost recovered. In general, each price will be a function of the time, the load, and the cost of the service. The basic issue is between effective allocation and the user's acceptance of accounting complexity.

Planning the Accounting Program

When the second version of the accounting procedures for the System 360 Model 195 installation at San Jose was started late in 1971, we wrote a programming specification in broad terms. The specification was designed to set forth general objectives, expose difficult or incomplete aspects of the method adopted, and serve as a reference against which program implementations could be measured. It was intended that the document be available to users or managers to whom detailed information on the accounting method was important or interesting. The programming specification was to be supplemented by separate memoranda documenting the programs and specifying the administrative procedures. It was successful in the sense that little revision seems necessary today. Much of the rest of this presentation is extracted from the specification.[22]

Our specific objectives were that

1. Each customer should be charged for the resources his or her work consumes. The charges should be based on job characteristics that the user can understand and control. For each job or terminal session, usage measures should be returned to the customer. In addition, there should be comprehensive summaries of appropriate scope for several levels of management and administration.

2. Under certain circumstances, there should be charges for denying resources to other users. The limiting case is a uniprogramming system, for which it is reasonable to charge on the basis of elapsed time. The best known practical example is stand-alone time, for which the user must pay the entire cost of the machine regardless of the use he or she makes of it.

3. Accounting should be supported on a cost center basis. That is, in specified accounting periods, the rates should be adjusted automatically so that all costs are apportioned among users in proportion to their consumption. The net profit or loss of the cost center is exactly zero. As an alternative, the program should also support fixed rates.

4. The charging system should be stable enough to permit prediction of charges, within reasonable limits (± 5 percent), so that users can plan their budgets.

5. No new data gathering package should be written. For OS/360 and OS/VS installation, the OS System Management Facility (SMF)[23] is the only IBM support available. If other data gathering tools are used, such as installation-generated SMF records or on-line storage records, the accounting program must be downward compatible to installations that have not installed such modifications or additions.

[22]A copy of the specifications is available from the authors.

[23]System Facility Management (MSF) is the name of the accounting package for IBM computers. Similar package is available on most other computers.

6. The program should be able to deal with peak and slack periods by applying shift differentials or permitting charges for priority service.

7. Each resource pool for which charges are made should be constructed to facilitate the use of pricing as an incentive for balancing resources usage or for signalling the desirability of changes in configuration. For example, if tape usage is heavy, the price per use will drop, indicating that it might be desirable to install more tape units.

8. The accounting program must handle arbitrary time periods; that is, the input data sets must be considered files without starts or ends. For example, it should be possible to summarize system usage between 12:35 P.M. on April 7, 1974 and 3:04 A.M. on June 20, 1974.

9. The accounting function should be automated, from measurement of usage to final posting of ledgers. It should be able to handle 1000 to 10,000 job steps a day, and it should include adequate error handling methods (e.g., rerun credit) and administrative adjustments. Each step requiring human intervention should be reexamined for necessity, and the exposure to human error should be identified.

10. In the event that an installation runs several computers, the program should support collation of charges from all machines. It should produce collated summary and project reports.

11. The accounting mechanisms must meet stringent auditing requirements, including written program specification and documentation; a file of source code listings and control of new versions of the program; separation of operational, programming, and accounting functions; regular distribution of usage reports to affected organizational functions; and an archival accounting data file of manageable size.

12. The implementation should be open ended in the sense that new services or improved data gathering tools can be incorporated easily.

13. There should be fail-safe mechanisms to prevent losses of accounting files, and procedures should be specified to account for tasks that are active at the time of a system crash or abnormally terminated by errors for which the installation is responsible. Since such mechanisms are not provided in the SMF package, the installation must provide them. It is not difficult to implement SMF exit routines that write duplicate copies of SMF data to a file that can be used if the primary SMF files are damaged or otherwise lost.

14. The total system summary must account for exactly 24:00:00 hours a day.

The difficulties and inconsistencies we were aware of included some that were intrinsic and some that were peculiar to the System/360 environment:

1. If the installation is a cost center, charges for the services necessarily fluctuate, depending on the overall load and how effectively the facility's management predicts the load and adjust costs and capacity. The usual technique for minimizing fluctuations is to average usage levels and costs over a suffi-

cient period to minimize extremes and permit publication of rates to customers. A moving average of several months is usually sufficient. This process, however, discourages the partitioning of resources into "subpools" apportioned according to usage levels, since the smaller the resource pool, the greater its chance of exhibiting widely fluctuating usage levels. It is an unfortunate attribute of the cost center that, regardless of the number of pools into which the resources are divided, the economic motivation of its pricing is always counterproductive: as the resource becomes lightly used, it falls into disuse, and the price per unit increases, further discouraging its use. (Fortunately, price is not the only motivation at work in apportioning resources; there are also such factors as turnaround responsiveness, which influences loading.) In practice, for resources whose usage levels may vary widely or be unreasonably priced (such as newly introduced service or resources), we compromised by lumping their costs into the overall cost center, and we make resource subpools of larger items such as CPU time and I/D facilities.

2. The complexity of a time-sharing, multiprogramming system seems to preclude a simple relationship among costs incurred by the installation, usage parameters that the customer can understand and control and load measurements that are available from standard measurement programs. For example, execution of channel programs requires storage space and CPU time as well as I/D paths and devices. This difficulty may be partly compensated for by adjusting the rates of related services, but some arbitrariness will remain in overhead estimation even in a careful approach.

3. Frequently, the usage measurement is imperfectly related to the actual activity. For instance, a channel program count is not proportional to either the amount of data transferred or the amount of time the channels and control units are busy. It should be recognized that the characterization, measurement, and prediction of the load on a system from a task or set of tasks are major areas for systems research. It seems inappropriate for the personnel of a service installation to do more than stay aware of the current state of the art and exploit the most significant advances on a conservative schedule. Many of these advances will involve basic changes to system architecture and to the accounting and data gathering component of the system. One should consider modifying the latter to be a project distinct from adjusting the accounting procedure.

4. In a complex environment, a task may generate considerably different usage measurements in repeated executions; for example, in a paging machine, the number of page replacements wil depend on paging activity interference from other tasks. Not only is this type of variation philosophically objectionable; very often it implicitly creates a price differential between peak load and off-shift periods. Sharpe[24] illustrates this with with the case of a time-sharing system in which CPU time and terminal contract time each have

[24]Sharpe, *Economics of Computers*, Chap. 11.

fixed rate prices: since response is slower during peak load periods, prime shift services not only will be less desirable, but they will be considerably more expensive than having the same work done at otherwise unattractive hours.

5. We have inadequate insight to relate prices for the same job run on different machines. It is often argued that prices should follow machine costs, permitting classical market forces to act, but this can lead to difficulties in a multiple-CPU installation where the user has some freedom to select among the various machines. Work tends to migrate to the machines with the best performance, leading to overloads on those machines and underutilization of others. If each machine is a separate cost center, there is economic motivation for some machines to be used more than others, making the loading even less stable.

6. Collecting accounting data and generating reports can become too expensive if too much detail is involved. For example, SMF can provide device usage for each unit employed by a job step, but to do so may require several million records a month for an installation processing 50,000 jobs a month; we are aware of one case in which data gathering alone consumed about 2 percent of the installation's capacity. Sometimes we can see only in retrospect that the data collected are too much or too little to provide the utilization and cost information needed. Fortunately, SMF allows widely varying levels of data collection.

7. The cost of some resources, such as CPU time, can reasonably be divided among users proportionally to their usage, since the cost is incurred whether the resource is used or not. For other resources, such as tape mounting, it can be argued that fixed rate per event is appropriate. A hybrid of fixed and varying rates is feasible, but not elegant.

8. It is common practice to base charges on measurements of machine usage and to include, as overhead, staff services (e.g., consulting, tape librarianship) that are seldom proportional to machine usage. This inequity can be dealt with in part by charging separately for the more expensive overhead services, with the disadvantage that this method requires manual data-entry steps. Another mechanism is to put a premium on machine services, such as volume mounting, that require human intervention.

9. Sometimes the data collection method omits information necessary for the implementation of consistent policy. For example, in OS/SMF, the usage measure for I/O activity is executed channel programs (*EXCPs*). Unfortunately, an *EXCP* may move widely varying amounts of data; a better measure would be channel bandwidth used, integrated over time. Singularly, the CPU time measured by SMF may vary widely due to paging activity and interruptions caused by the servicing of other tasks. (Curiously, the interrupted program is charged with some CPU time in OS.) A better measure would be instructions executed.

An Algorithm for Distributing Costs

In this section and the next, we describe a method for setting prices if an installation is run as a cost center. The following definitions apply. A resource is an identifiable service or machine for which an installation incurs costs. Some resources are not introduced explicitly and thereby become overhead. A usage measure, *u,* is a count (in specified units) made available by SMF for each service delivered.

For brevity, we will refer to any unit of service as a job step, *j.* This will include time-sharing sessions, unit record work, stand-alone time, or any other unit of service the installation wishes to define. A charge, *c,* is an apportionment, for a single job step, of the price of a resource. Each charge is calculated as a function of one or more usage measurements. Charges may be made at either variable or fixed rates. Variable charges are calculated as the user's equitable share of a pooled resource. Fixed charges are calculated at a rate independent of the load. Associated with each job step is a class identification, *C,* which can be used to implement differential charging policies. A class can identify either a service priority or a type of service, such as an APL terminal session.

The objective is to apportion resource costs among job steps according to their usage measures in an equitable, readily understandable way and to accumulate charges for each project. This can be done in four stages: determination of the fraction of each resource used by each job step, determination of the fraction of the installation's cost associated with each resource, accumulation of each customer's fractional use of the cost center, and finally, conversion of these fractions into dollar charges based on the expenses of the cost center. For resources that are to be charged for at a fixed rate, a modified method can be used: fixed charges can be accumulated separately and deducted from the cost center expense before the rate for variable charges is calculated.

Resources used

The resources used in our installation were problem program CPU time, problem program channel program count, problem program occupancy of main storage, direct access storage space, tape mounts, unit record output operation, unit record input operation, teleprocessing port connect time, job step initiation, graphic console time, stand-alone system time, off-line pack rental and other miscellaneous services, and spindle occupations for direct access devices. Of these, we chose to handle direct access storage, tape mounts, the graphic console, teleprocessing port usage, and unit record operations as fixed cost resources. For direct access storage, we decided that the most precious resource was long-term space usage. Consequently, rather than trying to monitor this resource on a job step basis, we decided to sample the on-line data base periodically to obtain a profile of the space used and to charge users according to this sampling. Several other resources were considered but not used in our implementation; they included plotting, data set allocation, and private direct access device usage.

It must be emphasized that, given the input data we discuss, it is a minor program change to adopt formulas other than those we outline next. For expository reasons, we have simplified some of the formulas that were actually used.

The charge for resources that are billed at variable rates is measured in arbitrary units called machine units. For the jth job step, the charge, $c(j)$, is the sum of subcharges for each of the resources used by that job step, as expressed by

$$c(j) = \sum_i s(i, j)$$

In this formula, $s(i, j)$ is the subcharge, in machine units, for job step j's use of the ith resource.

Each subcharge $s(i, j)$ is calculated as follows:

$$s(i, j) = TK(i) \frac{f(i)[u(i, j), p, C, t(j)]}{\sum_k f(i)[u(i, k), p, C, t(k)]}$$

Here, T is the total number of machine units (second of availability of the entire system) in the accounting period, $K(i)$ is the fraction of the system recovered by the usage of the ith resource, and $f(i)$ is a function of the usage measure, u, the class, C, the time of job step initiation, t, and externally supplied parameters, p. The denominator represents the sum of the usage of all job steps in the accounting period. For resources charged at fixed rates, the normalizing denominator is omitted in the formula, and the coefficient $TK(i)$ is replaced by a dollar rate per unit of service. For simplicity in exposition, these formulas and those that follow are written for an installation with a single machine. The result of extending the concept to multiple machines is obvious: subscripts proliferate.

Usage measure functions

Our usage measure functions follow. In each case, $d(t)$ is a shift differential function whose value depends on the time of day when the job step is started; it is piecewise constant, but it is not continuous. A mechanism is provided for charging weekend and holiday usage at third-shift rates. $D(c)$ is a premium factor for certain job classes. It allows resources to be priced differently for different usage classes. (For example, it may be desirable to induce users to make use of resources in a cost-effective way as by establishing a low price for low-priority background work and a high price for resources used in the time-sharing environment.)

1. CPU: $f(1) = d(t) \cdot D(c) \cdot$(problem program CPU time).
2. Channel programs: $f(3) = d(t) \cdot D(c) \cdot (EXCP$ count).
3. Direct access storage: $f(4) =$ (space occupied)$\cdot dt$. The direct access occupancy integral is measured by rectangular integration based on periodic sampling at unequal intervals (about once a week).
4. Tape mounts: $f(5) =$ number of tape mounts.

5. Unit record input/output: $f(6)$ = number of cards punched, local or remote, + number of lines printed, local or remote. We used HASP to provide the unit record usage statistics by writing installation defined records onto the SMF file from user exits provided by HASP. The unit record input load was omitted, since it is negligible compared with output. (It should be noted that in OS/VS, JES records are in SMF.)

6. Job step initiation and allocation: CPU, main storage, and I/O resources are all required whenever a job step is initiated. Most of the system operating cost is in accessing system data sets, allocating data sets, and the main storage occupied by the operating system during job step initiation. For the sake of simplicity, we chose to charge initiation as an I/O surcharge and a main storage occupation surcharge. Since the cost of any initiation increases with the number of data definition statements, n, an increment of the form $(a + bn)$ would be more precise.

7. TP port usage: $f(7)$ = length of time connected. SMF records the elapsed time of job steps from initiation to termination; for TP ports, this time approximates the actual connect time (for normal user behavior).

8. Graphic console time: $f(8)$ = (length of time graphic device is allocated) $\cdot d(t) = t(elp) \cdot d(t)$, where $t(elp)$ represents the actual elapsed time of a job step.

9. Main storage occupation: since the actual elapsed time varies for a job step executed at different times in a multiprogramming system, it is desirable, in the interest of consistency, to estimate the pseudoelapsed time—that is, the length of time a job step would occupy main storage if it were the only program in the system. In a spooled, disk-oriented system, a reasonable approximation is the sum of the CPU time and the product of the number of direct access I/O requested and the average delay on each request. The average delay is different for job steps in which the application is multitasked to overlap its own CPU and I/O time. For batch job steps involving interaction displays, the time in main storage is determined not by job characteristics, but by user response time, so that such job steps are best charged for according to total elapsed time rather than pseudoelapsed time. For the region size, it may be desirable to have varying rates so that, as an installation option, extremely large jobs can be penalized for reducing access to the CPU by other jobs; we avoid this extra complexity in the discussion. The pseudoelapsed time, $t'(elp)$, is

$$t'(elp) = \text{CPU time} + (\text{average time for an } EXCP) \cdot (EXCP \text{ count})$$

For any job, then, the elapsed time, g, is given by

$$g = t'(elp) + b \cdot \delta \cdot [t(elp) - t \cdot (elp)]$$

where $\delta = 1$ for a batch graphics job step and $\delta = 0$ otherwise, and where b is an installation parameter that could be used to reflect graphic device rental and overhead as well as main storage occupation costs.

The the main storage usage measurement function can be taken to be

$$f(2) = g \cdot d(t) \cdot D(c) \text{ (storage allocated in kilobytes)}$$

For interactive systems, the main storage formula can be modified to account for resident portions of the operating system dedicated primarily to time-sharing support:

$$f(2) = d(t) \cdot t(c) \cdot (TS \text{ region size } + TS \text{ monitor region size})$$

The foregoing largely presupposes that the computing environment includes a fixed capacity main storage, whose space is precious. In a virtual storage environment, the occupancy (in the sense of total virtual storage used) is less important. A measure more closely related to the utilization of a precious resource would be real storage occupancy and paging activity.

10. Finally, for each project, the total charge, c, in machine units is the accumulation over all job steps for that project:

$$c = \sum_j c(j)$$

For each project, there is also an accumulation of fixed prices, denoted by P. In addition to items already referred to, fixed prices include rental for terminals allocated to specific projects but managed by the computer facility, stand-alone machine time, set-up time, and special services. For each fixed price item, the rate generally includes administrative overhead as well as hardware rental costs.

Edit facility

The accounting program includes an input facility for charging for services not measured automatically and for crediting facility errors. It provides for credit and debit entries, charges in terms of machine units or dollars, and charges on either a prorated or an absolute basis. Input data can be repeated in appropriate output reports as an auditability feature.

Rerun credit

The program credits rerun costs automatically for jobs in execution at the time of a system failure and for jobs where the SMF entry is incomplete because of an SMF failure. In addition, when there is a known system problem that causes abnormal termination of a user program, the program can charge the affected runs to the rerun account automatically, and it can accumulate relevant statistics in a special output report. This facility reduces administrative overhead and obviates a remarkable number of minor complaints on the part of computer facility users.

Extension to virtual systems

In OS/VS 2 Release 2, SMF provides additional information regarding resource utilization: specifically, the algorithm might reasonably replace the usage measure functions for CPU time, channel programs, and main storage occupancy with functions for service units and paging activity, and the class, (C), with the performance group number. Of these functions, paging presents something of a problem. Generally, good accounting practice strives to minimize fluctuations in costs over which the user has no control. Paging activity represents such a cost since it depends on the configuration of active tasks in the system. On the other hand, the paging activity of a task may be vastly influenced by programming techniques, and it seems desirable to implement charging schemes designed to encourage good programming. Perhaps there is a trade-off to be made, or perhaps there is a technical solution that permits the paging activity to be measured independently of neighboring tasks. This is a subject that calls for further research.

Estimation of Resource Costs

In this section is described a method for estimating $K(i)$, the fraction of the system to be recovered in proportion to the ith usage measure. Note that it is not possible to ascribe system rental costs unambiguously to measured resources. For instance, one might inquire whether the system console should be regarded as part of the CPU, part of main storage, or part of the I/O configuration or apportioned somehow among those resources. For main storage and the CPU, parameters are given in the paragraphs that follow for apportioning such overhead. In the individual costs given, it is possible to include apportionments that represent salaries, materials, space rentals, and so on. Alternatively, they may appear as a burden expense proportional to the direct machine costs.

In view of the arbitrariness of some of the measures presented, the purpose of such a mathematical analysis may be questioned. Not all the measures are arbitrary, and those that are have limited ranges of reasonableness. The main point is that the type of analysis illustrated is an orderly exposition of which measures are arbitrary, and it makes for clear recognition of the relationship of prices to costs and to policy decisions. We have also found it effective as a background for discussion of prices with users and with upper management and for internal decision in the computer center.

CPU

SMF estimates the time used by the CPU for each job step while the program is in the problem state. The CPU also accomplishes overhead functions such as job, task, and I/O management. It may be desirable to recover part of this overhead in proportion to I/O activity rather than in proportion to CPU time. In the other direction, part of main storage is occupied permanently by system control programs; therefore, a desirable installation option is control of the proportions of main storage overhead recovered by assessment against CPU usage and I/O load. Accordingly, the adjusted cost of the CPU, $r'(c)$, can be expressed by the formula

$$r'(c) = r(c) \cdot [1 - x(c)] + r(M)\, x(M)$$

where $r(c)$ is the cost per month of the CPU, $x(c)$ is the fraction of the CPU cost to be recovered as I/O overhead, $r(M)$ is the cost per month of main storage, and

$x(m)$ is the fraction of main storage cost to be recovered as CPU overhead. The second term reflects the usage of the CPU for I/O overhead functions, and the third term reflects the portion of main storage assessed as part of the CPU.

Main storage

Typically, part of main storage contains modules required for source and sink I/O support (e.g., HASP). If this part is assessed against I/O usage, then the adjusted cost of main storage, $r'(M)$, can be expressed by

$$r'(M) = r(M)\cdot[1 - x(M) - x(IOSUP)]$$

Here, $x(IOUSP)$ is the fraction of main storage that supports external I/O devices. The second term compensates for the adjustments in the formula for $r'(T)$, and the third term reflects I/O support.

Tape mounts

The cost of tape drives can be recovered partly by a mount charge and partly by I/O counts. The part of the tape cost to be recovered by tape mount charges, $r'(T)$, can be represented as

$$r'(T) = x(T)\cdot r(T)$$

where $x(T)$ is the fraction of tape rental to be recovered by mount charges and $r(T)$ is the cost per month of tape drives and tape control units.

Unit record I/O

Where unit record I/O is measured, it is reasonable to include the cost of printers, card read punches, and associated control units and the cost of the part of the multiplexor channel, of the binary synchronous communications portion of a transmission control unit (TCU) used for remote job entry, and associated telephone costs, and of direct access devices used for spooling. In addition, it is reasonable to include the main storage cost of the spooling programs. Thus, the adjusted unit record I/O cost, $r'(pp)$, can be expressed as

$$r'(pp) = [r(pp) + r(BSC) + r(SPOOL) + r(M)\cdot x(IOUSP)]\, d(u)$$

where $r(pp)$ is the cost per month of printers and card read punches, $r(BSC)$ is the cost per month of telephone equipment and the BSC portion of the TCU, $r(SPOOL)$ is the cost per month of spooling devices, and $d(u)$ is the fraction of unit record machine rental recovered from I/O count assessment. Paper costs should be included in estimating the fixed charge for print and punch I/O.

Connect time

For terminal support, it is reasonable to include the cost of the terminals' portion of transmission control units, associated telephone equipment, and swapping or paging hardware. The adjusted connect time cost, $r'(con)$, then is

$$r'(con) = [r(ss) + r(SWAP)] \cdot d(c)$$

where $r(ss)$ is the cost per month of telephone equipment and the start-stop portion of the *TCU*, $r(SWAP)$ is the cost per month for swapping and paging hardware, and $d(c)$ is the fraction of transmission control rental recovered from connect time. Note that $d(u)$ and $d(c)$ can be calculated from summation of direct charges after an overhead ratio is included.

On-line storage

Long-term on-line storage is charged to the user at a fixed rate in a separate calculation. To avoid including the same resource twice, a deduction should be made from the cost of the peripheral equipment to reflect the portion of on-line storaged assigned to user libraries. Thus $r(ST)$, the long-term storage cost per month, is

$$r(ST) = \sum_{\substack{device \\ type}} [c(dev) \cdot m(dev)] \cdot x(ST)$$

where $c(dev)$ is the cost per megabyte-month for storage on a given device, $m(dev)$ is long-term storage on a given device in megabyte-month, and $x(ST)$ is the fraction of storage device cost recovered by long-term occupation.

Remaining I/O equipment

All remaining I/O equipment charges can be recovered by measurement of I/O activity. If the installation chooses not to charge directly for some of the foregoing resources addressed, their cost will be included as part of the residual I/O costs (see formula for $K(EXCP)$). The total cost per month for the peripheral I/O configuration, represented by $r(IO)$, is

$$r(IO) = r(T) + r(BSC) + r(SS) + r(PP) + r(SWAP) + r(CH) + r(SPOOL) \\ + r(DISK) + r(MISC)$$

Here, $r(CH)$ is the cost per month of channels, drums, and control units not otherwise included, $r(DISK)$ is the cost per month of direct access storage excluding long-term storage, and $r(MISC)$ represents a catchall term for rental costs not otherwise included.

Adjusted for main storage and CPU overhead terms, the I/O rental cost is

$$r'(IO) = r(IO) + r'(M) \cdot x(IOSUP) + r(c) \cdot x(c)$$

Then $r(p)$, the cost of the I/O equipment not covered by fixed rate charges, is

$$r(p) = r'(IO) - r(ST) - r(T) - r(con) - r(pp)$$

and the estimated rental cost of the entire system, r, is

$$\begin{aligned} r &= r'(IO) + r'(M) + r'(C) \\ &= r(IO) + r(M) + r(C) \\ &= r(p) + r(ST) + r(T) + r(con) + r(pp) + r(M) + r(c) \end{aligned}$$

The formulas can be combined to give the fraction $K(k)$ of the system recovered against the charge measure k:

CPU: $K(CPU) = r'(c)/r = [1/r] [r(c) - r(c) \cdot x(c) + r(M) \cdot x(M)]$

Main storage: $K(MSTOR) = r'(M)/r$
$$= [1/r] [r(M) - r(M) \cdot x(M) - r(M) \cdot x(IOUSP)]$$

Unit record: $K(UREC) = r'(pp)/r$
$$= [d(u)/r] [r(pp) + r(BSC) + r(SPOOL) + r(M) \cdot x(IOSUP)]$$

Tape mount: $K(TPMNT) = r'(T)/r = [1/r] [x(T) \cdot r(T)]$

Connect: $K(con) = r'(con)/r = [d(c)/r] [r(SS) + r(SWAP)]$

EXCP: $K(EXCP) = r'(p)/r$
$$= [1/r] [r(IO) + r(M) \cdot x(IOUSP) + r(c) x(c) - r(ST) - r(T) - r(con) - r(pp)]$$

$$\text{Note:}\quad \sum_k K(k) = 1$$

At installation option, any parameters x or d can be set equal to zero.

Reduction of Machine Charges to Dollars

For converting machine charge to dollars, the usage figures can be combined with costs as determined by the financial department. Also, adjustments can be made to exclude machine use by the computer facility for maintenance, since this is often considered an overhead item.

The dollar charge per job step, $\$(j)$, can be calculated as follows:

$$\$(j) = P(j) + c(j)\frac{E - \Sigma\, P(j)}{\Sigma\, c(j)}$$

Here, E is the total expense for the accounting period, including machine rental, labor, materials, and miscellaneous overhead expenses, $c(j)$ is the machine unit charge of the jth customer, and $P(j)$ is the dollar charge for resources billed at a fixed rate to the jth project. The set $[c(j), P(j)]$ is not to include computer facility overhead projects.

Implementation

Program structure and operation

The overall structure of the accounting program is depicted in Figure 9.6.

The data reduction program combines the SMF records, which may include installation defined records in addition to those provided by OS-SMF, and it drops data not needed by the accounting method, makes simply validity checks on the data and prints an exception list, and collects the job and step records of a single job. In addition, the program can combine SMF files from several systems. Each SMF record type is processed independently. Figure 9.7 summarizes the key output records, with a few of the less important details omitted.

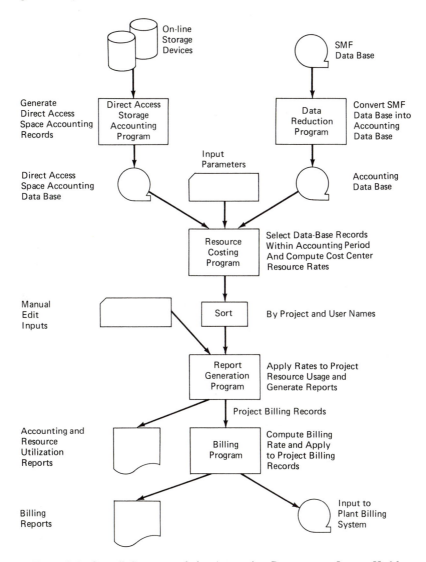

Figure 9.6 Overall Structure of the Accounting Program.   *Source:* H. M. Gladney, D. L. Johnson, and R. L. Stone, "Computer Installation Accounting," IBM *Systems Journal,* Vol. 4, 1975, pp. 314–38. Reprint by permission from *IBM Systems Journal.* © 1975 by International Business Machines Corporation.

We use installation-defined SMF records generated by HASP to account for and describe all non-OS time. The data reduction achieved is approximately 50 percent of the original SMF records. The output accounting data-base tape (actually a multireel volume of indefinite length) contains all the transaction records and cannot itself be edited by the accounting programs. After a grace period to permit examination of the exception listings, the SMF input data are destroyed so

Step Record

Record Type	Model No.	System ID	Job Name	Job Read Time	Job Read Date	Step Start Time	Step Start Date	Step ELP Time	Step CPU Time	Step Completion Code	Step EXCPS	Step Core	Tape Mounts	Step No.
3	2	2	8	8	6	8	6	8	11	3	7	4	1	2

HASP Record

Record Type	Model No.	System ID	Job Name	Job Read Time	Job Read Date	Page Count	Line Count	Punch Count	User Name	Project No.	Job Class
3	2	2	8	8	6	6	7	5	16	8	1

Job Record

Record Type	Model No.	System ID	Job Name	Job Read Time	Job Read Date	Job Start Time	Job Start Date	Job ELP Time	Job CPU Time	User Name	Project No.	Job Completion Code	Job Class
3	2	2	8	8	6	8	6	8	11	16	8	3	1

Direct Access Space Accounting Record

User ID	Run Date	Run Time	Device Type	No. of Data Sets	No. of Tracks
8	6	8	4	2	7

Figure 9.7 Key Accounting Data-Base Records. *Source:* H. M. Gladney, D. L. Johnson, and R. L. Stone, "Computer Installation Accounting," *IBM Systems Journal*, Vol. 4, 1975, pp. 314–38. Reprint by permission from *IBM Systems Journal.* © 1975 by International Business Machines Corporation.

that the corresponding section of the accounting tape cannot be reproduced. The accounting data-base tape must be stored as long as audit and tax regulations specify.

The direct access storage accounting program samples the on-line data base periodically, determining ownership of data sets from the first qualifier of the name (a convention that must be enforced by data-base maintenance procedures and programs). This program produces a data base that is similar to the accounting data base. These two data bases, along with the cost parameters, are the input to the resource costing program.

The resource costing program is structured (as is the data reduction program) with a separate procedure for each type of input record, so adaptation to new records and formats is facilitated. Input parameters include formula constants, accounting period dates, factors for service levels, and rates for fixed rate resources. This program computes the denominators and prefactors in the formula for calculating the value of $s(i, j)$. If all rates are fixed, this step can be omitted.

Following a sort by project and user names, the report is generated. We have done this on a weekly and monthly schedule. Figures 9.8 and 9.9 indicate the output format. Although not shown, all manually entered records and input parameters should be printed on the output. These records include adjustments for rerun credit (job aborted because of computer facility error) and administrative adjustments such as one-time charges for new hook-ups and bills for dedicated equipment. To provide timely information for users, the report necessarily estimates the costs. Later, when financial information for the accounting period is available, the billing program generates precise charges based on the cost of operation. At this time, input of suitable format for the corporate accounting system is generated.

Reports and their use

Figure 9.8 shows the part of the report that summarizes system activity and gives a dollar breakdown. Although most of the information is self-explanatory (as it most emphatically should be), a comment is in order: system performance information is useful not only to persons in a position to do something about it, but also to the user community at large. We found that a brief summary of machine uptime and utilization, published for the user community on a regular basis, makes for good "customer relations." Thus, when system performance and reliability are good, everyone can see that it is; and when it is not good, the pressure (even embarrassment) of public knowledge provides a powerful incentive to make things better.

The breakdown of usage by departmental groups is useful in at least two ways: it can show user groups that they are getting their rightful share of the resource (as properly determined by upper management), and it allows computer facility overhead to be compared with the quantity of resource delivered to more directly productive work.

METER TIME IS FROM MAY 15, 1973 TO JUNE 22, 1973   SJRL SMF V3 2/1/72

ACCOUNT PERIOD 09:00:00   73:135 TO 08:59:59   73.173

ELAPSED TIME	911:59:59		
METER TIME	0671.44.40 -	73.6% OF E.T. - 2418280	MACHINE UNITS
MACHINE DOWN TIME	7:19:45 -	1.3% OF E.T.	
PM TIME	0016.00.00 -	1.7% OF E.T.	
TOTAL ACTIVE	545:53:33	CPU UTILIZATION 81.2%	

PROJECT STATISTICS:

GROUP NAME	JOBS	CPU TIME HH:MM:SS	EXCPS	CORE MBS	% OF TOT MU	FIXED CHARGES	TOTAL CHARGES
PROJECT A	2840	134:40:44	082246	600158	16.5%	$1105.55	$127368.45
PROJECT B	761	1:03:47	904678	23384	0.5%	$3336.80	$6642.25
PROJECT C	3241	11:14:42	12338120	157029	4.7%	$21291.93	$54576.93
PROJECT D	117	0:22:54	137889	3418	0.1%	$675.20	$1248.65
PROJECT E	840	1:17:13	317549	17788	0.3%	$3945.33	$6066.68
PROJECT F	592	2:04:21	661334	12390	0.4%	$3012.17	$5592.82
PROJECT G	253	0:53:15:	223822	13318	0.2%	$1545.99	$3087.09
OTHER	3873	106:28:38	12049072	368156	11.6%	$15258.09	$96822.44

RATES:

RESOURCE	RATES	UNITS
CPU	0.34911	MU PER CPU SEC
CORE	0.22426	MU PER MBYTE SEC
EXCP	0.00525	MU PER EXCP
CONNECT	$8.00	DOLLARS PER HOUR
UNIT RECORD I/O	$0.0015	DOLLARS PER LINE
TAPE MOUNTS	$3.00	DOLLLARS PER MOUNT
DIRECT ACCESS STORAGE		
2314	$63.00	DOLLARS PER MEGABYTE MONTH
3330	$63.00	DOLLARS PER MEGABYTE MONTH
2250 TIME	$0.00	DOLLARS PER HOUR

CLASS	TOTAL E.T. HH:MM:SS	ACTIVE HH:MM:SS	EXCPS	CORE MBS	JOBS	1ST	SHIFT 2ND	3RD	% OF TOT MU	PAGES	LINES	CARDS
A	213:05:41	8:35:11	7139294	69212	6852	4384	1387	1081	2.6%	266813	12575740	104919
B	76:18:07	11:00:28	2538017	30366	1118	624	319	175	1.4%	38389	1689553	1330
C	61:21:53	8:59:34	1133541	15680	548	294	141	113	0.9%	19417	853264	8602
D	169:36:08	18:47:40	12709810	107325	3708	2267	1075	366	4.7%	143008	5985327	26041
E	163:34:16	18:24:18	10876956	77314	4263	2571	1199	493	4.0%	112467	4883418	109734
F	31:13:48	2:25:20	944417	17505	415	266	97	52	0.5%	9686	442125	9
G	270:20:23	23:08:18	9532834	148583	4413	2966	874	573	4.6%	220543	9401991	41899
7	152:04:36	31:50:07	8685182	236086	77	1	12	64	5.7%	3818	205403	1853
8	168:18:23	45:09:12	5724499	229893	50	0	4	46	5.7%	3399	163127	1169
9	93:17:23	21:58:06	1201579	111372	34	0	8	26	2.4%	17109	988290	2632
RRUN	20:48:46	2:50:28	751869	22876	184	77	23	84	0.5%	999	39766	350
TOTALS			126349633	3058450	35728	22326	8530	4872		1362059	59602165	563240

SHIFTS	JOBS	% OF TOTAL JOBS	CPU HH:MM:SS	% OF TOTAL CPU	EXCPS	CORE MBS	TAPE MOUNTS
1ST	22326	62.4%	125:25:14	22.9%	40528972	998272	3421
2ND	8530	23.8%	182:58:14	33.5%	37341582	843580	3895
3RD	4872	13.6%	237:30:05	43.5%	48479079	1216599	2622
TOTAL	35728	99.8%	545:53:33	99.9%	126349633	3058450	9938

DIRECT ACCESS SUMMARY

DEVICE	TRKDAYS	BILLED MBYTE MONTHS	BILLABLE MBYTE MONTHS	% BILLED	RECOVERY
2314	319678	377.68	526.93	71.7%	$23632.31
3330	1735277	753.11	2062.13	36.5%	$47445.31

RUN DATES

73.135
73.143
73.172

Figure 9.8 A Summary Report.   *Source:* H. M. Gladney, D. L. Johnson, and R. L. Stone, "Computer Installation Accounting," IBM *Systems Journal,* Vol. 4, 1975, pp. 314–38. Reprint by permission from *IBM Systems Journal.* © 1975 by International Business Machines Corporation.

PROJECT NO.   PROJECT NAME   .   PROJECT MGR.   SJRL SMF V3 2/1/72

AAA-1234   INFO. SYS. ARCH   E. MCFURD

PROGRAMMER

METER TIME IS FROM MAY 15, 1973 TO JUNE 22, 1973
ACCOUNT PERIOD IS FROM 09:00:00 73.135 TO 08:59:59 73.173

A. SMITH

CLASS	1ST	2ND SHIFT	3RD	ELP TIME HH:MM:SS	CPU TIME HH:MM:SS	EXCPS	CORE MBS	UNIT RECORD I/O PAGES	LINES	CARDS	TAPE MOUNTS
D	33	16	0	1:59:06	0:08:36	74466	815.37	1382	60351	0	0
E	15	6	0	0:46:51	0:01:48	14698	205.90	2264	89637	0	0
A	10	7	0	0:09:50	0:00:03	2803	69.42	172	5737	0	0
H	3	0	0	0:17:05	0:03:31	4737	144.76	83	3564	0	0
U	13	0	0	0:19:06	0:00:13	2146	61.88	13	777	0	0
TSO	33	12	0	58:09:43	0:23:12	3350	8660.78	0	0	0	0
TOTAL	123	54	0	65:19:45	0:47:36	212340	11600.40	5566	253090	0	0

ABEND	NUMBER	PCT OF TOTAL CPU TIME
BOA	4	0.21%
O3B	2	0.01%
913	1	0.01%
622	2	1.01%
TOTAL	53	2.11%

DEVICE	DATASETS	TRK DAYS
2314	5	16720
3330	26	8774

P. SMYTHE

CLASS	1ST	2ND SHIFT	3RD	ELP TIME HH:MM:SS	CPU TIME HH:MM:SS	EXCPS	CORE MBS	UNIT RECORD I/O PAGES	LINES	CARDS	TAPE MOUNTS
TSO	2	2	0	1:28:25	0:00:30	260	178.73	0	0	0	0
TOTAL	2	2	0	1:28:25	0:00:30	260	178.73	0	0	0	0

DEVICE	DATASETS	TRK DAYS
3330	2	389

133

PROJECT TOTAL	SHIFT	JOBS	ABENDS	CPU TIME HH:MM:SS	EXCPS	CORE MBS	MACHINE UNITS
	1ST	125	33	0:36:11	161055	9073	3638
	2ND	56	20	0:11:55	51545	2707	1127
	3RD	0	0	0:00:00	0	0	
	TOTAL	181	53	0:48:06	212600	11779	4765

COST CENTER RATES

RESOURCE	RATE	UNITS
CPU TIME	0.34911	MACHINE UNITS/CPU SEC.
CORE	0.22400	MACHINE UNITS/MEGABYTE SEC.
EXCPS	0.00525	MACHINE UNITS/EXCP

FIXED RATE CHARGES
RESOURCE

CONNECT TIME   59.636 HRS AT $8.00 PER HR = $476.27
UNIT RECORD I/O   253090 LINES at $0.0015 PER LINE = $378.54
DIRECT ACCESS SPACE

16720 TRK DAYS ON 2314 = 4.0629 MBYTE MONTHS AT $63.00 PER MYBTE MONTH = $255.32
9181 TRK DAYS ON 3330 = 3.9845 MBYTE MONTHS AT $63.00 PER MBYTE MONTH = $249.67

TOTAL ESTIMATED CHARGES

TOTAL FIXED RATE CHARGES $1359.80
COST CENTER CHARGES   4765 MACH UNITS = 1.324 HRS AT $1050.00 PER HOUR   = $3902.40
    TOTAL ESTIMATED CHARGE TO PROJECT AAA-1234   = $15262.20 ± 5%
    SUBJECT TO COST CENTER FLUCTUATIONS

Figure 9.9 An Individual User and Project Report. *Source:* H. M. Gladney, D. L. Johnson, and R. L. Stone, "Computer Installation Accounting," IBM *Systems Journal,* Vol. 4, 1975, pp. 314–38. Reprint by permission from *IBM Systems Journal.*

The breakdown by job class provides a 24-hour-a-day picture of system util-ization. Trends in amount and types of usage can be identified, so job class distinc-tions can be refined, hardware can be ordered or released, and so forth.

The report illustrated in Figure 9.9 is sent to each project manager, enabling him or her to see at a glance which persons in his or her project are doing what kind of work. The cost center rates are printed here as a convenience, to facilitate future planning as well as to help in figuring the values of various usage trade-offs.

Future plans

In retrospect, several aspects of the implementation could bear improve-ment. The output from the direct access accounting program should be merged with the output from the data reduction program, thereby reducing the physical size of the accounting data base, the amount of clerical support needed, and the opportunity for error. For better security, it would be preferable that the manu-ally entered records and the input parameters be entered into the accounting data base, thus consolidating the accounting information in a single untamperable data set. Also, our implementation did not take into account that a user assigned to one project might legitimately charge runs to another project.

The reports generated would be more helpful if year-to-date totals for se-lected information were provided. To go a little farther, budget tracking could be nicely provided for with a plotted curve of cumulative dollars spent versus a planning line for the various projects.

Although the publishing of cost center rates in the user report is helpful, it could be carried a step farther: a brief summary of the charge algorithm could be provided so that the user need not refer to separate documentation when verify-ing or analyzing his charges.

Our future plans call for a substantial revision of this accounting system. These minor revisions can be incorporated, but major changes in our computing environment dictate a major rewrite. The computing facility has undergone a mas-sive consolidation, integrating some dozens of systems and several major cost centers, with a flexible netting and load-sharing capability among many of the machines. Not all the accounting ramifications of these changes are yet understood, and we are looking forward to a period of challenge and new enlightenment.

Performance

No attempt has been made to optimize the program's performance. To process a monthly input generated by 30,000 jobs, the program typically requires 4 minutes of CPU time on the Model 195 and 40,000 EXCPs in a 300 Kbyte region. A new version could be much more economical.

CONCLUDING REMARKS

Administrating the allocation of a computer resource can be segmented into several responsibilities, with fairly well-defined subjects of common concern: the policy of the parent organization and strategies to realize the overall objectives by allocating computer resources and assessing results, tactics of users to maximize value per unit price, control functions to demonstrate compliance with externally imposed regulations, planning and assessment within the computer facility, and technology of load measurement. It is possible to design an installation accounting package that does much to decouple these varied functions. We have described an implementation that is quite successful in this regard.

It is possible and desirable to design and implement a single accounting package that would be acceptable for the majority of medium to large installations and that would have a well-defined set of options and alternatives and clear identification of areas in which installation-written procedures could be added to implement unusual policies. The program should be structured to take advantage of new measurement methods and to support new services. We believe that the implementation presented here is valuable as a guide for an entirely fresh design.

SELECTED READINGS

BOROVITS, I. "Pricing of Computer Services." *Data Processing Journal,* Vol. 16, no. 3 (1974), pp. 160–163.

CORTADA, JAMES W. *EDP Costs and Charges: Finance Budgets and Cost Control in D.P.* Englewood Cliffs, N.J.: Prentice-Hall, 1980.

DEARDEN, J., AND R. L. NOLAN. "How to Control the Computer Resources." *Harvard Business Review,* Vol. 51, no. 6 (1973), pp. 66–78.

HIRSCHLEIFER, J. *Internal Pricing and Decentralization Decisions, in Management Controls: New Directions in Basic Research.* New York: McGraw-Hill, 1964.

NOLAN, RICHARD L. "Effects of Chargeout on User/Manager Attitudes." *Communications of the ACM,* March 1977, pp. 177–185.

NUNAMAKER, J. F., AND A. WHINSTON. "Design of a Corporate Computer System: From Problem Statement to Cost Allocation" (USA AD-724161, Army Research Office, Springfield, Va.: National Technical Information Services, 1972).

SHARPE, W. F. *The Economics of Computers.* New York: Columbia University Press, 1969.

10

Recruiting, Training, and Development

INTRODUCTION

Motivating and managing data processing personnel as well as motivating the users are important factors in a successful implementation of computerized information systems. In a study conducted by Couger and Zawacki, it was found that there are five major factors that cause the backlog in new systems development and implementation.[1] These factors are (1) increasing complexity of systems, (2) increasing quantity of systems, (3) turnover of computer personnel, (4) increasing maintenance cost, (5) shortage of qualified personnel. Both the third and fifth factors, concerning the shortage of qualified personnel, are interrelated. It is difficult to recruit new qualified personnel because of the shortage, and the turnover rate is also affected by the shortage of qualified personnel.

Therefore, recruiting and training have become important issues and will require a large share of the organization's budget as well as time from key personnel who otherwise may devote their time to development of new systems.

RECRUITMENT OF DATA PROCESSING PERSONNEL

Introduction

Currently, one of the major problems faced by companies that use computer technology is the difficulty they have in recruiting qualified data processing personnel. Unfortunately, this human resource problem is basically one of supply

---

[1]J. Daniel Couger and Robert A. Zawacki, *Motivating and Managing Computer Personnel* (New York: John Wiley, 1980), pp. 2–5.

and demand. The spiralling growth of data processing has created a severe demand for data processing professionals. However, the current supply of skilled personnel is inadequate to meet this demand.

To satisfy their data processing staffing needs, companies have been forced to develop more aggressive, creative, and systematic recruiting programs. The objectives of the following discussion are to provide the reader with comprehensive guidelines and techniques for the recruitment, assessment, and selection of competent data processing job applicants.

If a company is going to be successful in recruiting qualified data processing personnel, it must launch and maintain an aggressive, imaginative, and systematic recruiting program. Such a program also saves time and money.

The successful data processing recruiting program is a system composed of sequential stages. These stages are the following:

1. Determining accurate and realistic staffing specifications
2. Undertaking effective applicant recruiting
3. Assessing the applicants
4. Making a final evaluation of the applicant

These stages are discussed now in detail. It is hoped that this information will assist readers in developing and implementing a recruiting program for their organizations.

Determining Accurate and Realistic Staffing Specifications

Before recruiting for a vacant data processing position, the manager must have a thorough knowledge of the position's duties and requirements. Two tools that are useful in providing this information are the job description and the job specification.

The job description

The first step in determining accurate and realistic staffing specifications is to prepare a job description (as discussed in Chapter Four). The purpose of this description is to delineate what it is that an employee is to do in the prospective position. It must contain the following information:

1. Duties to be performed
2. Level of complexity and responsibility
3. Physical environment and related working conditions
4. Equipment, machinery, or tools to be used
5. Extent of supervision and direction received

6. Extent of independent judgment and initiative required

7. Terms of employment

The job specification

After the job description is developed, the next step is to prepare the job specification. Its purpose is to outline the specific qualifications that an applicant must possess to perform the job duties successfully. The job specification must include the following:

1. Level of education
2. Specialized skills
3. Essential personality characteristics
4. Extent of prior work experience
5. Level of intelligence

Job specifications should be realistic. As an aid in determining which job specifications are truly realistic, the recruiter should identify the critical job requirement. Certain credentials, qualifications, or personal characteristics may be completely superfluous.

Another method of identifying the truly critical factors in a position is to conduct a differential analysis of the qualifications possessed by employees who have been successful in the job against those who have failed in the job. Such a "success-failure" analysis requires a commitment from the company in terms of time and money. However, it is useful in empirically identifying important and vital applicant qualifications.

The personnel requisition

In many companies, when a department desires to fill a given position, an approved personnel requisition is prepared and forwarded to the personnel department, authorizing it to set the staffing wheels into motion. Such a requisition usually contains the job information contained in the job description and job specification. At this point, it is essential that the data processing manager who initiated the requisition work very closely with the personnel department.

The more the personnel department knows about the data processing job, about the managers for whom the applicant will be working, and the advancement opportunities that are available, the better their chance of recruiting the most qualified professionals.

In general, the full-time personnel specialist will be responsible for implementing the first three stages of the data processing recruiting program. The personnel specialist screens out the unqualified candidates and recommends one or several qualified individuals to the hiring data processing manager for a final decision. However, in some companies, the data processing manager may not have the services of an on-site personnel department and must handle the entire employment function without such assistance.

Effective Applicant Recruiting

The objective of effective applicant recruiting is to attract a large number of well-qualified job applicants to the company. The achievement of this objective depends on the recruiting sources selected.

Several recruiting sources are available to the personnel specialist. A sampling of these are

1. Newspaper advertisements
2. Recommendations and referrals
3. Employment agencies
4. Unsolicited applicants
5. Direct-mail solicitations
6. Executive search firms
7. Advertising in trade, professional, or business journals
8. Colleges, universities, and vocational schools

This list is not inclusive. Generally, trial and error may be the only means for testing before deciding which source to use for a given type of job opening. However, when recruiting for data processing personnel, certain sources are preferred to others.

Colleges, universities, and trade schools

There are several types of schools and training centers from which companies can obtain data processing employees. These include junior and community colleges, universities, and trade schools.

When considering recent or upcoming graduates of a data processing training program, the recruiter should evaluate at least two aspects of the school's program: curriculum and equipment used. Generally, an individual will receive a well-rounded data processing education if the curriculum emphasizes several computer languages, up-to-date techniques, and subjects of current interest (e.g., data-base management). Students have to have hands-on experience in a programming course. However, the equipment they use should be equipment that they would find in industry, not obsolete operating systems.

For a company to be successful in hiring recent graduates, it is essential that management develop an effective and mutually beneficial relationship with the schools. The academic and vocational institutions must get to know the company and its job requirements so that only reasonably qualified candidates will be referred. The company can help facilitate this relationship by conducting the following activities: providing the schools with informative literature about the company, offering summer or field employment to students, providing speakers for various educational programs, and participating in on-campus recruiting activities.

Recommendations and referrals

Another recruiting source of data processing personnel is people already familiar with the company. Past and present employees, customers, vendors, contractors, and suppliers may recommend applicants. The quality of applicants recommended by people who know the company is usually of higher than that of candidates coming from a totally unscreened source such as a newspaper advertisement. Because the referral candidate is considered a reflection of the person who recommended him or her, people tend to be selective in whom they refer to the company.

Former applicants

Another excellent recruiting source for data processing professionals is former applicants. The personnel specialist or data processing manager should maintain a file of former candidates who did not qualify for specific jobs. In a year or two, those individuals will have accumulated additional experience, perhaps in a speciality in an area where someone is needed.

Newspaper advertisements

Advertising is a relatively inexpensive and quick way to recruit applicants. Instead of requesting the reader to submit a letter or résumé, invite the candidate to call in to obtain further information about the job and to be considered for the position. This technique attracts not only the unemployed applicant but also a relatively large number of employed and generally contented candidates who ordinarily would not respond to the traditional ad because they are not really in the job market.

Internal recruitment

Search firms lure away data processing professionals by somehow knowing the highly competent employees and either contacting those who are unhappy in their present jobs or selling individuals on a "better" opportunity.

A similar system can be established within a company. This internal search function can seek out competent employees and offer them the choice of other opportunities within the company if they so desire. An alternative to the internal search system is to post all data processing vacancies internally and invite all current employees to apply for consideration. It is important for a company to be consistent and fair when recruiting internally. Disparate treatment can result in affirmative action complaints and possible lawsuits.

Assessing the Applicants

Once a company has attracted several promising job applicants, the next stage for the personnel specialist is to screen out the unqualified applicants. It is important that every applicant be treated fairly and courteously.

The applicant assessment stage involves three major steps:

1. Initial applicant screening
2. Checking applicant's employment references
3. Structured selection interview

Initial applicant screening

The initial applicant screening is best accomplished through the use of the screening (mini) interview. Basically, two purposes are served by the screening interview: determining whether the applicant possesses the critical specifications for the position and tactfully expediting the departure of unqualified applicants.

The screening interview is not intended to elicit any real depth of background information from the job applicant, nor should it be construed as a final selection interview. The interview usually takes no more than a few minutes.

How to conduct the screening interview

One or more of the four approaches described next should be used to screen job applicants.

Visual Screening. At times, merely looking at a candidate can determine desirability. Individuals who can be identified visually as warranting no more than a screening interview are those whose appearance and dress are unacceptable.

Even if the applicant is obviously undesirable, the interviewer should at least ask the candidate a few questions related to past job experience and as soon as possible thank the applicant for his or her interest in the company and mention that other candidates will be interviewed within the next few days. The candidate should be informed that the company will notify him or her by mail or telephone if the candidate is to be considered further.

The interviewer must appear sincere and interested in the applicant. No applicant should ever be rejected or told that he or she is not qualified during the course of the screening interview. The interviewer may end up in a lengthy, unproductive debate.

Use of Critical or Knockout Questions. Most data processing jobs have specifications that are absolutely critical. If the candidate lacks these qualifications, he or she should be immediately eliminated from further consideration. The screening interview can determine very quickly if the candidate is qualified.

This type of screening interview can be conducted by asking the applicant key or "knockout" questions. These questions are directly related to the skills and characteristics needed for successful performance in the positions.

Review of the Application Form. Most data processing professionals are not actively seeking other employment. Therefore, the interviewer who says, "Here is our application, please fill it out," before the screening interview is in error. The average data processing professional does not believe this request applies to him or her and perceives it as a put down. The interviewer should make the data processing professional feel that he or she is more important than the piece of paper. An application can always be completed later.[2]

On the other hand, entry-level data processing candidates should be requested to complete application forms prior to the screening interviews. A review of the candidate's application can often indicate whether or not a more comprehensive interview is warranted. Furthermore, the interviewer should not allow a résumé to substitute for the application form. A candidate's résumé usually tells the interviewer only what the candidate wants the interviewer to know.

Briefly Describe the Job to the Applicant Another way to eliminate unqualified applicants is to describe the job briefly to them. Applicants may be completely unfamiliar with the job requirements for which they are applying. For example, some data processing jobs require irregular work schedules. A willingness to accept shift assignments may be a condition of employment.

After receiving a brief description of some of the job's key aspects during a screening interview, the candidate may find the described employment conditions unacceptable and remove him- or herself from further consideration.

Use of Skill and Ability Tests to Screen Out the Unqualified. Skill and ability tests are objective means for determining whether a job applicant has the basic competence to perform the duties of a position.

Once a decision is made to use aptitude tests, the data processing manager must select the appropriate tests. For this selection process, the data processing manager should consider the following guidelines: tests should be relevant, reliable, and predictive of on-the-job success.

Relevancy. A relevant test measures those abilities that are critical to job success. These factors, called job criteria, differ greatly for the various data processing jobs. This difference means that the same aptitude test should not be used for all data processing jobs. The abilities necessary for success as a computer operator seldom assure success as a programmer. Therefore, a test should be designed to measure the abilities of each job.

Reliability. A reliable test should be shown to have predicted success on the job over a long period of time and in a wide range of applications.

Predicting on-the-job success. The data processing manager should ensure that the tests are valid for the job skills that they are being used to evaluate. A validation study should demonstrate the "close agreement" by statistical measures of test scores and supervisory rating of performance on the job by the candidate.[3]

Checking the applicant's employment reference

After a candidate successfully completes the initial screening and aptitude testing processes, the candidate's employment references should be checked. The information obtained from these reference checks will provide further insight into the candidate's qualifications.

[2]Scott Upp, "How to Interview for Scare DP Pros," *Computer Decisions*, Vol. 12 (July 1980), p. 54.

[3]Allan M. Bloom, "Test the Test for Programming Applicants," *Data Management*, Vol. 16 (October 1978), p. 37.

In some cases, the applicant will not permit a prospective new employer to check with his or her present company for fear of jeopardizing his or her present job. In this situation, the recruiter should inform the applicant that an offer of employment is contingent on receiving a satisfactory reference from the present employer.

Reference checks can be accomplished in one of three ways: in person, by mail, or by telephone.

The most useful method for reference checking is via the telephone. Unlike the other two methods, the telephone reference check obtains information immediately at a relatively low cost.

The telephone reference check should be treated as an interview. It is important to note not only what the applicant's former superior says about him or her but how the superior says it.

If a job applicant does not receive a favorable reference from one employer, he or she should not be automatically rejected. Failure in one position does not necessarily forecast failure in another one.

The structured selection interview

The most important step in the application assessment stage is the structured selection interview. Only applicants who have survived the initial screening interview and employment reference check will participate in this phase.

The structured selection interview should be conducted by the data processing manager, not the personnel specialist. This interview is the final step in evaluating the applicant. To conduct a successful interview, the data processing manager should follow the guidelines outlined in the paragraphs that follow.

Prepare for the Interview.   The interviewer should review the job description, job specifications, and all the data obtained on the applicant. The interviewer should also determine any areas of further inquiry.

At this time, interview location should be determined. If possible, the interview should be conducted at the company so that the candidate can get a feel for the organization. However, some data processing professionals may be apprehensive about the possibility of being seen by others who currently work for the prospective employer. Under such circumstances, a place outside of the work site should be selected.

The interviewer should allocate enough time for the interview. Also, care should be taken in preventing disturbing interruptions.

Personal Introduction, Welcome, and Small Talk.   To establish good rapport with the applicant, the data processing manager should begin the interview by introducing himself or herself to the applicant and extending a warm and sincere welcome. Afterward, a few minutes of small talk will help to relax the applicant.

Obtain Relevant Information.   The most essential part of the interview is to obtain relevant and job-related information. Three areas need to be explored thoroughly: work experience, educational background, and personal factors directly related to the position.

The data processing manager should prepare specific questions to ask the applicant during the interview. These questions should focus on the three key areas already cited.

Discuss the Company and the Position.   Once the data processing manager has obtained all the necessary information regarding the applicant, it is time to give the applicant comparable and full facts about the company and the position. Staffing is a two-way street. The company must be convinced that the applicant is truly qualified for the position that is open, and the applicant must feel that the company and the position meet his or her career goals and needs. Unless there is an appropriate fit, neither party will be satisfied.

The data processing manager must therefore be as candid and as informative with the applicant as he or she expects the applicant to be with him or her. The negative as well as the positive aspects of the job must be discussed.

Respond to the Applicant's Questions.   The applicant probably has several questions that he or she would like answered. Often a degree of give and take ensues between the interviewer and the applicant in which additional areas are clarified by both parties.

Ending the Interview.   When there are no more questions asked by either the applicant or the interviewer, the interviewer should end the meeting. The interviewer should thank the applicant for his or her time. The applicant should also be informed of the procedure by which the company will arrive at its selection decision.

Evaluating the Applicant and Reaching a Decision

By this stage, a great deal of valuable information has been accumulated. If properly evaluated, it should help the data processing manager to arrive at an objective and accurate final selection decision.

Evaluating the applicant

In arriving at a decision, it is advisable to have some concept of the "ideal" applicant. After the real candidate has left, his or her credentials can be compared with those of the "ideal" applicant to see how closely they match.

To arrive at an objective and accurate final evaluation, the data processing manager should evaluate the candidate's qualifications against an established rating scale.

Final selection

After the finalist is selected, a firm offer of employment must be extended to this individual. To accomplish this, the data processing manager should arrange another meeting with the individual.

At the meeting, the offer is made and a decision is called for. Once an employer has come up with a dollar figure, it should be understood that this is a one-time offer. When an offer is not acceptable to the prospect, go on to the next candidate.

In data processing, most employees who resign receive a counteroffer from their employer. It is a danger that the prospective new employer must guard against. During the interview, the data processing manager should explore this openly and stress that if the prospect decides to leave his or her present organization, it is a firm commitment.[4] It is also important to agree on a firm start date.

Conclusion

According to experts, if a company is going to be successful in recruiting qualified data processing personnel, it must launch and maintain an aggressive, imaginative, and systematic recruiting program.[5]

In this discussion, a practical recruiting system for obtaining qualified data processing professionals was presented. This system, currently used by a large number of organizations, is based on following each of the four sequential stages in the system as follows:

1. Determining accurate and realistic staffing specifications
2. Undertaking effective applicant recruiting
3. Assessing the applicants
4. Making a final evaluation of the applicant

It is hoped that the information provided in this discussion will assist the recruiter to develop or improve a recruiting program for data processing personnel.

TRAINING AND DEVELOPMENT

Introduction

The current trends in information systems technology seem to indicate that in the near future, a sizable part of the work force will have some type of involvement with information technology. And from this involvement stems a need to teach people not only how to use the technology but how to exploit it and cope with the changes it will bring.

Training is not just limited to the end user, however. The rapid changes in technology itself with new capabilities, enhancements, and releases coming at a faster pace result in a continuing need for ongoing education and training of data processing professionals, such as programmers, system analysts, operators, data processing management, and so on.

---

[4]Dale Rhodabarger, "How to Hire the People You Want," *Computer Decisions*, Vol. 13, (February 1981), p. 185.

[5]Dale Rhodabarger and David Roman, "Developing an Aggressive Recruiting Program," *Computer Decisions*, Vol. 13 (August 1981), p. 154.

The focus of this discussion is on both these issues and how organizations must recognize the needs of both groups if information technology is to have a truly positive impact on the organization.

The Need of Training

With the proliferation of data processing applications and equipment throughout organizations, users find themselves trying to achieve a firm's objectives with technological tools. But many still regard the computer as an object of mystery or even fear. At first, this hostile attitude toward computerization was thought to be a fear of losing one's job or an irrational unwillingness to accept change. However, the evidence seems to be pointing to the fact that the problem has to do with the introduction of the computer system into the working environment; it is almost always the human ways of thinking, acting, and communicating that must be altered, not the computer's.

It appears that the novice's behavior in using the computer to solve a problem does not agree with the way the data processing professional thinks he or she should act. Designers of computer systems are not paying enough attention to the effect of the computer on the people whose livelihoods depend on eliciting useful responses from a computer. So, naturally, it is the user who must adapt to this "thing" that has invaded his life.

The problem of person-machine interface, or how human beings relate to computers, has focused primarily on the physical design of the equipment and the language used to communicate with the computer system. Concern over what little knowledge there is about the psychological aspects of the person-machine interface has prompted computer manufacturers to fund a number of experiments and research projects aimed at making computers easier to use by nonexperts. One of these studies, which was conducted by the United Kingdom's Medical Research Council, found that the majority of people view the computer as "an alien creature, isolating the user, mocking him with images of the world and its resources, to which he must haplessly conform."[6]

Users have traditionally placed a lot of importance on the possible impact a new computer might have on organizational structure and work style. As the organization adapts to the change the computer brings, these factors are diminished and the important question becomes, "How easy is the computer to use?"

The occasional user, most often a manager or other professional, wants to be able to use a computer with a minimum amount of training and will usually have some choice over whether or not to use it. If a manager finds the computer difficult to use, he or she will probably find another way of solving the problem, even if it is less efficient or less accurate. In many instances, the lack of awareness on the part of programmers and system designers of users' needs has led to a

[6]Malcom Peitu, "Making a Match Between Man and Machine," *International Management* (September 1979), p. 56.

barrier occasioned by the skills that the user has to master before taking advantage of the system.

Another problem closely related to ease of use is the language of computer systems. Language is broken down into three types of communicating with computers. At the primary level is the vocabulary of commands a user gives to the system. At the next level is the dialogue that takes place between the user and the machine. And, finally, there are the languages needed to program the computer to carry out its functions. The casual user is likely to use only the first two types of communicating, but the language with which the user deals in communicating to the computer frequently has little relationship to normal language one would use in daily life.

The relationship between people and machines has always posed problems. And programmers and system designers seem to have created systems with no regard for the human aspect in the design phase, placing people in situations in which they must change their thinking, acting, and communicating if they are to use the computer. Systems need to be designed with the user in mind. Moreover, the "law of divergence" is often the result: divergence between a delivered system and the user's real requirements increases proportionately to the length of time taken for the development of the system.[7]

Regardless of how accurate and complete the data gathering process is, users' needs are bound to change before the system is installed. If there is no mechanism to incorporate these changes into the system, the system that is finally implemented will not satisfy users' needs, and there will be little or no motivation for the user to accept, much less use, the system.

Training current and potential users could take a lot of persuasion. Until now, data processing technology has been limited to those committed to it or to those who had no alternative but to accept the automated systems. But managers and executives do have the power to reject automation of their office.

The struggle to implement computer systems may be a long-term one. Many of the top business schools are requiring their students to take computer classes, but organizations cannot afford to wait for a new breed of young people to enter management before they can automate. What companies must do is create an environment in which managers are encouraged and want to use computerized systems. In addition to the executives and managers who will benefit from using a computer, there are also the people who use the system on a day-to-day basis. These people may input information into the system, receive and interpret output, or do both. This is the largest segment of users and the ones needing the most training. They probably use the computer everyday, but they are most likely afraid of it and have no knowledge about it.

It is clear that the organization should develop a strategy for introducing data processing into the workplace, dealing with the above-mentioned problems, of which training is part.

---

[7]Thomas R. Conroy and Jacque Bieber, "Educating the Manager to Use New Office Technology," *Administrative Management* (November 1981), p. 41.

Implementation Strategy

User involvement at all stages of implementation, via awareness, education, training, and consulting, is probably the best way of creating a system that meets the user's needs and is one that he will want to use. *Involvement* on the part of the user is a key word.

In the beginning, users are introduced to the technology and how data processing applications will be implemented throughout the organization. The users will also have to be made aware of the changes that this new technology will have on how individuals, departments, and the corporation will operate.

The educational segment of the strategy will have to provide users with tools to analyze their work flow and to understand the technologies available to perform their work. It will also have to provide users with the tools to plan, design, and develop automated systems to perform that work. Training programs should also provide users with the necessary hands-on skills to use the computerized system. Training executives, managers, and users would not meet the opposition so prevalent in the past since the users have now been involved in the system design.

Ongoing consulting programs that provide user information support is the final element of this strategy. There would be consultants readily available to answer any questions and to integrate and coordinate the efforts of all user groups. The consulting department would also arrange seminars and make available to users newsletters, bulletins, and research reports. A data processing library would also be needed along with individual consultation.

Users must be educated and trained if they are going to accept and use a computer system. And along with this training and education must be user involvement in all phases of analysis, design, and development of the application system.

Ongoing Education and Training

There is no doubt that a company will have a large investment in hardware and software, but an even bigger investment is the cost of finding, hiring, and training data processing personnel. There is no question that ongoing training is needed for the data processing personnel, operators, programmers, systems analysts, and managers.

In-house training for data processing personnel was at one time considered a waste of time. But now it has become an absolute necessity in today's job market. Data processing people demand to keep abreast in their field, especially with the frequent changes that are occuring. Ongoing education and training is probably one of the most important factors in attracting and keeping data processing people. A 1979 study by Booz, Allen and Hamilton found that their company had a turnover rate of only 11 percent for professionals who received ongoing education and training versus a 52 percent turnover rate for those who did not.[8] There is strong evidence that ongoing training is needed, but it does not seem to be taking place. Training could also improve the data processing department's effectiveness in dealing with the other users of the organization.

Successful training programs direct training toward the attitudes, interests, and abilities of the individual and in turn create a desire to perform at a higher level. Training courses for data processing professionals must not only expose them to the current developments in their field, but try to broaden the individual personally and managerially in areas such as time management, decision making and other management skills. A list of such courses is presented in the appendix.

Training for a data processing professional can come from four sources:

1. Learner-paced, vendor-supplied courses
2. In-house seminars run by outsiders
3. Internally developed in-house seminars
4. Off-site vendor seminars

A solid program would utilize all four of these sources at one time or another.

Learner-paced courses are usually some combination of text, audio, video, and the computer. The course is structured in such a way that students can study at their own pace, an approach that has been found to be more effective than the traditional "teacher tells and student listens" situation. There should be someone available to answer questions raised by the student.

On-site vendor-supplied seminars are effective when a large number of people need to be trained on a specific subject in a short period of time.

Internally developed seminars are effective when there is no possibility of obtaining training anywhere else and current staff can adequately teach the course. This type of seminar can be more tightly controlled, but time must be spent for developing the course, which requires internal resources.

Off-site vendor seminars are best when the subject is highly technical and the number of people requiring this training is small. A variation of this type of training would be to have several key people attend the off-site seminar and then have them share the information with others in their group. One disadvantage of this type of training is the cost involved.[9]

Continuing education and training are critical factors in the development and retention of a highly skilled staff. And just as important as the commitment from the data processing manager is the commitment from top management to look beyond the immediate horizon at all the reasons to develop and support a strong training program.

[8]"Ongoing Training," *Infosystem* (February 1982), p. 43.

[9]Barbara K. Pavelle, "Continuing Education in DP—A Necessary Perk," *Data Management* (March 1982), p. 37.

SELECTED READINGS

BERTUZZI, ALBERTA. "How Good Are Trade Schools?" *Data Management,* Vol. 16 (October 1978), pp. 31–32.

BLOOM, ALLAN M. "Test the Test for Programming Applicants." *Data Management,* Vol. 16 (October 1978), pp. 37–39.

COUGER, J. DANIEL, AND ROBERT A. ZAWACKI. *Motivating and Managing Computer Personnel.* New York: John Wiley, 1980.

HENAULT, DAVID. "Trade School Approach Helps Managers Seeking New Employees." *Data Management,* Vol. 16 (June 1978), pp. 40–42.

"Ongoing Training." *Infosystem,* February 1982.

PAVELLE, BARBARA K. "Continuing Education in DP—A Necessary Perk." *Data Management,* March 1982.

RHODABARGER, DALE. "How to Hire the People You Want." *Computer Decisions,* Vol. 13 (February 1981), pp. 184–185.

———, AND DAVID ROMAN, "Developing an Aggressive Recruiting Program." *Computer Decisions,* Vol. 13 (August 1981), p. 154.

UPP, SCOTT. "How to Interview for Scare DP Pros." *Computer Decisions,* Vol. 12 (July 1980), pp. 54–60.

Appendix

Courses in Data Processing

The following is a listing of recommended courses and the types of people who should attend those courses. As mentioned previously, these courses may be given in house or taken outside. The list of courses in this appendix is only a partial one. A large number of courses is offered by a number of organizations, and it is the responsibility of the person in charge of training to survey the market continuously to develop a good education program for the organization.

Selecting, Estimating, and Justifying New Applications

This course should cover the early phases of application development. The primary topics are establishing standard procedures for new applications analysis and definition, cost-benefit analysis, selecting the proper mix of skills necessary for staffing, organization structures, and decision-making techniques.

This type of course should be attended by data processing and user personnel responsible for the initiation of new applications.

Project Management and Implementation

The participants should be taught practical techniques and skills that enable them to provide leadership in a complex project environment, develop project plans with appropriate phases and milestones; estimate project costs, schedules, and personnel; measure and control progress; coordinate the project team activities; improve software and hardware documentation; and manage the resources.

This course is for managers and supervisors who are responsible for data processing projects. Key technical people, such as senior analysts and chief programmers, should participate in this course.

Project Planning and Control for Users

This course is similar to the previous one. However, the emphasis is on the role of users in developing and using data processing applications. The participants should be taught the application development project life cycle, its importance and value and the user's role in each phase, the role of the user in maintaining existing programs, and working with data processing operations people.

This course is for nondata processing people responsible for working with the data processing department.

Structured Design and Programming

This course should present the practical, systematic tools and techniques of structured design and programming. Some of the topics to be taught in this course are structured software design methods, structured programming, increase programming productivity, reliability, testing and documentation, and reduction of software development and maintenance costs.

This course is intended for programmers, systems analysts, and users who are responsible for planning, design, and implementation of complex application programs.

Programming Techniques

Topics to be covered in this course should include the design process, testing strategies, debugging strategies, data structures, data handling techniques, program optimization, and advanced programming tools.

This course should be attended by programmers, analysts, designers, and data processing managers.

Structured Testing

Students should be taught the various testing methodologies, where they should be applied, and under what circumstances, developing a complete test plan, setting up guidelines for enforcement of testing standards, and developing of test plans appropriate to the software development life cycle.

This course may be valuable for designers, programmers, and all levels of management concerned with the design/programming process.

Structured Documentation

This course should discuss the concepts and techniques of structure development of documentation, designing of the individual manuals and documents, testing the document, reviewing the document for clarity and readability, and developing documentation standards.

This course should be attended by programmers, analysts, documentation specialists, technical writers, and data processing managers and supervisors.

Data Processing Operations Management

This course should cover concepts, techniques, and skills to provide leadership within data processing and the production process; understand how production can support the organization's objectives; and implement, enhance, and control the key processes that support production—recovery, capacity planning, problem, change, and performance management. Other topics may be the role of computer operations management, effective management of people resources, establishing effective computer operations organization, conversion planning and control, planning for distributed systems, work schedule alternatives, and planning for meeting current and future work loads.

This course is for managers and supervisors of data processing centers and data processing operations, managers of scheduling, and data control, data-entry, and technical support.

Design and Implementation of Database

This course should cover the characteristics of a data-base system for a shared environment and its impact on the organization, the design methodology for developing integrated data-base structure, and the data-base administration functions and organizational considerations. The emphasis should be on clearly identifying the real needs of the organization and on adapting the data base to them.

The following should participate in such a course: data processing professionals responsible for the data-base system, systems analysts, data processing auditors, and application development programmers.

Distributed Information Systems Planning and Design

This course should be designed to present the design process of an overall distributed information system, identifying information needs, determining information handling activities and service level requirements, developing alternative strategies, and physical selection criteria. Other topics that should be taught in this course are multicomputer system elements, distributed versus central processing, architecture design, hardware considerations, communication hardware, and special-purpose devices.

This course should be attended by those responsible for developing long-range systems plans, systems analysts, programmers, and technical managers.

Data and Physical Security and Control

Topics covered by this course include designing security controls into information systems, evaluating application processes, assessing exposure and risk, cost-benefit analysis, and understanding the operational aspects of data security administration.

This kind of course is intended for data processing personnel (programmers, analysts, designers, management) and for people external to data processing (auditors, DP auditors, security administrators, management).

Auditing and Control in Data Processing

This course should cover the following subjects: audit requirements for data processing, understanding and improving of the audit-data processing relationship, using the computer as an audit tool, and developing data processing audit plan for the installation.

This course is for auditors who are responsible for data processing auditing, data processing and user personnel with responsibility for data processing auditing, systems analysts and designers, and security officers and managers with data processing responsibility.

Computer Performance Measurement and Evaluation

The participants should be taught the techniques and tools for capacity planning, performance measurement, and the measurements analysis and evaluation.

This course is intended for systems, technical, and operating personnel.

Data Processing Concepts for Management and Users

This course should cover introduction to data processing, computing processes and hardware, peripherals, software, data communications, methodologies for computer systems development, and if possible simple language, such as BASIC.

It is recommended that many people in the organization be exposed to this course.

Developing Writing Skills

Data processing professionals have to communicate with users as well as with other data processing people. Therefore, this course should cover the writing skills for getting a message across, system documentation, minutes, status reports, RFPs, user manuals, and simple correspondence.

This course should be attended by all, since almost everybody has to communicate with others regardless of his or her position or profession.

Index